From the time of its creation in the writings ⟨of⟩
contemporaries, the story of Pocahontas has
a flexible discourse that has been put to mult
dictory agendas. Pocahontas was the most frequently and variously
portrayed female figure in antebellum literature. She served as the
prototype for both the beautiful "Indian princesses" of the frontier
romances and for the heroines of numerous "rescue" scenes. In
Pocahontas: The Evolution of an American Narrative, Robert S. Tilton
draws upon the rich tradition of Pocahontas material to examine
why her half-historic, half-legendary narrative has engaged the imaginations of Americans from the earliest days of the colonies to the
present.

Pocahontas: The Evolution
of an American Narrative

Books in the series

87. Rita Barnard, *The Great Depression and the Culture of Abundance*
86. Kenneth Asher, *T. S. Eliot and Ideology*
85. Robert Milder, *Reimagining Thoreau*
84. Blanche H. Gelfant, *Literary Reckonings: A Cross-Cultural Triptych*
83. Robert Tilton, *Pocahontas: The Evolution of an American Narrative*
82. Joan Burbick, *The Language of Health and the Culture of Nationalism in Nineteenth-Century America*
81. Rena Fraden, *Blueprints for a Black Federal Theatre, 1935–1939*
80. Ed Folsom, *Walt Whitman's Native Representations*
79. Alan Filreis, *Modernism from Right to Left*
78. Michael E. Staub, *Voices of Persuasion: The Politics of Representation in 1930s America*
77. Katherine Kearns, *Robert Frost and a Poetics of Appetite*
76. Peter Halter, *The Revolution in the Visual Arts and the Poetry of William Carlos Williams*
75. Barry Ahearn, *William Carlos Williams and Alterity: The Early Poetry*
74. Linda A. Kinnahan, *Poetics of the Feminine: Authority and Literary Tradition in William Carlos Williams, Mina Loy, Denise Levertov, and Kathleen Fraser*
73. Bernard Rosenthal, *Salem Story: Reading the Witch Trials of 1692*
72. Jon Lance Bacon, *Flannery O'Connor and Cold War Culture*
71. Nathaniel Mackey, *Discrepant Engagement: Dissonance, Cross-Culturality and Experimental Writing*
70. David M. Robinson, *Emerson and the Conduct of Life*
69. Cary Wolfe, *The Limits of American Literary Ideology in Pound and Emerson*
68. Andrew Levy, *The Culture and Commerce of the American Short Story*
67. Stephen Fredman, *The Grounding of American Poetry: Charles Olson and the Emersonian Tradition*
66. David Wyatt, *Out of the Sixties: Storytelling and the Vietnam Generation*
65. Thomas Strychacz, *Modernism, Mass Culture, and Professionalism*
64. Elisa New, *The Regenerate Lyric: Theology and Innovation in American Poetry*
63. Edwin S. Redkey, *A Grand Army of Black Men: Letters from African-American Soldiers in the Union Army, 1861–1865*

Continued on pages following the Index

POCAHONTAS: THE EVOLUTION OF AN AMERICAN NARRATIVE

ROBERT S. TILTON

Queens College, City University of New York

CAMBRIDGE
UNIVERSITY PRESS

Published by the Press Syndicate of the University of Cambridge
The Pitt Building, Trumpington Street, Cambridge CB2 1RP
40 West 20th Street, New York, NY 10011-4211, USA
10 Stamford Road, Oakleigh, Melbourne 3166, Australia

First published 1994

Printed in the United States of America

Library of Congress Cataloging-in-Publication Data
Tilton, Robert S.
Pocahontas: The Evolution of an American Narrative. / Robert S. Tilton.
p.   cm. – (Cambridge studies in American literature and
culture : 83)
Includes bibliographical references and index.
ISBN 0-521-46189-8 – ISBN 0-521-46959-7 (pbk.)
1. American literature – Colonial period, ca. 1600-1775 – History
and criticism.   2. American literature – 19th century – History and
criticism.   3. Pocahontas, d. 1617 – Legends – History and criticism.
4. Women and literature – United States – History.5. Pocahontas, d.
1617 – In literature.   6. Indians in literature.   7. Narration
(Rhetoric) I. Title. II. Series.
PS173.I6T55   1994
813.009'352042 – dc20
94-4607
CIP

A catalog record for this book is available from the British Library.

ISBN 0-521-46189-8 Hardback
0-521-46959-7 Paperback

This book is dedicated to the memories of my grandparents, Harry and Josephine Boylan, my aunt, Margaret Mary Boylan, and my mother, Joan Marie Boylan Tilton.

CONTENTS

Acknowledgments   *page* ix

List of Illustrations   xiii

Extracts   xv

Introduction   1

1   Miscegenation and the Pocahontas Narrative in
    Colonial and Federalist America   9

2   The Pocahontas Narrative in Post-Revolutionary
    America   34

3   The Pocahontas Narrative in the Era of the
    Romantic Indian   58

4   John Gadsby Chapman's *Baptism of Pocahontas*   93

5   The Figure of Pocahontas in Sectionalist
    Propaganda   145

    Postscript   176

    Notes   187

    Bibliography   227

    Index   245

ILLUSTRATIONS

Figure 1. Frontispiece from John Davis, *Captain Smith and Pocahontas*.   *page* 95

Figure 2. John Warner Barbar, a version of the Rescue from *Interesting Events in the History of the United States*.   96

Figure 3. Edward Corbould, *Pocahontas Rescues Captain John Smith*.   98

Figure 4. Engraving after Alonzo Chappell, *Pocahontas Saving the Life of Capt. John Smith*.   99

Figure 5. Antonio Capellano, *Preservation of Captain Smith by Pocahontas*.   100

Figure 6. John Trumbull, *Signing of the Declaration of Independence*.   100

Figure 7. John Gadsby Chapman, *The Baptism of Pocahontas*.   101

Figure 8. John Gadsby Chapman, *Hagar and Ishmael Fainting in the Wilderness*.   103

Figure 9. Unidentified artist, *Matoaks als Rebecka* – "*The Booton Hall Portrait*."   106

Figure 10. Simon Van de Passe, *Matoaks als Rebecka*.   107

Figure 11. Unidentified artist, after Simon Van de Passe, *Matoaks als Rebecka*.   109

Figure 12. Unidentified artist, *"The Sedgeford Hall Portrait."* 110

Figure 13. Mary Woodbury, *Pocahontas.* 111

Figure 14. *Pocahontas.* Engraving after Robert Matthew Sully's copy of *"The Turkey Island Portrait."* 113

Figure 15. Thomas Sully, *Pocahontas.* 114

Figure 16. Robert Matthew Sully, *Pocahontas* (Virginia). 115

Figure 17. Robert Matthew Sully, *Pocahontas* (Wisconsin). 116

Figure 18. Charles Bird King, *Hayne Hudjihini (Eagle of Delight).* 117

Figure 19. John Gadsby Chapman, *Pocahontas Saving the Life of Captain John Smith.* 118

Figure 20. Robert W. Weir, *Embarkation of the Pilgrims.* 124

Figure 21. Joseph Mozier, *Pocahontas.* 129

Figure 22. George Catlin, *Pigeon's Egg Head (The Light) going to and returning from Washington.* 132

Figure 23. William H. Powell, *Discovery of the Mississippi River.* 133

Figure 24. Joseph Mozier, *Indian Girl's Lament.* 138

Figure 25. Tompkins H. Matteson, *The Last of the Races.* 139

Figure 26. *Tenskwatawa.* Engraving after Charles Bird King. 141

Figure 27. Pocahontas figurehead, attributed to William Rush. 147

Figure 28. "The Noble Virginians Going To Battle" and "The Noble Virginians In The Heat Of Battle," from William Hillhouse, *Pocahontas; A Proclamation.* 150

Figure 29. "Virginia." Frontispiece from Henry Howe, *Historical Collections of Virginia.* 163

Figure 30. Pocahontas fan. 167

Figure 31. Flag of the Powhatan Guards. 170

Figure 32. Horatio Greenough, *The Rescue.* 177

Figure 33. Victor Nehlig, *Pocahontas and John Smith.* 181

Figure 34. Paul Cadmus, *Pocahontas Saving the Life of Captain John Smith.* 182

Figure 35. David McFall, *Pocahontas.* 183

Figure 36. R. L. Morgan Monceaux, *Matowaka.* 185

ACKNOWLEDGMENTS

The dissertation from which this book developed would never have been completed without a great deal of scholarly and moral support. Jay Fliegelman, through his extraordinary knowledge of colonial and antebellum culture and energetic encouragement at crucial moments, was the driving force behind this book. George Dekker witnessed the birth of the dissertation and subsequently used his considerable skills as a reader and advisor to keep it alive. Albert Gelpi's steadfast belief in the importance of this project provided great quantities of intellectual and emotional energy for its often languid author. These men were and continue to be models of professionalism and dedication to their work and their students. What talents I have as a scholar and teacher are due largely to their advice and example.

There are other members of the Stanford University family to whom I am extremely grateful. First among these is Wanda Corn, who signed on for one chapter and ultimately was kind enough to read through the entire text. I must also thank Helen Brooks, Monica Moore, my erstwhile housemates Ron and Priscilla Davies, and all of the members of the old and new squads in the Humanities/ Special Programs office. While your provision of employment kept me eating, your contributions to my spirit were at least as valuable. Thomas C., Sr., Joyce, and Margot Moser provided good wishes and pleasant walks throughout the course of this project. And while I owe thanks to librarians and researchers all over the country, special mention must be made of the efforts of Jim Knox, Eric Heath, and Sonia Moss at Stanford's Green Library, who tirelessly responded to my increasingly bizarre questions and quests.

At Cambridge University Press, T. Susan Chang wisely and cheerfully saw this sometimes troublesome project to its fruition. Janet Polata miraculously kept the versions, illustrations, and official paperwork under control. The brilliant copyediting talents of Christie Lerch made it a far better read, if not a far better book. And Camilla T.K. Palmer patiently put up with that special mania generated by a first-time author, fielded all late night and early morning telephone calls with a minimum of hostility, and generally kept things moving forward against occasionally long odds. Thank you one and all.

From among those who supported this project I must also thank Steven F. Kruger, the kind of friend everyone should have, who read through various versions of various sections of this book during its evolution. His suggestions about it, and most other things, were consistently on the mark. Thomas C. Moser, Jr. and Catherine Bledsoe provided wonderful accommodations, genial fellowship, sage advice, and great quantities of single-malt scotch. Richard and Anne Connolly, Mary Ericksen, and Cliff and Rita Randolph were tireless in their encouragement. And finally, I must thank Rita Connolly-Tilton for her unflagging support, unbelievable patience, and unwavering belief in this book and its author.

What is useful in the following pages is due in large part to the efforts of these friends and colleagues. What is amiss should be blamed squarely on the author.

EXTRACTS

After some six weeks fatting amongst those Salvage Courtiers, at the minute of my execution, she hazarded the beating out of her owne braines to save mine, and not onely that, but so prevailed with her father, that I was safely conducted to James towne, where I found about eight and thirtie miserable poore and sicke creatures, to keepe possession of all those large territories of Virginia, such was the weaknesse of this poore Common-wealth, as had the Salvages not fed us, we directly have starved.

– John Smith, 1624[1]

Good Heaven! What an eventful life was hers! To speak of nothing else, the arrival of the English in her father's dominions, must have appeared (as, indeed, it turned out to be) a most portentous phenomenon. It is not easy for us to conceive the amazement and consternation which must have filled her mind and that of her nation at the first appearance of our countrymen. Their great ship, with all her sails spread, advancing, in solemn majesty to the shore; their complexion; their dress; their language; their domestic animals; their cargo of new and glittering wealth; and then, the thunder and irresistible force of their artillery; the distant country announced by them, far beyond the great water, of which the oldest Indian had never heard, or tho't, or dreamed – all this was so new, so wonderful, so tremendous, that I do seriously suppose, the personal descent of an army of Milton's celestial angels, robed in light, sporting in the bright beams of the sun and redoubling their splendor, making divine harmony with their golden harps, or playing with the bolt and chasing the rapid lightning of Heaven, would excite not more astonishment in Great Britain than did the debarkation of the English among the aborigines of Virginia.

– William Wirt, 1803[2]

Two large stones were brought in and placed before Powhatan, and Smith was dragged up to them and his head was placed upon them, that his brains might be beaten out with clubs. The fatal weapons were already raised, and the stern executioners looked for the signal, which should bid them descend upon the victim's defenseless head. But the protecting shield of divine Providence was over him, and the arm of violence was arrested. Pocahontas, the King's favorite daughter, – at that time a child of twelve or thirteen years of age, – finding that her piteous entreaties to save the life of Smith were unavailing, rushed forward, clasped his head in her arms, and laid her own upon it, determined either to save his life, or share his fate. Her generous and heroic conduct touched her father's iron heart, and the life of the captive was spared, to be employed in making hatchets for himself, and bells and beads for his daughter.

The account of this beautiful and most touching scene, familiar as it is to every one, can hardly be read with unmoistened eyes. The incident is so dramatic and startling, that it seems to preserve the freshness of novelty amidst a thousand repetitions. We could almost as reasonably expect an angel to have come down from heaven, and rescued the captive, as that his deliverer should have sprung from the bosom of Powhatan's family. The universal sympathies of mankind and the best feelings of the human heart have redeemed this scene from the obscurity which, in the progress of time, gathers over all, but the most important events. It has pointed a thousand morals and adorned a thousand tales. Innumerable bosoms have throbbed and are yet to throb with generous admiration for this daughter of a people, whom we have been too ready to underrate. Had we known nothing of her, but what is related of her in this incident, she would deserve the eternal gratitude of the inhabitants of this country; for the fate of the colony may be said to have hung upon the arms of Smith's executioners.

– Jared Sparks, 1839[3]

Pocahontas is one of those characters, rarely appearing on the theatre of life, which no age can claim, no country appropriate. She is the property of mankind, serving as a beacon to light us on our way, instruct us in our duty, and show us what the human mind is capable of performing when abandoned to its own operations.

– William Watson Waldron, 1841[4]

INTRODUCTION

The subject . . . is one of such exciting interest, that it should cast a
halo around the page which it adorns, and be sufficient of itself to
disarm all criticism, with regard to the words wherein it is invested,
whether delivered in prose or verse.[1]

In all history and in all romance it would be difficult to find a more
perfect character than Pocahontas; and taking her as she has come
down to us, it appears to me to be impossible to say wherein it could
have been improved.[2]

In *Regeneration Through Violence,* his landmark study of the Daniel
Boone narrative, Richard Slotkin points out what was perhaps the
most crucial reason for the emerging power of this particular representation of life on the American frontier.

> The power of Filson's myth lay, not in an ability to alter existing
> conceptions of the frontier drastically and suddenly, but in the
> ease with which it could be assimilated to such preconceptions,
> and made to adjust to new fashions, conceptions, and ideolog-
> ical requirements.[3]

It mattered little where or when the narrative was reproduced because of the facility with which "the image of Boone was made to
serve as the embodiment of local values or cultural assumptions and
as the vicarious resolver of the dilemmas that preoccupied that culture."[4]

A group of texts that is similar to the Daniel Boone tradition in
their ability to express multiple and at times contradictory agendas
are the various incarnations of Pocahontas, the prototypical Indian
princess. Her act of bravery in saving the life of Captain John Smith
was recast and retold more often than any other American historical
incident during the colonial and antebellum periods. The Pocahontas narrative provided literary and visual artists with a flexible discourse that came to be used to address a number of racial, political,
and gender-related issues. In this book I discuss a selection of these

texts in order to account for the cultural usefulness, and hence, the pervasiveness, of this favorite American tale.

Judging by the number of books published in recent years with the name "Pocahontas" in the title, one might suspect that such a project would be unnecessary. Yet, an examination of some of these works finds that for the most part they are not actually about Pocahontas or her narrative. For example, Helen C. Rountree's *Pocahontas's People* (1990) tells the story of the Powhatan Indians over the course of four hundred years.[5] Pocahontas herself virtually disappears from the book after the third of the ten chapters. Asebrit Sundquist's *Pocahontas and Co.* (1987) is a study of all fictional American Indian women in nineteenth-century literature.[6] Pocahontas is certainly treated as an important and exemplary member of this group, but she is by no means the focus of the book. Mary Dearborn uses events from the Pocahontas narrative to present the problems faced by authors who found themselves doubly removed from what they perceived to be the cultural mainstream in her study of ethnic women writers, *Pocahontas's Daughters* (1986).[7] Again, Pocahontas provides a useful thematic model but is not the principal subject. The monumental genealogy, *Pocahontas' Descendants* (1985), compiled by Stuart E. Brown, Jr., Lorraine F. Myers, and Eileen M. Chappell (and to which two supplements have since been added), is for the most part simply a listing, with an introduction and some commentary, of the thousands of individuals who have descended from Thomas Rolfe, and therefore from Pocahontas and John Rolfe, and ultimately from Powhatan and the hereditary rulers of America.[8]

Although neither Pocahontas nor her narrative is the primary concern of any of these texts, the authors, especially of the first three books, presumably included her name in their titles because it would have an immediate resonance with their target audience. In each instance, as would have been true during the antebellum period, her name acts as a lure to attract readers, and, as was also often true, in each case a different type of resonance is sought. Indeed, Pocahontas's name and narrative are as multivalent today as in the nineteenth century. Since its creation in the works of John Smith and his contemporaries, through the colonial and Federalist eras, and into the nineteenth century, part of the power of the Pocahontas myth has been based on the multiplicity of correspondences available to the author who invokes the name of the heroine of Jamestown.[9]

I should say at the outset that I will not be spending a great deal of time examining the texts that document the Virginia plantation, such as the narratives of John Smith, Ralph Hamor, William Stra-

chey, Edward Maria Wingfield, and Alexander Whitaker. In Chapter
1 and occasionally thereafter I invoke the primary documents, particularly Smith's *Generall Historie*, but for the most part my study is
confined to eighteenth- and nineteenth-century interpretations of
these sources. At least in part because so much attention has recently
been paid to Smith and his contemporaries, commentators have generally ignored the vast literature that was generated by those who
reformulated the early representations of the daughter of Powhatan.
One of the principal goals of this book is the recovery and analysis
of this tradition, in the service of a reassessment of the importance
of the figure of Pocahontas during the antebellum era.

My study begins with the eighteenth-century Virginia historian
Robert Beverly, whose *History and Present State of Virginia* contains the
first important colonial attempt to reconstruct the Pocahontas narrative. During this period her relationship to John Rolfe, whom she
married, was often seen as being as important as her rescue of John
Smith. Commentators could muse that had other Europeans followed Rolfe's example and intermarriage become commonplace
from the outset of the colonial enterprise, the ongoing, apparently
irreconcilable, conflict between the Anglo-American colonists and
the native cultures might have been avoided. This retrospective theory, which amounted to a fantasy of the absorption of the established
peoples into the culture of the newcomers, was revived during the
Jeffersonian era, but always in the form of either a nostalgic looking
back to the earliest days of the colonies when it could have happened, or a looking ahead to when it might someday occur. There
was clearly no room in the present for such a union.

My second chapter deals with the post-Revolutionary War period.
The primary focus here is on the work of John Davis, who first recognized the potential of the narrative to be the germ of a great
romance. Davis is also the first to subordinate Pocahontas's relationship with Rolfe to her more dramatic tie to Smith, and to posit that
it was her love for the captain that accounted for her heroism. In
this chapter I also deal with the growing popularity of the Pocahontas narrative in the forty years after the Revolutionary War, and compare the rescue of John Smith to the other great mythic incident
that emerged during this period, the story of George Washington
and the cherry tree, which was invented by Mason Locke Weems for
his biography of the first president, and talk briefly about the importance of the narrative to the engendering of the American romance.

Chapter 3, "The Pocahontas Narrative in the Era of the Romantic
Indian," focuses primarily on texts produced between 1820 and
1850. Literary artists who reconstituted the Pocahontas narrative

during this period focused almost exclusively on her relationship to Smith. I argue that this was necessitated by their desire to avoid the theme of miscegenation. The alternatives available to those who wanted to make use of this well-known tale were either to provide Pocahontas-like scenes (usually rescues) in romances that were otherwise unrelated to her story (such as Paulding's *Koningsmarke,* Sedgwick's *Hope Leslie,* and Caruthers's *The Cavaliers of Virginia*), or to make adjustments to the narrative that deemphasized her marriage and motherhood, as was done in a number of the "Pocahontas dramas." I also examine other personae of the princess, including Pocahontas as the foiler of conspiracies, and discuss how characters like Prescott's Doña Marina are in many ways based on the archtypal protectress of European men. In the end I turn to the anthropologist Adolphe Bandelier, who, toward the conclusion of the nineteenth century, equated Pocahontas figures with Cooper's Indian braves and argued that both types of fictional, "romantic" natives must be eliminated in order to clear a path for the scientific representations of Indians prepared by scholars like himself and Lewis Henry Morgan.

In my fourth chapter I focus on visual representation. My central text here is John Gadsby Chapman's painting, *The Baptism of Pocahontas.* I examine the early career of this young Virginia artist and move to a discussion of his attempt to create an alternate persona for the Indian princess in his painting for the Rotunda of the Capitol in Washington. Chapman's painting the *Baptism* is examined in terms of both its relation to the rescue of John Smith, the far more often reproduced scene from the narrative, and its relation to other contemporary paintings of Native Americans. *The Baptism of Pocahontas* seems to allow for the salvation of some Indians, but, because their survival is based on the adoption of Anglo-American Christian culture, the Manifest Destiny dimension of the painting is also evident. Chapman makes clear what will happen to those Indians who do not abandon their cultural heritage and adopt a white way of thinking. Also, because the survival of the Indian race is thematically ensured through this mythic absorption of Pocahontas into the white colonizers, others of "her people" who were perceived as standing in the path of American expansion could be guiltlessly eliminated.

My last chapter, "The Figure of Pocahontas in Sectionalist Propaganda," concerns the political uses of the Pocahontas material during the years that preceded the Civil War. As early as 1820 her name is invoked as a pseudonym by abolitionist writers, in part because she symbolized safety for the endangered captive and the possible peaceful coexistence of two distinct races, but also because as a "princess of Virginia" and progenitrix of many members of the planter aristocracy she made a convenient and widely recognizable target. Conversely, it was in part because of Pocahontas, and her provision for the South of an alternative aristocracy (through her descendants) and an alternative history (through her actions in the service of John Smith and Jamestown), that the Confederacy was able rhetorically to coalesce into a nation and to formulate a culture that was independent of the New England Puritan history on which the larger nationalist narrative had traditionally been based. Her story gave southerners a common historical point of origin and a common heroine, and therefore it is not surprising that at this critical juncture it came under attack. There can be little doubt that the attempts of John Gorham Palfrey, Charles Deane, and Henry Adams to undercut the historicity of Pocahontas's rescue of John Smith were politically motivated. I conclude by arguing that by the second half of the nineteenth century the Pocahontas narrative was so ingrained in the American consciousness that its authenticity had ceased to be an issue of any significance.

For modern critics, however, the authenticity of the rescue of John Smith is still a subject of considerable interest. Historians of the early colonial period, led by Philip Barbour, and biographers of Pocahontas, such as Frances Mossiker and Grace Steele Woodward, have all tried to find explanations for the events surrounding Smith's internment.[10] The most convincing argument, which was first formulated by Barbour in *The Three Worlds of Captain John Smith,* is that the apparently lifesaving action of Pocahontas was in fact part of an adoption ritual that was misinterpreted by Smith. This reading, with various modifications, has been accepted by a number of recent scholars, including Mossiker, Karen Ordahl Kupperman, Jean Fritz, Peter Hulme, and most recently J. A. Leo Lemay. Helen Rountree, however, has argued against this interpretation. She suggests that we do not have enough information about Powhatan adoption rituals to make this case and points out that Smith provides no convincing corroboration for this theory. Only Alden Vaughan, among modern scholars, steers clear of this controversy. He argues that we will probably never have a definitive explanation about what, if anything, happened while Smith was a prisoner.[11]

The debate about the authenticity of the rescue story is outside of the scope of this book, which deals primarily with the period before the first serious uncertainties about Smith's account of this incident surfaced. Indeed, the doubts raised by Charles Deane and his followers, and their effect or lack of it, mark the end of my discussion. In the eighteenth and for most of the nineteenth century, the rescue of John Smith by Pocahontas was generally accepted as a mythohistoric fact. It was this historical status, coupled with the resonance that her romantic tale had for American readers, that made it so apparently irresistible to so many antebellum artists.

Philip Young has pointed out that some aspects of the Pocahontas narrative have sources that date to the classical age.[12] The stories of the salvation of Jason through the efforts of the enamored barbarian princess Medea, and of the engendering of the Roman race through the joining of the foreign soldier Aeneas to the indigenous princess Lavinia, certainly contain aspects of the later myth. However, neither these possible models, nor the medieval sources mentioned by Young, nor even Smith's story of his salvation through the good offices of the Lady Tragabigzanda, which is sometimes seen as a prefiguration of his rescue by Pocahontas, are discussed here. Although some structural and/or narrative similarities exist, the crucial elements of the Pocahontas narrative – the New World setting, the ambiguous relations between the colonists and the Indians, the youth and innocence of Smith's protector, and the fact that Pocahontas does not marry the man whom she saves – serve to set the narrative apart from its thematic models. The unnamed daughter of Ucita (the "Lord of the Floridians") who rescues Juan Ortiz seems a likely precursor of Smith's Pocahontas, but I will not elaborate on this connection here.[13] Questions about the ultimate sources of the narrative are not answered in this book, although in Chapter 2 I talk briefly about the importance of the *Aeneid* to those who wished to compose an American epic for the young nation.

I should also mention here that I do not invoke the "squaw," the female Indian figure who is now often seen as an alternative to the Pocahontas figure. Although I do discuss alternative personae, my study is for the most part confined to Pocahontas and to the "Indian princesses" who I believe were based primarily on her model.[14] Nor am I, by stressing the importance of the Pocahontas narrative, attempting to privilege the Jamestown founding or to get involved in the long-standing debate concerning the relative importance of the Jamestown and Plymouth/Massachusetts Bay colonies. If anything, my study constitutes something of a corrective, by arguing that the importance of the Virginia colony was widely accepted during the antebellum era, if only because of the popularity of its marquee figures.

Finally, it must be mentioned at the outset that the wealth of available materials for a project such as this is great. Therefore, no claim is made to total coverage. I understand that for every text that I discuss it would be quite easy to point to others that I have neglected. My goal is not to be exhaustive. Rather, it is simply to identify and examine some of the dominant themes of the reformulations of the

Pocahontas narrative that appeared at crucial moments during the colonial, Federalist, and antebellum periods.

At this point I should take a moment to explain my choice of terms. For the most part, I have used the misnomer "Indians" as my generic locution for Native Americans. Its use in no way endorses the prejudices that the term often implied. This identification simply conforms with the practice of the periods I am discussing and thus avoids confusion. Discussions of "mixed-bloods" and "half-breeds" again in no sense endorse the racial theories suggested by these terms, but merely reproduce historical usage and prejudices. I have also used "miscegenation" and "Manifest Destiny" throughout the book, even though neither was coined until the mid-nineteenth century.[15] Each is simply the clearest way to express that particular idea.

From the beginning of the colonization of the New World, Europeans used their standard terminologies to describe those whom they perceived to be in positions of power and influence among the native people. Powhatan was therefore a "king" or an "emperor," and his daughter was a "princess." In this book I often refer to Pocahontas by her bestowed title. She is by far the most often mentioned "princess," and so all such references, unless otherwise specified, are to her. Also, the rescue of Captain John Smith is the best-known, and arguably the most important, event in the Pocahontas narrative. Therefore, it will be alluded to quite often. When I refer to the Rescue (capitalized) without further explanation, I mean the rescue of Smith by Pocahontas. Finally, I have chosen to capitalize "North," "South," "East," and "West" when they are used as nouns to represent the regions of the United States.

It may also be of use here to outline briefly the major events in the life of the historical Pocahontas. Sharon Larkins, in her recent discussion of methods of teaching the Pocahontas narrative, provides a useful chronological sketch of the crucial moments.[16]

1. Her birth about 1595.
2. The traditional story of her rescue of Captain John Smith in 1607 and her continued relationship with him and help to the people of Jamestown.
3. Her abduction by Captain Argall in 1612 and subsequent captivity at Jamestown.
4. Her conversion to the Christian faith in 1613 while living in Jamestown.
5. Her marriage to John Rolfe in 1614 and the birth of her [their] son [Thomas] in 1615.

6. Her trip to England in 1616 including her success there as an Indian princess. [This would include her reception at the court of King James I and Queen Anne, her attendance at *The Vision of Delight*, the Twelfth Night masque staged by Ben Jonson, and her sitting for the Simon Van de Passe engraving of her portrait, the only likeness of Pocahontas known to have been executed during her lifetime.]

7. Her death [and burial] at Gravesend in 1617.[17]

These are, in fact, the only events about which there are extant accounts. The other material in the sometimes lengthy biographies of Pocahontas is, at best, based on studies of Powhatan Indian culture, of the founding of the British colonies in the New World, or of the Stuart period in England. At worst, it is pure conjecture.

By the early nineteenth century, American romancers, followed closely by poets and dramatists, began to stray farther and farther from the "facts" as presented by John Smith and his contemporaries. Their own knowledge of the Pocahontas material, however, was often mediated through the fertile imaginations of eighteenth-century historians, who actually began the process of augmenting the primary documents. As we shall see in Chapter 1, the emphasis in many of these historical presentations was often as much on the relationship between Pocahontas and her actual husband as on that with her mythic compatriot.

1

MISCEGENATION AND THE POCAHONTAS NARRATIVE IN COLONIAL AND FEDERALIST AMERICA

─────

[W]hat will it avail you, to take that perforce, you may quietly have with love?[1]

It is not probable that this sensible and amiable woman, perceiving the superiority of the Europeans, foreseeing the probability of the subjugation of her countrymen, and anxious as well to soften their destiny as to save the needless effusion of human blood, desired, by her marriage with Mr. Rolfe, to hasten the abolition of all distinction between Indians and white men; to bind their interests and affections by the nearest and most endearing ties, and to make them regard themselves as one people, the children of the same great family?[2]

As the Chevalier de Chastellux was traveling through eastern Virginia in April 1782, he was informed that his presence was expected at the home of Mary Marshall Tabb Bolling, second wife and widow of Robert Bolling, whom Chastellux describes in his *Travels in North America in the Years 1780, 1781, and 1782* as "one of the greatest landholders in Virginia, and proprietor of half the town of Petersburg."[3] Upon his arrival he was greeted by Mrs. Bolling, her young daughter Anne, and her son Robert, Jr., who was accompanied by his cousin and new bride, Mary Burton Bolling. There can be no doubt as to which of this young couple more impressed the Chevalier.

> The young gentleman appears mild and polite, but his wife, of only seventeen years of age, is a most interesting acquaintance, not only from her face and form, which are exquisitely delicate, and quite European, but from her being also descended from the Indian Princess *Pocahunta*, daughter of King *Powhatan*, of whom I have already spoken. We may presume that it is rather the disposition of that amiable American woman, than her exterior beauty, which Mrs. Bowling [Bolling] inherits.[4]

9

Chastellux goes on to give a brief, imaginative rendering of the life of Pocahontas, which often strays from the accounts of John Smith, Ralph Hamor, and the other seventeenth-century creators of her narrative, as well as from the texts of the eighteenth-century historians who had paraphrased, and in some cases greatly modified, the "history" that was presented in the primary documents. The Chevalier then concludes with a brief genealogy. "She [Pocahontas] left an only son, who was married, and left only daughters; these daughters, others; and thus, with the female line, the blood of the amiable Pocahunta now flows in the veins of the young and charming Mrs. Bowling."[5] Chastellux was clearly enchanted by Mary's "European" appearance. All visible manifestations of her Indian genetic heritage had apparently been bred out over the five generations between Mary and Pocahontas, but the Chevalier speculates that the "disposition" of the princess, which here means more character than temperament, had been passed down to this "amiable" young woman.

In 1787, the year that the first English translation of Chastellux's *Travels* was published, a corresponding view was expressed by Samuel Stanhope Smith in *An Essay On The Causes Of The Variety Of Complexion And Figure In The Human Species*. Arguing against Lord Kames's assertion that "Uniformity is the offspring of nature, never of chance," Smith chooses an interesting example of the process that can bring about such apparent uniformity.

> There resided in the college of New-Jersey, in the years seventeen hundred and eighty-five, six and seven, . . . two young gentlemen of one of the most respectable families of the state of Virginia. They were descended in the female line from the indian emperor Powhatan, and were in the fourth descent from the princess Pocahuntis, a high-spirited and generous woman. Although all their ancestors in Virginia had retained some characteristics, more or less obvious, of their maternal race, in these young gentlemen they appeared to be entirely obliterated. The hair and complexion, of one of them in particular, was very fair, and the countenance, and the form of the face, perfectly Anglo-American. He retained only the dark and vivid eye which has distinguished the whole family, and rendered some of them remarkably beautiful.[6]

In both of these cases the inheritance from Pocahontas is clearly seen as a boon to the young people involved. To Chastellux it is the "disposition" of the princess that he posits as having been handed down. In Smith's text it is manifested by the "dark and vivid eye" that makes some members of this family particularly attractive; the "respectability" of those who had descended from this mixing of an

English settler with the royal family of the aboriginal population; and, by implication, the "high spirit" and "generosity" of their famous forebear. Such inheritances were thought to be the natural legacy of the woman who had been so instrumental to the survival of the first permanent Anglo-American colony in the New World.

In neither instance is her English husband John Rolfe mentioned. To do so in this context would have necessitated an attempt to distinguish his particular Caucasian gifts to his descendants, which would have been next to impossible because of the large number of Anglo-American family members, each of whom would ostensibly have contributed to the European features of their offspring. It is also clear, however, that in these cases it was important to de-emphasize any colonial contributions, since the surprise expressed by both Chastellux and Smith is based specifically on their subjects' being descended from Pocahontas.

Such noble descendants were always distinguished from others of Indian-white descent during the colonial and early national periods. Many of the latter group were often referred to generically as "half-breeds" because of their unclear racial identity and/or political affiliation, or labeled "part savage," no matter how small that part may actually have been. And although William Scheick points out that not everyone "saw half-bloods as the embodiment of 'the worst traits of both races,'" as Albert Keiser had earlier suggested, it is certainly fair to say that such people were often feared and mistrusted by Anglo-Americans.[7] Interestingly, it was a "hidden side," which both nonconnected mixed-bloods and the descendants of Pocahontas were thought to possess, that served to differentiate them. Whereas in those traditionally defined as "half-breeds" a "savage" was potentially lurking somewhere beneath the visible surface, especially of those who could "pass for white," so the nobility and "disposition" of Pocahontas, which was based as much on her royal lineage as on her apparently pro-English actions, was often believed to have been transmitted to her descendants, even if the individual in question seemed in all other respects to be Caucasian. Their connection to Pocahontas was a source of great pride for the Bollings, the Randolphs, and a good many other members of the colonial Virginia aristocracy. Thomas Jefferson, although not a direct descendant himself, was said to have expressed satisfaction over the fact that both of his daughters married descendants of the famous Indian princess.[8]

By the end of the eighteenth century, Pocahontas was already beginning to take on a mythic significance based on John Smith's representations of her as his heroic rescuer and the savior of the fledgling Jamestown colony. During the colonial and early national periods, however, she was as importantly remembered as a real, flesh-and-blood Indian woman, who, as Europeans saw it, had turned her back on her people and her title. Pocahontas had converted, married an Englishman, and produced a son, and many of her descendants had become influential, highly visible members of southern society.

The marriage of Pocahontas and John Rolfe came to be seen as a model that, to the detriment of both Indians and whites, had not been followed during the earliest years of the English colonial enterprise. It was interpreted as a proof that a merging of the two peoples and cultures was, or at least had been, possible. If this aspect of her narrative had been reenacted on a larger scale, then perhaps the continual animosity between the races, which appeared to many commentators in the eighteenth century to be an unavoidable legacy to their own descendants, might have been averted. When contemporary historians nostalgically theorized about this missed opportunity, they generally invoked the marriage of Pocahontas and John Rolfe, which Bernard W. Sheehan calls "the great archetype of Indian-white conjugal union."[9]

The subject of their marriage, and of intermarriage in general, is often raised in historical descriptions of the founding of Jamestown. And by the early eighteenth century it was the rare historian who could resist the temptation provided by this aspect of the Pocahontas narrative to editorialize on the missed opportunity for a general intermarriage modeled on the successful union of Pocahontas and Rolfe. Although in such comments the details of her story were sometimes rearranged or new material was added to help dramatize the presentation, the consistency of such commentary suggests that Indian-white intermarriage was an important topic of discussion, if no longer a practical option, for the chroniclers of the Virginia colony and the early republic.

In this chapter I will examine colonial American attitudes toward what has since come to be known, usually by those who oppose intermarriage, as "miscegenation."[10] Although most Anglo-Americans took what became the dominant view that intermarriage was morally wrong and even "unnatural," there were colonial writers who from the beginning suggested that it would have been beneficial for both peoples. Later historians pointed out that such a policy would have allowed for the easier acquisition of Indian lands by the Anglo-American colonists, helped to keep the peace between the races, and helped to "civilize" the Indians, to the point where, in the course of a few generations, the sight of "charming" young white people like Mary Bolling, who were descended from such unions, would not have been a great surprise to European visitors to America.

Although to colonial Anglo-Americans the first two advantages would have seemed to benefit the colonists and the third the Indians, in fact all of these aspects of intermarriage would have benefited the Europeans by permitting an eventual absorption of the native cultures and their lands. By the eighteenth and early nineteenth centuries such unions had come to represent a foregone golden opportunity for a mixing of the two races into a single "American" people. And when such instances were discussed, it was often Pocahontas – not as the rescuer of Smith, but rather as the wife of John Rolfe and the mother of Thomas – who was invoked.

A wholesale amalgamation of the Indian and white peoples was never considered a real option by the early Anglo-American settlers. Many colonists were warned, even before they left England, to avoid intermarrying with the people of the New World. Thus, on April 25, 1609, one group that was about to leave for the privations and temptations of colonial life was admonished by William Symonds to avoid certain specific pitfalls associated with their enterprise.[11] In this sermon Symonds used as his primary text the popular Genesis 12:1–3, which describes God's calling of Abraham. His explication is quite precise concerning any mixing of God's chosen people with the natives of the new lands.

> Out of these arguments, by which God enticed *Abram* to goe out of his Country, such as goe to a Christian Plantation may gather many blessed lessons. *God Will Make him a Greate Nation.* Then must Abrams posteritie keepe them to themselves. They may not marry nor give in marriage to the heathen, that are uncircumcised. And this is so plaine, that out of this foundation arose the law of marriage among themselves. The breaking of this rule, may breake the neck of all good successe of this voyage, whereas by keeping the feare of God, the Planters in shorte time, by the blessing of God, may grow into a nation formidable to all the enemies of Christ, and bee the praise of that part of the world, for so strong a hand to be joyned with the people here that feare God.[12]

Symonds here makes one of the earliest cases for the power of racial purity, which he believed would ensure the prosperity of the Virginia colony. Such expressions of the fear of miscegenation, as well as of any type of "unnatural mixing," become a constant feature of colonial and early American thought. As Scheick puts it, "for a variety of reasons (most not very rational) white society in general frowned upon racially mixed marriage or cohabitation; the former was civilly, and the latter morally, dubious to an apparent majority of white settlers."[13]

Notwithstanding the clear pronouncements of Symonds and those like him who felt that any mixing was tantamount to the dooming of the Jamestown settlement, John Rolfe, in an act that truly ensured the "good successe" of the colony, married "Rebecca" – formally known as "Matoaka" or "Pocahontas" – the favorite daughter of Powhatan, who was the most powerful leader of the Tidewater Virginia tribes.[14] Rolfe explains, in a letter in which he asks Governor Thomas Dale's permission to marry the princess, that his purposes were apparently quite noble: "*but for the good of this plantation, for the honour of our countrie, for the glory of God, for my owne salvation, and for the converting to the true knowledge of God and Jesus Christ, an unbeleeving creature, namely* Pokahuntas."[15] Indeed, this letter is often cited as an expression of the general fear of such marriages because Rolfe is at some pains in it to convince Governor Dale of his own proper intentions, as well as of the good that will come to the colony through this joining.

Few southern colonists followed their example during the decades when they could legally have done so. By 1662, Virginia had a law that expressly prohibited interracial marriage, which was amended in 1691 to remove any doubt that Indians were included in this ban. In New England, the response of the Plymouth colony to what they saw as the improper relations between Indians and whites at Thomas Morton's Mare-Mount makes clear the attitude of the earliest colonists of that region to this apparent threat to their errand. The question of intermarriage came up for debate in the Massachusetts Bay Colony in 1634, but, although it was "referd to after consideration," it was not mentioned again in the Massachusetts Assembly for some time. In 1705, Samuel Sewall could boast that he had "got the Indians out of the Bill" before Chapter 10 of the Province Laws prohibiting marriage between whites and non-Caucasians was passed, but it should be noted that by 1786 a law specifically banning intermarriage between Indians and whites was on the books in Massachusetts.[16] Other states also had such statutes, some explicitly prohibiting marriage between Indians and whites, and others marriage where one of the parties was classified as "colored," a designation usually reserved for the offspring of black-white relationships, but that could be applied, when necessary, to those of mixed Indian-white blood as well. In all cases it was made clear to whites that for their own good, and the good of their respective colonies, they should not take nonwhite partners.[17]

Laws, however, were not all that kept the races apart. David H. Fowler provides a good synopsis of some of the other obstacles that would have to be overcome before they might mix freely.

> There were, in addition to striking differences in physical appearance, great cultural disparities between the two races. The Indians spoke languages strange to Europeans, had neither a technology advanced beyond the Stone Age nor a literature, depended on hunting and fishing more than crop cultivation for subsistence, and often appeared to the colonists as unpredictable, treacherous, cruel, and dirty. The fact that the aborigines were also pagans was a cultural difference of great importance to the Christian newcomers.[18]

These "cultural disparities," which were clearly delineated in many of the popular captivity narratives of the period where great emphasis was often placed on the apparent savagery of the Indians, were too much for many European colonists. And there was also the added, equally potent fear that for the Christian involved this sort of mixing was sinful no matter what the circumstances.

Miscegenation fears were often expressed in terms of the presumably horrible results. The 1705 Massachusetts law was entitled "An Act for the Better Preventing of a Spurious and Mixt Issue." The 1691 Virginia law, specifying "that for the time to come whatsoever English or white man or woman being free shall intermarry with a Negro, mulatto, or Indian man or woman, bound or free, shall within three months thereafter be banished and removed from the dominion forever," was similarly put in place "for the prevention of that abominable mixture and spurious issue which may hereafter increase in this dominion."[19] Such sentiments express another reason why intermarriage, and indeed all sexual intercourse between the races had to be banned. The relationship itself was bad enough, but the thought of the issue that might be produced by such unions was even more alarming.

Although this was the majority view, in fact some of the most prominent of the early Virginia settlers had looked upon the Pocahontas-Rolfe marriage as an extremely positive event. Alexander Whitaker calls the conversion and marriage of Pocahontas the best thing to have happened in the colony.[20] Dale himself mentions that "she lives civilly and lovingly with him [Rolfe], and I trust will increase in goodnesse, as the knowledge of God increaseth in her"; about her conversion he states, "were it but the gayning of this one soule, I will thinke my time, toile, and present stay well spent."[21] And William Alexander, writing in 1630, eight years after the massacre of 1622, is even more effusive, although he makes a strange error concerning the place of Pocahontas in the Powhatan royal family. He states that the peace in the early Virginia colony had been ensured by "a Marriage of their Kings sister with one of the Co-lonie."[22] As Karen Ordahl Kupperman points out, "Alexander wrote praising the Rolfe-Pocahontas marriage precisely because he hoped intermarriage would erase distinctions and 'by admitting equalitie remove contempt.' "[23]

The possibility even existed for a second intermarriage during the first years of the Jamestown colony, but, according to Ralph Hamor, it was Powhatan who refused to sanction that next proposed union. The emperor would not give his consent for a second, younger daughter to be married to an Englishman.[24] In this case, however, the "groom" would have been Governor Dale himself, who already had a English wife and children. Hamor, while reporting from the English perspective, perhaps unwittingly convinces his readers of the love of Powhatan for his daughter, as well as of the purely political motivations of Dale; he makes clear that material advantages, rather than love, were all that were at stake for the English.

The issue of intermarriage becomes central to considerations of the Pocahontas material in the eighteenth century. The first serious attempt to reproduce the Pocahontas narrative from the primary documents is contained in Robert Beverley's *History and Present State of Virginia* (1705). Here the reader is introduced to the princess by a report of her kidnapping by Captain Samuel Argall, but this is followed, later in the same sentence, by the news of her marriage to Rolfe, "which *Powhatan* taking to be a sincere Token of Friendship, he vouchsafed to consent to it, and to conclude a Peace."[25] This gives Beverley the opportunity to digress on the subject of intermar-riage, and his comments were to become the model for many later chroniclers.

> Intermarriage had been indeed the Method proposed very often by the *Indians* in the Beginning, urging it frequently as a certain Rule, that the *English* were not their Friends, if they refused it. And I can't but think it wou'd have been happy for that Coun-try, had they embraced this Proposal: For, the Jealousie of the *Indians*, which I take to be the Cause of most of the Rapines and Murders they committed, wou'd by this Means have been altogether prevented, . . . the Colony, instead of all these Losses of Men on both Sides, wou'd have been increasing in Children to its Advantage; . . . and, in all Likelihood, many, if not most, of the *Indians* would have been converted to Christianity by this kind Method; the Country would have been full of People, by

the Preservation of the many *Christians* and *Indians* that fell in the Wars between them.[26]

In Beverley's terms, it is the "Jealousie of the *Indians*" that is at the root of their violent actions. Like Alexander's "contempt," this type of bad feeling between the two peoples is what intermarriage could have overcome.

Beverley allows John Smith himself to tell the story of his Rescue and of the other beneficent deeds of Pocahontas toward the colony by reproducing the letter he ostensibly wrote to "introduce" Pocahontas to Queen Anne. After a brief account of the princess's life in England, Beverley ends his section on Pocahontas with a remark about her descendants: "She left Issue one Son, nam'd *Thomas Rolfe*, whose Posterity is at this Day in good Repute in *Virginia*."[27] Beverley's comment on the character of her family is one of the earliest instances of what became a customary bow to her many powerful descendants.

In Beverley's *History,* the material about the marriage of Pocahontas and Rolfe and the notice of her descendants form a frame around Smith's letter, which itself takes up almost three pages in Louis B. Wright's modern edition of the text. The importance of the idea of intermarriage here is emphasized by its placement at the beginning of Beverley's remarks, by the reference to the issue of the marriage at their end, and by the fact that Beverley takes the time to digress from his *History* to expand on the general idea of intermarriage. This aspect of the Pocahontas narrative allowed Beverley and many of the eighteenth-century historians who followed him to editorialize on the "Indian question," which was a constant concern of the political leaders of the period. The particular, highly successful marriage of Pocahontas and Rolfe had provided the early colonists with an opportunity that they failed to grasp, and by the eighteenth century was providing historians with the opportunity to discuss this wonderful chance that had been missed at the beginning of the colonial enterprise. In these remarks Beverley also became the first commentator to deflect the blame for contemporary conflicts between Indians and whites from his own generation back to the original founders. He thereby attempted to alleviate the guilt occasioned by the perceived need to carry out alternative, usually violent, strategies against the Indians in his own day.

This discussion of Pocahontas and Rolfe also allowed Beverley to point out what had become the critical difference between their marriage and other such relationships. Her son, and his descendants, were highly visible and in "good Repute," whereas others of "mixed blood," especially the products of contemporaneous interracial un-

ions, were by definition and by law "spurious issue." The early Anglo-American interpreters of the Pocahontas narrative, out of respect
for her actions as well as her "royal" status, consistently felt this need
to celebrate her family and thereby to segregate it from the offspring
of other similar but less "noble" unions.

Perhaps the most influential addition that Beverley makes to the
Pocahontas narrative is his description of the strong reaction of
James I to the marriage of Pocahontas and Rolfe.

> Upon all which Occasions she [Pocahontas] behaved her self
> with so much Decency, and show'd so much Grandure in her
> Deportment, that she made good the brightest Part of the Char-
> acter Capt. *Smith* had given of her. In Body, so much that the
> poor Gentleman her Husband had like to have been call'd to
> an Account for presuming to marry a Princess Royal without the
> King's Consent; because it had been suggested that he [Rolfe]
> had taken Advantage of her being a Prisoner, and forc'd her to
> marry him. But upon a more perfect Representation of the Mat-
> ter, his Majesty was pleased at last to declare himself satisfied.[28]

This anecdote is probably based on Smith's comment, in his letter
to Queen Anne, that Pocahontas should be treated well in England
because "this Kingdom [England] may rightly have a Kingdom by
her Means."[29] Beverley presents King James as becoming angry when
he heard that the commoner John Rolfe had had the audacity to
marry the lady Rebecca, princess of Virginia. Presumably the English
king was offended at this apparent corruption of the "royal blood"
of America, but beneath this lay a different fear – that Rolfe or his
half-Indian son might assume the title to the new lands through the
royal side of the family. Nothing comes of this – Rolfe does not claim
Virginia for his son, nor does the English king, "upon a more perfect
Representation of the Matter," choose to press charges – but this
interesting anecdote was appropriated and enhanced by later re-
corders of Virginia, colonial, and ultimately U.S. history.[30]

Some twenty-three years after Beverley's *History*, William Byrd
clearly defined the three crucial aspects of intermarriage that would
become central to those who would nostalgically muse about such
unions in this now famous passage from his *History of the Dividing
Line*.

> They had now made peace with the Indians, but there was one
> thing wanting to make that peace lasting. The natives could by
> no means persuade themselves that the English were heartily
> their friends so long as they disdained to intermarry with them.
> And, in earnest, had the English consulted their own security

and the good of the colony, had they intended either to civilize or convert these gentiles, they would have brought their stomachs to embrace this prudent alliance. . . .

Besides, the poor Indians would have had less reason to complain that the English took away their land if they received it by way of a portion with their daughters. Had such affinities been contracted in the beginning, how much bloodshed had been prevented and how populous would the country have been, and, consequently, how considerable! Nor would the shade of skin have been any reproach at this day, for if a Moor may be washed white in three generations, surely an Indian might have been blanched in two.[31]

Although Byrd does not mention Pocahontas and Rolfe specifically, he certainly would have known of their marriage, and his analysis here is apparently a wish that what had been gained by their particular intermingling of the races could have been achieved on a larger scale. In any case, he suggests that intermarriage would have helped to sustain the fragile peace, would have made the acquisition of Indian lands much easier, and could possibly have brought about a "blanching" of the Indians' skin. Presumably, with their shade of skin would have gone both the Indian culture and what had come to be thought of as "savagery," which often referred as much to what would have been considered a "savage" attitude as it did to the actual performance of any real actions.

Roy Harvey Pearce, in his discussion of Adam Ferguson's *Essay on the History of Civil Society*, clarifies the European position as a need to believe "that men in becoming civilized had gained much more than they had lost; and that civilization, the act of civilizing, for all of its destruction of primitive virtues, put something higher and greater in their place."[32] Although some of these "primitive virtues" would be necessary for the success of the westward migration, and romantic white figures such as Daniel Boone and later Natty Bumppo would come to be identified with them, these men would themselves always be outsiders who were unable to come to terms with the civilized world. For most Anglo-Americans, however, the savagery that apparently lurked on their borders, while it was more often sensed than directly experienced, needed to be eradicated. It seemed reasonable to many in the eighteenth century that civilizing the Indians would put an end to the threat (if not the idea) of savagery, and that interbreeding would have been a fairly painless way of accomplishing this task. If the races had interbred from the outset, then all that was savage would have begun to fade, and might perhaps have disappeared over the course of a few generations. And if this practice

had become standard on the frontier, it would have removed the
constant threat of armed reprisals from the Indians as the Europeans
moved westward.

Intermarriage would also have been an orderly and apparently
legitimate way to acquire Indian lands. There was no doubt that
certain Indian tribes owned, in a European sense, particular parcels
of land.[33] As Francis Paul Prucha points out, one of the problems
that the new Americans faced after the Revolution was to find ways
to "extinguish in an orderly way the Indian title to the land so that
the expanding settlements might find unencumbered room."[34] Intermarriage, as Byrd suggests, between white men and Indian
"daughters," would have allowed for these lands to be acquired and
ultimately cultivated, as many Anglo-Americans believed God had
intended.

In fact, the idea that incorporation through intermarriage might
work as a strategy for land acquisition was based on an incomplete
knowledge of the Indian sense of landownership. The Anglo-
American understanding was that, although whole tribes certainly
did control certain territories, no individual Indian believed that anyone could actually own the soil itself. If Indian tradition did not
recognize private ownership of lands held communally by the group,
then tribe members would not feel the need to lay claim to such
lands after the death of a chief or other tribal leader. If an intermarriage had occurred, however, and the offspring had been raised
"English," the white side of the family could be waiting to take control of any newly "available" properties. All that apparently needed
to be done was to have white men marry Indian women who were
in a position to inherit such lands. Clearly we are talking here about
Indian "princesses," and the only widely known "Indian princess"
in the eighteenth century was Pocahontas. Indeed, in her life we
find a model scenario for this type of belief, in that a peace, though
short-lived, had been achieved through her marriage; she, her child,
and their descendants had become "civilized"; and the former "wilderness" home of her people was by the early eighteenth century
firmly under English control.

John Smith had first implied that a strategy of land acquisition
through inheritance might work in his letter to Queen Anne, and
Beverley would have us believe that James I also thought that acquisition through inheritance was a possibility. John Oldmixon, in the
1741 edition of his history, *The British Empire in America,* provides
another example of the belief that Indian lands could have been
handed down to mixed-bloods and their ultimately white progeny.
He first comments on the failure of the policy of intermarriage,
which, "was proposed at the time as a sure means of continuing the

Peace with the *Indians*."[35] Oldmixon is not clear about who first made this proposal, but he infers that it was the Indians, as we are then told that "the *English* were not fond of taking *Indian* Women to their Beds as Wives" – this even though, "By *Powhatan's* Alliance with the *English*, and Mr. *Rolfe's* marrying an *Indian* Princess, a great Nation were made Friends to the Colony."[36] He concludes his section on Pocahontas with this brief word about her descendants. "She had one Son by Mr. *Rolfe*, whose Posterity are at this Day in good Repute in *Virginia*, and inherit Lands by descent from her."[37] If her progeny were in good repute, then clearly they were no longer savages, and if they had inherited their lands from her, surely other children of such marriages could inherit the lands originally belonging to the Indian side of their families as well. Oldmixon's comment about inheritance, which is not in the 1708 edition of *The British Empire in America*, also validates the great wealth and position achieved by many of her descendants during the early part of the eighteenth century.[38] The fact that it was through Pocahontas that they acquired both the seeds of their great fortunes and their aristocratic place in colonial society served to legitimize their status.

The Reverend Peter Fontaine of Virginia, in a letter to his brother Moses, dated March 30, 1757, first blames the English monarchy's treatment of John Rolfe for the lack of intermarriages early in the colony's history.

> Now, to answer your first query – whether by our breach of treaties we have not justly exasperated the bordering nations of Indians against us, and drawn upon ourselves the barbarous usage we meet with from them and the French? . . . I shall only hint at some things which we ought to have done, and which we did not do at our first settlement amongst them, and which we might have learnt long since from the practice of our enemies the French. I am persuaded we were not deficient in the observation of treaties, but as we got the land by concession, and not by conquest, we ought to have intermarried with them, which would have incorporated us with them effectually, and made of them staunch friends, and, which is of still more consequence, made many of them good Christians; but this our wise politicians at home [in England] put an effectual stop to at the beginning of our settlement here, for when they heard that Rolfe married Pocahontas, it was deliberated in Council, whether he had not committed high treason by doing so, that is, marrying an Indian Princess; and had some troubles not intervened which put a stop to the inquiry, the poor man might have been hanged up for doing the most just, the most natural,

the most generous and politic action that ever was done this
side of the water. This put an effectual stop to all intermarriages
afterwards.[39]

Here we see what by mid-century had become a fairly standard rendition of the opportunity that had been missed by the early settlers.
Fontaine also uses the incident created by Beverley to put forward
another possible reason for the lack of intermarriages following that
of Rolfe and Pocahontas. He would have Moses believe that no other
Englishman would place himself in the kind of jeopardy that Rolfe
did, and so now those in the colonies, white and Indian, are suffering
the consequences.

Fontaine goes on, though, and soon gets to the heart of his argument. He points out why Indian-white intermarriage should not
necessarily be seen as problematic, as well as what would be gained
by such alliances.

But here methinks I can hear you observe, What! Englishmen
intermarry with Indians? But I can convince you that they are
guilty of much more heinous practices, more unjustifiable in
the sight of God and man . . . for many base wretches amongst
us take up with negro women, by which means the country
swarms with mulatto bastards, and these mulattoes, if but three
generations removed from the black father or mother, may, by
the indulgence of the laws of the country, intermarry with the
white people, and actually do every day so marry. Now, if instead
of this abominable practice which hath polluted the blood of
many amongst us, we had taken Indian wives in the first place,
it would have made them some compensation for their lands.
They are a free people, and the offspring would not be born in
a state of slavery. We should become rightful heirs to their lands,
and should not have smutted our blood, for the Indian children
when born are as white as Spanish or Portuguese, and were it
not for the practice of going naked, in the summer and be-
smearing themselves with bears' grease, etc., they would continue white; and had we thought fit to make them our wives,
they would readily have complied with our fashion of wearing
clothes all the year round; and by doing justice to these poor
benighted heathen, we should have introduced Christianity
amongst them. Your own reflections upon these hints will be a
sufficient answer to your first query. I shall only add that General Johnson's success was owing, under God, to his fidelity to
the Indians, and his generous conduct to his Indian wife, by
whom he hath several hopeful sons, who are all war-captains,

the bulwarks with him of the five nations, and loyal subjects to their mother country.[40]

Fontaine speaks here of Sir William Johnson of New York, who was largely responsible for keeping the Iroquois nations on the English side during the French and Indian War. His wife was Molly Brant, a Mohawk woman and sister of Joseph Brant of Revolutionary War fame.

Good colonial Virginian that he was, Fontaine argues that one should differentiate between the offspring of Indian-white unions and those of the black-white relationships that he sees around him. He contends that rather than shun the offspring of the former mixture, we should look proudly on those like Thomas Rolfe and his descendants, who were prominent citizens of Fontaine's home state of Virginia, and the sons of General Johnson, who at that moment were fighting for England against the French and their Indian allies. (One could debate about whether they were really fighting for their "mother country.") If nothing else, he saw these beings as far preferable to the "mulatto bastards" who often go on to "smut" the "blood" of the white race. Fontaine's case is that the progeny of Indian-white relationships would quickly become members of the Anglo-American culture, both in color and in political affiliation, and he stresses what he believes to be the qualitative differences between them and the children of black-white unions. Pocahontas and Rolfe are again the model for a successful intermarriage, and her descendants, like the sons of General Johnson, prove that assimilation was originally, and to Fontaine possibly was still, a viable option, although it clearly would have been best had such relationships been encouraged from the beginning of the colonial enterprise.

Another reason used to explain the lack of intermarriages was that prejudices may have come to exist on the Indian as well as the English side. This is suggested by William Robertson in his presentation of the Pocahontas material in *A History of the Discovery and Settlement of America* (1796). As we have seen, Robert Beverley had spoken of the "Jealousie of the *Indians*" that resulted from the English refusing to intermarry with them.[41] Robertson expands on this idea.

> But notwithstanding the visible good effects of that alliance [Pocahontas and Rolfe], none of Rolfe's countrymen seem to have imitated the example, which he set them, of marrying with the natives. Of all the Europeans who have settled in America, the English have availed themselves the least of this obvious method of conciliating the affection of its original inhabitants. . . . The Indians, courting such a union, offered their daughters in marriage to their new guests: and when they did not accept of the

proffered alliance, they naturally imputed it to pride, and to their contempt of them as an inferior order of beings.[42]

Robertson restates here the idea that the Indians of the period of the first contacts with the English were able to perceive the racist attitudes of the colonists through their refusal to intermarry. As had been first suggested by William Alexander, Robertson would have his readers believe that this "contempt" shown by the British engendered any subsequent animosity on the part of the Indians.

By reaffirming that the racism of the eighteenth century was based, at least in part, on that of the early founders of the colony, Robertson allows for the type of reappraisal of the human species that was taking place in his own day. Anthropologists like Samuel Stanhope Smith were reconsidering the relative attributes of the races and concluding that what colonists perceived as Indian inferiority was not inherent but resulted from their circumstances and environment. Even Thomas Jefferson got involved in this debate. In his attempt to refute the Count de Buffon in *Notes on the State of Virginia,* Jefferson takes great care with his answer to Buffon's charge that the species of the New World are not as highly developed as those found in Europe. Included in Jefferson's argument is a defense of the Indian; he points out that when the all of the facts are in, "we shall probably find that they are formed in mind as well as in body, on the same module with the 'Homo sapiens Europaeus.' "[43] Robertson drives home the point that it was the first English colonists who formed the racist opinions, and he thereby leaves the door open for the enlightened Americans of his own day to refute both the old colonial prejudices and the contemporary continental racist theories in one blow. While doing so, he too mentions the single son of Pocahontas and Rolfe, and quotes Virginia historian William Stith's version of the standard, brief description of their aristocratic descendants.[44]

It was Thomas Jefferson and his followers in the early nineteenth century who were the last to speak of an amalgamation of the races as a real possibility. In 1808, in an effort to convince them of the suitability of their adopting Anglo-American laws and agricultural practices, the president told a visiting part of Delawares, Mohicans, and Munries, "you will mix with us by marriage, your blood will run in our veins, and will spread with us over this great island."[45] As the whites spread out over the continent the Indians will be with them, but, interestingly, they will be *inside* of them, in the blood, rather than *beside* them. Jefferson also wrote of the Indians to Benjamin Hawkins, "the ultimate point of rest and happiness for them is to let our settlements and theirs meet and blend together, to intermix, and become one

people. Incorporating themselves with us as citizens of the United
States, this is what the natural progress of things will of course, bring
on, and it will be better to promote than retard it.''[46] His words here
recall a more famous document, where he states that sometimes "in
the course of human events, it becomes necessary for one people to
dissolve the political bands which have connected them with another.''[47] Jefferson's point in both cases is that such blendings and dis-
solutions are part of a natural historical progression. They will work
themselves out in their own manner and time and are in many ways
completely beyond human control. Therefore, because this combin-
ing of the Indian and white races will eventually happen, it can be
speculated about without anyone having to take any concrete steps toward its fruition in the present. The ultimate result of such a mixture,
of course, would be the creation of a white, landowning race, the
members of which would possess an Indian presence "in the blood,"
and perhaps even certain attractive Indian character traits, but would
for all intents and purposes be Caucasian.[48] The Enlightenment fantasy of absorption would actually be nothing less than a quiet geno-
cide of the native population, which would ultimately be more
effective than any military campaign.

Jefferson's inconsistent responses to the Indian question signal a
failure to come to grips with the present situation, while showing an
urgent need to alleviate the guilt that this situation causes. Just as
Jefferson attempted to allay the guilt over the rebellion of the colonies in this manner in the Declaration of Independence, so he
similarly attempted to allay some of the national guilt over the destruction of many of the eastern Indian tribes by positing an amalgamation of Indians and whites at some point in the probably distant
future. He makes such a mixture the custody of the future, as the
eighteenth-century historians had made it the custody of the past,'
but either way, there was clearly no time for it in the present.

At the turn of the nineteenth century, as Americans became more
sure of themselves and their national destiny, many such apparently
humanitarian suggestions concerning Indian-white relations were
similarly relegated to the past or the future.[49] When the Indians had
to be dealt with immediately, force was still the method of choice. The
need for land for the exploding Anglo-American population had become much more immediate, and the Louisiana Purchase, though in
the long run meant to provide new lands for white settlement, provided a wonderful short-term answer to the Indian question. The Indians could simply be moved out into these vast open spaces, out of
contact with the civilized world, and therefore away from any whites
other than explorers and "mountain men." This must have seemed
to be an excellent solution, because land "trades," which of course

paid no attention to the inseparability of tribal lands and tribal life, soon became a feature of most treaties, with the threat of an armed alternative, however terrible it might be for all concerned, lending a great deal of weight to the white side of any bargaining. There was no longer the need to think about an actual incorporation of the Indians, and intermarriage, with its advantage of the seemingly legitimate appropriation of Indian lands, was too great a sacrifice when the natives could simply be pushed out of the way or otherwise forcibly removed. Dispossession was clearly a much quicker, and a much more sure, way of being rid of the Indians, as one did not have to wait two or three generations to see its result.

A second, more subtle, factor that contributed to the end of the idea of intermarriage as a solution to the Indian problem was the loss of the example of Pocahontas, whose crucial role in American lore was in the process of shifting from "wife of Rolfe" to "savior of Smith." In her former persona Pocahontas was an ideal model for nostalgic, pro-intermarriage sentiments, but as the nineteenth century progressed, the birth of Thomas Rolfe, the most positively portrayed representative of the issue of a successful mixing of the races, had steadily begun to be relegated to the status of a minor incident in her life, when it was mentioned at all. John Smith had emerged as an American hero shortly after the birth of the new nation, and by the first decade of the nineteenth century, with the publishing of the first admittedly fictional versions of her story by John Davis and the production of James Nelson Barker's *The Indian Princess,* the first of the "Pocahontas dramas," the emphasis in representations of her narrative had begun a relentless shift.[50] Her role as an actual mother and ancestor gave way to her persona as a mythic protector, which she gained by demonstration rather than procreation.

Her saving of Smith grows to be paramount, to the point where whatever happened afterward in the narrative becomes at best anticlimactic, and at worst the spoiling of this romantic, exemplary fable. In fact, by 1804 John Burk can discuss how her marriage to Rolfe rather than to Smith might lead one to disbelieve the entire narrative. The truth comes to haunt the Pocahontas story, and what should provide the most solid evidence of its believability, in that descendants of their marriage abounded, now gives it the aura of a badly conceived romance.

> Indeed, there is ground for apprehension, that posterity in reading this part of American history, will be inclined to consider the story of Pocahontas, as an interesting romance. . . . It is not even improbable, that, considering every thing related to cap-

tain Smith and Pocahontas as a mere fiction, they may vent their spleen against the historian, for impairing the interest of his plot, by marrying the princess of Powhatan to a Mr. Rolfe, of whom nothing had previously been said, in defiance of all the expectations raised by the foregoing parts of the fable.[51]

The marriage to Rolfe adds doubt, rather than veracity, to the narrative. Burk's sense is that those who will read the more romantic accounts of the story, which heighten the drama and elevate the characters beyond the bounds of common humanity – accounts very much like that composed by Burk himself – will be disappointed by the ending. As the events of her life began to assume the status of a folk tale, the failure of Smith and Pocahontas to live happily ever after became in some ways the narrative's greatest weakness.

Richard Slotkin has made the point that "the most potent recurring hero-figures in our mythologies are men in whom contradictory identities find expression: the white man with a knowledge of the Indians, the outlaw who makes himself an agent of justice or even of law."[52] He could easily have included in this group the "good Indian," who, though maintaining his or her exotic qualities, somehow discerns the correctness or inevitability of white conquest of America. Rayna Green describes this type of individual as an Indian who "acts as a friend to the white man, offering them aid, rescue, and spiritual and physical comfort even at the cost of his own life or status and comfort in his own tribe to do so. He saves white men from 'bad' Indians, and thus becomes a 'good' Indian."[53]

During this period the figure of Pocahontas becomes one of the great representations of the good Indian, and as her story is retold, her early actions rather than her later choices begin to be stressed. Indeed, one could argue that her relegation to the camp of the literary good Indian, at the cost of the actual woman who, perhaps under some duress, did ultimately choose English culture over that of her own people, can be seen as something of a diminishing of her actions. This generic "goodness" removes the power of choice from her, and when she becomes simply a representation of a good Indian – the quality almost taking precedence over the racial identification – those telling her story with confident hindsight remove any doubt as to her "choice." Whether Pocahontas was portrayed as having abandoned savagery, or perhaps as having never really been a savage at all, she ultimately came to be seen as the great alternative to those of her race who would slow the settlement of the new nation. As Angie Debo, one of the great historians of the American Indian, put it, in early America, "except for Pocahontas, the gap between opposing life ways was too vast to be bridged by giving the Indians Christianity, education, and vocational training, at least by the method conceived at the time."[54] The Powhatan princess was always the exception; there was never any real possibility that in her marriage to Rolfe she could have served as an effective exemplar.[55]

As has been mentioned, a customary feature of many of the eighteenth-century constructions of the Pocahontas narrative was a mention of her descendants. Interest in them was such that Benjamin Latrobe, having traced the family lineage during a visit to the home of William and Rebecca (Bolling) Murray in 1796, worked his notes into a paper that he presented to the American Philosophical Society in February 1803.[56] In his earlier *Journal* account, after commenting humorously on the astonishing increase in the ratio of living to dead descendants, Latrobe chooses an interesting way of telling his readers about what he sees as the virtues of the family.

> Should Monarchy and its concomitant, *Nobility of blood,* ever come again into fashion in this Country, an event which at this moment is most seriously apprehended by, and disturbs the sleep of many of our *good citizens,* I hope the blood of Powhatan will not be neglected, unless the great good sense, and merit of many of his descendants whom I know, should be thought less necessary to a man of title, than to a plain commoner.[57]

Latrobe, like his contemporary Samuel Stanhope Smith, continues the genealogy past Pocahontas to her father, and he attributes a type of "common" nobility to this family, which he ironically comments might not be appropriate to the traditional European monarch. This type of sentiment was not unusual where the descendants of Pocahontas were concerned. As James Kirke Paulding put it some years later, when writing about John Randolph and Bolling Robertson, "if I were to choose a pedigree for myself, I would prefer this to a descent from any one of William the Conqueror's barons, or William the Conqueror himself."[58]

The descendants of Pocahontas are generally said to be at least "in good repute" but often are given more extensive praise, to the point where Burk can summarize what he sees as the dominant attributes of the family. Burk points out that while no great generals, artists, or statesmen have emerged from her heirs, "the virtues of mildness and humanity, so eminently distinguished in Pocahontas, remain in the nature of an inheritance to her posterity."[59] In attempting to find a way to explain why no great political figures had emerged from the family (a statement that no doubt would have brought some disagreement from various members of the Randolph

clan), Burk does so in terms of their wealth: "affluent circumstances
... generally take away the motive to exertion and enterprize."[60]
Theirs, of course, is the rare family about whom enough information
was extant for such generalizations to be made. Discussions of the
founding of Jamestown had almost universally included a mention
of Pocahantas's marriage and an acknowledgment of her descendants, who "boast of their descent from the race of the ancient
rulers of their country."[61] And while one could of course argue that
it was their position in colonial and early national society that ensured the positive mentions of her descendants, there can be no
doubt about the importance of Pocahontas to their aristocratic
standing.

It is therefore hardly surprising that colonial lawmakers conveniently chose to ignore, or at best forget, Pocahontas, Rolfe, and their
descendants when they were formulating their antimiscegenation
legislation. The intermarriage aspect of the Pocahontas narrative
was, however, to play a role in the rescinding and revising of some
of these statutes. When George Brandburn addressed the Massachusetts House of Representatives in 1841 as one of the speakers for a
petition put forward by William Ellery Channing, among others, to
repeal the Massachusetts miscegenation laws, it is Pocahontas and a
well-known but unnamed descendant (John Randolph) whom he
invokes: "One of America's most distinguished orators and statesmen was accustomed to boast that he owed his birth to the union
of Pocahontas and a certain Anglo-American, – a union from which,
history tells us, have 'descended some respectable families of Virginia.' "[62] And there can be no doubt about who was in mind when
"An Act to Preserve Racial Integrity" was passed by the Virginia
Assembly in 1924. The following curious definition testifies to the
intent of those who authored this bill:

> It shall hereafter be unlawful for any white person in this State
> to marry any save a white person, or a person with no admixture
> of blood than white and American Indian. For the purpose of
> this act, the term "white person" shall apply only to the person
> who has no trace whatsoever of any blood other than Caucasian;
> but persons who have one-sixteenth or less of the blood of the
> American Indian and have no other non-Caucasian blood shall
> be deemed to be white persons.[63]

The Virginia statue was written in this way for the sole purpose of
ensuring that the descendants of Pocahontas would be classified as
white.[64] Writing in 1966, Walter Wadlington noted, however, that
"If John Rolfe and Pocahontas were to be married in Virginia today,
they would probably be guilty of a felony. . . . Moreover, their chil-

dren might be unable to marry white persons. . . . It is also possible that their children would be considered illegitimate."[65] (The Virginia miscegenation laws were not repealed until 1968.)[66]

Although John Rolfe is an important player in some nineteenth-century renditions of the Pocahontas narrative, such as Charlotte Barnes's drama *The Forest Princess* and Mary Jane Windle's novel *Life At The White Sulpher Springs*, for the most part the emphasis in later versions focuses on the heroic/romantic relationship between Pocahontas and John Smith.[67] Rolfe is generally a tangential character, who, even when he is permitted to stay onstage long enough to assume the role of the love interest of the princess, is rarely an important protagonist. His contribution to the resolution of most antebellum texts, other than as a prospective match, is generally minimal. And while he remains important to his descendants, any national significance that Rolfe may have had fades, to the point where, in the early twentieth century, Vachel Lindsay, speaking for the dominant Anglo-American society, can categorically state:

> John Rolfe is not our ancestor.
> We rise from out the soul of her
> Held in native wonderland,
> While the sun's rays kissed her hand,
> In the springtime,
> In Virginia,
> Our Mother, Pocahontas. (I, 27–33)[68]

From time to time during the antebellum period, however, Pocahontas still appeared, as in Brandburn's speech, in her role as family matriarch. Herman Melville, who had twice mentioned the comments of "John Randolph of Roanoke" in his examination of the conditions aboard a man-of-war in *White-Jacket* and had invoked the Randolphs as one of the three "old established" families in "Loomings," returns to this clan in his discussion of American genealogies at the beginning of *Pierre*.[69] When speaking of the great age of some native families, Melville makes sure to include "the old and oriental-like English planter families of Virginia and the South; the Randolphs for example, one of whose ancestors, in King James's time, married Pocahontas the Indian Princess, and in whose blood therefore an underived aboriginal royalty was flowing over two hundred years ago."[70] Although he is a bit off in his dating of when the Randolphs married into the family, Melville, as suggested by his use of the Randolphs in *Moby-Dick* and *Pierre*, saw them as a noteworthy "old family" whose antiquity was based, at least in part, on their link to Pocahontas and *her* ancestors.

Another such case is in Ebenezer Baldwin's 1834 treatise, *Obser-*

vations on the Physical, Intellectual, and Moral Qualities of Our Colored Population. In the following passage Baldwin discusses the problematic nature of cultural interrelations between the races.

> No amalgamation producing a unity of feeling and identity of interest, can take place, until difference of complexion is obliterated by inter-marriage. It need hardly be said that this plan is not feasible, even if it were desirable. . . . And yet the derelish for Indian alliances is by no means as strong as exists in regard to Africans. The *Randolphs* of Virginia are proud of the blood of *Pocahontas,* and their white kindred do not feel ashamed to acknowledge the descendants of *Eunice Williams.*[71]

(Eunice Williams was a young woman who had been taken captive by the Mohawk Indians, with whom she apparently led a happy, productive life. Her story is one of the sources of the Faith-Oneco subplot of Catharine M. Sedgwick's *Hope Leslie.*) Baldwin, like Peter Fontaine, differentiates between Indian-white and black-white relations, and interestingly theorizes that the physical differences among all three races will have to be broken down before the cultural aspects of assimilation can be addressed.

It is ironic that in Baldwin's day such an "obliteration" was occurring among the Pamunkeys, Pocahontas's own people. Helen C. Rountree, in *Pocahontas's People,* the second of her two fascinating studies of Powhatan Indian culture, points out that "By 1830 the core people among the Powhatans had Anglicized so much that they were no longer easily recognizable to outsiders as 'real' – that is, pre-Contact – aborigines."[72] "Father William" reports that by 1854, "Few of them deserve the name of Indians, so mingled are they with other nations by intermarriage. Some are partly African, others European, or rather, I should say Virginian . . . it [the settlement] is inhabited by the most curious intermixture of every color and class of people."[73] And by 1894 J. G. Pollard could state: "No member of the Pamunkey tribe is of full blood. While the copper colored skin and straight coarse hair of the aboriginal American shows decidedly in some individuals, there are others whose Indian origin would not be detected by the ordinary observer."[74] The inability of Chastellux and Smith to discern visually Pocahontas's apparently white descendants because of the dilution of her blood one hundred years before can be seen as prophetic of what would happen to some members of her tribe through the assimilation process. As of 1989, one faction of the few remaining Pamunkeys, who live on their reservation east of Richmond, Virginia – none of whom is of "full blood" – were fighting to keep control of their traditional, male-dominated culture in the face of pressures from within as well as outside the tribe. As

Chief William Miles assessed the situation, "I think we'll change. I think we have to change. If we don't, we're going to totally disappear even faster."[75] It is interesting to read his comments and then take note of the huge hardbound volume of *Pocahontas' Descendants,* to which two supplements have now been added.[76] Many thousands of people, the great majority of them white, are proud to be able to prove their ancestry from Pocahontas, and therefore from Powhatan, whereas the guardians of Powhatan's gravesite are in a constant battle to maintain their cultural heritage.

In 1800 John Davis, a young Englishman traveling in America, published his second work of fiction. *The Farmer of New-Jersey; or, A Picture of Domestic Life,* tells the story of a Mr. Cheeseman and his family. Cheeseman, a former American patriot and soldier, is also the narrator of the story. He and his brood lead a delightful family life on "a pleasant spot of twenty-five acres" on the Hudson River. This domestic bliss, which ultimately would be put to the test, and the life of a country farmer are the main subjects of this short novel. At the outset Davis describes a Christmas dinner in the Cheeseman home, after which the assembled group, which include the host's family and that of his neighbor, Colonel Brandywine, gather around the turf fire. It is proposed and accepted that stories be told to pass the evening, and the narrator's young son Harry begins with a fanciful version of the rescue of John Smith, in which "Pocahuntas" is described as an "Indian queen," and Smith is to be burned at the stake before her intervention. As the boy finishes his tale, Colonel Brandywine offers what seems an odd toast: " 'Bravissimo!' cried colonel Brandywine. 'Here is a health to the descendants of the tender Pocahuntas.' "[77]

Harry's story, of course, had nothing to do with her descendants, but at the turn of the new century her persona as a matriarch was still an important aspect of her character, and Davis, who had already toured Virginia and the Federal District and would be visiting again soon, perhaps thought it best to pay this brief homage to some of the more wealthy and powerful families of the Tidewater region. He was only beginning to mine the Pocahontas narrative, however, and in the next few years Davis would be the primary agent in the removal of her story from the exclusive purview of historians.

It did not take Davis long to realize that the Rescue segment of the narrative had a great deal of potential and, in the right hands, could be the seed of a wonderful romance. As we shall see, his attempt to create one in his *Travels* and his subsequent embellishings of the tale in *Captain Smith and Princess Pocahontas* and *The First Settlers of Virginia* were the first American versions of the story to focus on the love of Pocahontas for Smith as the explanation for her surprising actions. These texts led the way for the prodigious number of romantic reconstructions of the narrative in the nineteenth century.

This change that Davis originates, which refocuses the emphasis of the narrative from living to literary memorials of the princess, could only have been successfully effected after the Revolution, when Americans had begun to scan the colonial past in search of figures like Pocahontas and Smith who could be rewarded retroactively for their proto-nationalist sentiments. There had to be a United States of America before the ultimate implications of the Rescue could be recognized and before her individual act of rebellion and sacrifice could be seen as a saving of, and even a precedent for, the citizens of the new nation. In Chapter 2 we shall see how Davis seizes this apparent opportunity, attempts to create a name for himself by making something greater of the Pocahontas narrative, and thereby plays an important role in the continuing rise of American literary nationalism, as well as in beginning the era of the Romantic Indian.

THE POCAHONTAS NARRATIVE IN POST-REVOLUTIONARY AMERICA

"A monument to her memory"[1]

After the death of George Washington in December 1799, his nephew Bushrod Washington chose another great Virginian, Chief Justice John Marshall, to write the authorized biography of the hero of the Revolution and first president of the United States.[2] In *The Life of George Washington* (1804–7), Marshall includes not only events from the life of "the Father of His Country" but also a narrative of the events that foreshadowed Washington's presence on the world stage.[3] Conscious that this prefatory material might have seemed a peculiar inclusion in his biography, Marshall takes the time to explain his reasoning:

> [T]he history of general Washington, during his military command and civil administration, is so much that of his country, that the work appeared to the author to be most sensibly incomplete and unsatisfactory, while unaccompanied by such a narrative of the principal events preceding our revolutionary war, as would make the reader acquainted with the genius, character, and resources of the people about to engage in that memorable contest.[4]

Among the events in this chronology are three moments from the life of Pocahontas: her rescue of Smith, whom Marshall calls "one of the most extraordinary men of his age"; her kidnapping by "Captain Argal" [Argall]; and her marriage to "Mr. Rolf" [Rolfe], which we learn stabilized the relations between the early settlers of Virginia and the neighboring tribes.[5] Marshall presents these incidents as being crucial to the success of the Anglo-American colonial enterprise; they are necessary links in the chain that had led to the recent Revolution against England – an event that was guided by Washington, a Virginian and thereby a figurative descendant of the Jamestown planters.

Marshall also takes a moment to add a bit of editorial commentary to his description of the most famous incident of the Pocahontas narrative.

> At the place of execution, with his head bowed down to receive the blow, he [Smith] was rescued from a fate which appeared to be inevitable, by that enthusiastic and impassioned humanity which, in every climate, and in every state of society, finds its home in the female bosom. Pocahontas, the king's favourite daughter, . . . rushed between him and the executioner, and folding his head in her arms, and laying hers upon it, arrested the fatal blow.[6]

In this rendition, it is her natural "humanity," or feelings of benevolence toward all human beings, which to Marshall is present in all women, that emerges and causes her to protect the helpless prisoner. Marshall is not specific about the feeling that this humanity engendered in Pocahontas, but earlier in the first decade of the nineteenth century her emotion had been identified as romantic love by John Davis, a young British expatriate writer, who had sensed that the Rescue was the scene with the most potential interest for the growing, largely female, audience for fiction in America. In this chapter I will examine the Pocahontas period of Davis's literary career, concentrating on his *Travels In The United States of America During 1798, 1799, 1800, 1801, And 1802*. This was the text in which he first posited that it was her romantic love for Smith, rather than just a general feeling of benevolence or charity for all men, that prompted her heroic action.[7] Before examining this work, however, it will be necessary to look briefly at some earlier, post-Revolutionary War treatments of this popular narrative. I will then discuss the enhancements made by Davis and the reformulations made by a sampling of the writers who followed his lead in their own interpretations of the Rescue. In the hands of Davis and his successors, the events of the Pocahontas narrative simultaneously served to promote the cultural coalescence of the fledgling nation and to inspire a tremendous amount of literary activity. Indeed, Davis can now be seen as having provided a precocious expression of what would come to be known as American Romanticism.

After his almost fifty-page digression on the life of Pocahontas, which radically intrudes on the progress of his *Travels*, John Davis takes a moment to consider his accomplishment.

> Thus have I delivered to the world the story of *Pocahontas;* nor can I refrain from indulging in the idea, that it was reserved for my pen, to tell with discriminating circumstances, the tale of

this *Indian* girl. No Traveller before me has erected a monument to her memory, by the display of her virtues; for I would not dignify by that name the broken fragment which is to be found in the meagre page of Chastellux.[8]

From his self-congratulatory comment, we can see that Davis has little doubt about his standing as the primary purveyor of the Pocahontas story. This description of his rendition of the narrative as a "monument to her memory" would have seemed appropriate to readers of a nation whose writers, artists, and architects had become obsessed with memorializing and monument building and were busily trying to create a history for a country that was only twenty-seven-years old when Davis's *Travels* was first published. His sense of his text being a monument to the "memory" of Pocahontas, rather than to the actual woman, indicates that by the early nineteenth century the princess herself had begun to become less important than what her primary action, the saving of John Smith, had come to represent in the collective memory of the new nation. Finally, he chooses to contrast his creation not with Smith's version or with those of the eighteenth-century historians, but with the brief rendering provided by Chastellux in the Frenchman's earlier *Travels*. Davis's intent will become clear, and the ultimate success of his effort to supplant Chastellux as the most important purveyor of the Pocahontas narrative of the period will be explained by his maintaining much of what had made the chevalier's version popular, while shifting the emphasis of the tale to the emotional entanglements of the protagonists, so as to make the narrative more attractive to a wider, particularly female, audience.

This idea of a monument to Pocahontas was not original in Davis's day, however. In fact, almost seventy years earlier, an anonymous correspondent to the *Boston Gazette* had made his or her feelings on this subject quite clear.

> For my own part I don't recollect any of the celebrated Heroines of Antiquity of half so just a behaviour or that any way exceed her [Pocahontas] in virtue or true greatness of Mind. How many Statues and Medals would have been made by the *Romans* in memory of such a Lady? Not a Woman of Fashion but wou'd have had her impression on a Jewel or a Seal: To shew your selves the most Elegant of all the Settlements, you shou'd Subscribe for her STATUE, to set up in the beautifullest Places of the Publick Walks where your Company meets.[9]

Although it seems as though this individual would clearly like to see the image of princess become a subject for many of the craftsmen of his age, the close proximity of a passage from an early literary monument, Robert Beverley's *History and Present State of Virginia,* casts some doubt on the trustworthiness of these sentiments. (See my further discussion of this "letter" in Chapter 4.) The raising of such a statue would have been a fitting acknowledgment of Pocahontas's efforts on behalf on the English settlers and would have helped to promote her to what this correspondent saw as her rightful place in the public's perception.

In Davis's own day, the Virginian William Wirt, in his *Letters of the British Spy,* which purports to be letters written by a young Englishman traveling in America to a member of Parliament back home, has his mysterious correspondent note with surprise that there had yet to be any sort of public acknowledgment of the important role played by Pocahontas in the founding of Wirt's home state.

> I wonder that the Virginians, fond as they are of anniversaries, have instituted no festival or order in honor to her memory. For my own part I have little doubt, from the histories which we have of the first attempts at colonizing their country, that Pocahontas deserves to be considered as the patron deity of the enterprize. . . . [T]here is the strongest reason to believe that, but for her patronage, the anniversary cannon of the fourth of July, would never have resounded throughout the United States.[10]

This canonization of Pocahontas as a founder both of Virginia and (as her connection to the Fourth of July celebrations attests) of the nation was in part an attempt to elevate Virginia history to the stature already achieved by the narratives of the first settlers of New England. The early Puritans were by Wirt's time beginning to be acknowledged as the group that had laid the moral and intellectual groundwork for the Revolution. Virginia, however, had been the earliest successful Anglo-American settlement, as well as the state that had produced more than its share of the leading patriots, including Jefferson, Madison, Henry, Mason, and, of course, Washington, the actual leader of the revolutionary forces and first president of the United States. And since literary as well as stone, bronze, and canvas memorials were being produced to honor Washington and many of his contemporaries, it is not surprising that there was a call for similar treatment for earlier "American" heroes. Wirt wants the Virginia planters to get their due, and so it is not surprising that he has his correspondent express consternation at the lack of an appropriate festival.

It should also be mentioned that Davis had recently journeyed through Tidewater Virginia and was planning to return in the near future. It is not surprising that he describes his accomplishment as a monument when he sets out to honor the great heroine of Virginia, for he no doubt hoped to ensure cordial greetings from her wealthy descendants, and perhaps even to ensure that future efforts in this vein would meet with approval and (more importantly) sponsorship.

One reason Davis compared his composition to that of Chastellux was that in the Chevalier's *Travels* the Pocahontas narrative was presented as only a brief, tangential interlude in his lengthy journey. He had simply touched on the Pocahontas material and then continued his *Travels*. Davis, however, took the time to interrupt the course of his travel narrative to expand on this interesting tale. Chastellux also did not represent her actions as being particularly important in the history of Virginia or of the United States. Davis had realized the tremendous potential of the Pocahontas narrative for this type of interpretation and for expansion into a romance that could stand on its own. His attack on Chastellux can therefore be seen as an effort to create a space for a rendition that would join the historical importance of her life to a romantic depiction of the principal moment.

Another, more practical, reason, however, was simply that Chastellux's rendition of the Pocahontas material was the one most familiar to many early American readers and therefore represented the competition that Davis had to overcome. When the editors of the *Columbian Magazine* chose to recount the Pocahontas narrative in July 1787, they simply copied the story from the contemporary translation of Chastellux's *Travels*.[11] When Noah Webster decided to insert the Pocahontas narrative into his already successful reader, *An American Selection of Lessons in Reading and Speaking,* again it was the translation of the Chastellux narrative that was used.[12] In the years following the Revolutionary War this text became something of a standard, which, while always available in its original form, was also readily accessible in excerpts.

Henri Petter points out, however, that by Davis's time a number of other versions of the Pocahontas narrative were available.[13] For example, many readers encountered the story in the long section on John Smith in Jeremy Belknap's popular *American Biography;* most of the earlier histories of the British colonies were still in print, and contemporary texts such as those of Robertson and Burk were available; and the published works of John Smith himself were not unknown, although they were apparently hard to come by in America during this period, as this excerpt from a January 20, 1797, letter from Mason Locke Weems to his publisher Mathew Carey attests: "If you coud get a copy of Smith's History of Virginia, you wd do well to reprint it, I could sell you many a thousand of that curious work. N B, it shd have one or two Romantic Engravings in it. Bishop Madisson desird me to reprint it. Many have expressd a wish to have a copy of it."[14] It is probably safe to say that the demand for Smith's *Generall Historie* was high because readers had seen incidents from it, including the Rescue, described in other texts. And there can be little doubt about what scene one of the engravings that Weems requests would have depicted.

With so many other versions of the narrative available, one might ask why Chastellux's presentation was so often reproduced. The two features that made it so attractive to an American audience were most likely the Frenchman's clearly Anglophobic and antimonarchical sentiments. The latter is first expressed in his description of the pride of Powhatan in exhibiting Smith, and is especially evident in his commentary on Powhatan's response to Pocahontas's actions at the moment of Smith's rescue: "All *savages* (*absolute sovereigns* and *tyrants* not excepted) are invariably more affected by the tears of infancy, than the voice of humanity."[15] Such tyrants cannot be convinced by words (i.e., reason) but can be affected by either emotional appeals (particularly those, one would suspect, of their own children) or by dramatic actions. In insisting that the subjects of such monarchs make a mistake when they resist with words rather than actions, Chastellux seemed to be reinforcing the lesson that had been learned by those who had taken part in the American Revolution. Also, in his argument for the power of the passions the Chevalier champions the emerging awareness of sentimentality as a force. Such feelings, when aroused and focused, could far surpass reason or logical argumentation in potency and effect.

Readers familiar with Beverley's *History and Present State of Virginia* could also compare the earlier historian's fairly mild description of the "problem" faced by John Rolfe at the court of James I with the Chevalier's caustic account, which blamed any mistreatment of Rolfe and Pocahontas on the king's arrogance.[16]

> She ["Pocahunta"] was treated with great respect [by the English, after her kidnapping] and married to a planter of the name of *Rolle* [*sic*], who soon took her to England. This was in the reign of *James the First;* and, it is said, that this monarch, pedantic and ridiculous in every point, was so infatuated with the prerogatives of royalty, that he expressed his displeasure, that one of his subjects should dare to marry the daughter even of a savage *King.* It will not perhaps be difficult to decide on this occasion, whether it was the savage King who derived honour from finding himself placed upon a level with the English

prince, or the English monarch, who by his pride and prejudices
reduced himself to a level with the chief of the savages.[17]

It is not surprising that this portrayal of an English monarch would
have found an appreciative audience in a republic that had so recently won its freedom from George III, who had been widely depicted by the American revolutionaries as exactly this type of proud,
despotic ruler.

Another important feature of the Chastellux version is a long foot-
note on Indian savagery, which is injected into the narrative by the
unnamed translator, who identifies himself simply as an "English
Gentleman Who Resided in America At That Period." (This was
almost certainly George Grieve.)[18] Some of the details of this passage
were violent enough for Noah Webster to choose to omit this note
from his text, presumably because it would not have been appropriate for his young audience. Grieve chose Smith's captivity to direct
his readers' attention to the fact that Indians were better known for
their cruelty than their kindness to their prisoners. By way of illustration he recounts the horrific story of Colonel Crawford and his
party, which had been recently edited by Hugh Henry Brackenridge,
a man well known for his anti-Indian sentiments. This tale of the
torture and death of Colonel Crawford and his son, and of the mi-
raculous survival of the "surgeon" who relates the story, reminded
readers of the more usual result of a captivity experience, as opposed
to the fate of John Smith. And when Grieve promulgates the idea
that it is the Indian women who are the most vicious to their victims,
it becomes clear that Pocahontas is an amazing exception to those
who were normally thought to be ready to practice the worst type of
savagery. Her actions could then be appreciated without one's having to alter one's well-established hatred and fear of Indians. Grieve
possibly included this tale to balance the pro-Indian feelings expressed by Chastellux in this section of his narrative, but more likely
it was simply a way of including the type of horrific account that sells
books.

When John Davis decided to augment the few incidents that had
made up the traditional Pocahontas narrative, which, as we have
seen, he had first used as a Christmas fireside tale in *The Farmer of
New-Jersey,* he followed the model of Chastellux and injected the Pocahontas material into the memoirs of his own journey through the
new nation.[19] Concerning this long digression within his travelogue,
Davis asserts that he had "adhered inviolably to the facts," but this
is provided more as the standard disclaimer of the early writer of
historical fiction than as a demand that each detail of his text be
believed (321). In lengthening the narrative Davis does fill in some

of the gaps left by Chastellux, but his main contribution to the tale is to make the love of the princess for Smith the primary motivation for her most famous action.

This was, in truth, not a totally original idea. A modern historian, Richard Beale Davis, mentions a version of the narrative produced in England in 1755 called *A Short Account of the British Plantations in America*, in which the author [Edward Kimber] attributes the success of the Jamestown settlement to "the love this young girl had conceived for Capt. Smith."[20] It was John Davis, however, who first provided in great quantity the trappings of a bad romance. His version of the Rescue was clearly far more a product of his own imagination than of any of the early historical accounts.

In Davis's version, the women of Orapakes first make the captive Smith run a rather gentle gauntlet. (Their weapons are twigs.) We are quickly told, however, that "Cruelty was succeeded by kindness," and thereby provided with a clue concerning the effect that the captain has on native women (290–1). He is then led through the countryside, first to Opechancanough's settlement and ultimately to Werowocomoco, the seat of the "Emperor" Powhatan. Davis then begins his rendition of the Rescue by mentioning that the great majority of the Powhatan Indian women at the court were apparently sympathetic to the plight of the "extremely prepossessing" prisoner (296). This description immediately distances his text from the cruelty of the Indian women portrayed in Grieve's note. He goes on to say that Smith notices that in one heart there seemed to be a stronger than normal response to his predicament: "[B]ut his attention was principally attracted by the charms of a young girl, whose looks emanated from a heart that was the seat of every tenderness, and who could not conceal those soft emotions of which the female bosom is so susceptible" (296–7). The upshot of these emotions becomes clear in Davis's presentation of the Rescue itself.

> The next day a long and profound consultation was held by the King and his Privy Council, when a huge stone was brought before Powhatan, and several men assembled with clubs in their hands. The lamentations of the women admonished *Smith* of his destiny; who being brought blindfolded to the spot, his head was laid on the block, and the men prepared with their clubs to beat out his brains. The women now became more bitter in their lamentations over the victim; but the savage Monarch was inexorable, and the executioners were lifting their arms to perform the office of death, when *Pocahontas* ran with mournful distraction to the stone, and getting the victim's head into her arms, laid her own upon it to receive the blow. Fair spirit! thou

ministering angel at the throne of grace! If souls disengaged from their earthly bondage can witness from the bosom of eternal light what is passing here below, accept, sweet Seraph, this tribute to thy humanity. (297–8)

As John Marshall later commented, it is her humanity that makes her brave action inevitable. But in Davis's rendition of this scene Pocahontas is not the only one who is portrayed positively:

Powhatan was not wanting in paternal feeling; his soul was devoted to his daughter *Pocahontas;* and so much did his ferocity relent at this display of innocent softness in a girl of fourteen, that he pronounced the prisoner's pardon, and dismissed the executioners. Indeed, every heart melted into tenderness at the scene. The joy of the successful mediator expressed itself in silence; she hung wildly on the neck of the reprieved victim, weeping with a violence that choked her utterance. (298)

This is the rare occasion where the reader is provided with a sense of the emotions felt by Powhatan at this dramatic turn of events. His devotion to his daughter is shown to be far more powerful than any feelings of "ferocity" toward the prisoner.

This rescue scene is perhaps only surpassed in melodrama by the moment that Davis later recounts, when John Rolfe discovers Pocahontas "strewing flowers over the imaginary grave of Captain *Smith.*"[21] She, surprised, faints into his arms, and he "clasped the *Indian* Maid to his beating heart, and drank from her lips the poison of delight" (312). William W. Jenkins calls this episode "Davis's major contribution to the Pocahontas legend, for in none of the accounts that were composed either by Smith or his contemporaries does one find a Rolfe with such ardor or a Pocahontas with such a willingness to be wooed."[22] Davis, perhaps as a concession to his female readers, makes it clear that the crucial element in each of the important relationships described in his account – Pocahontas-Powhatan, Pocahontas-Smith, and Pocahontas-Rolfe – is love.

Davis even goes so far as to predict that his "fair readers" will "hug with the tenderest emotion to their bosoms" his "story of Pocahontas, whose soft simplicity and innocence cannot but hold captive every mind."[23] These "fair readers," then, when immersed in the narrative, are actually in the same captive position as John Smith. The hearts of the readers are among those that "melt into tenderness," and just as Smith is freed and the colony saved by the benevolent actions of the princess, so the female reader could engage in, and then be freed by, the catharsis that the story of the Rescue provides. In this, Davis is clearly following more in the footsteps of Richardson and the eighteenth-century tradition of sentimental fiction than in those of Smith or the historians who had previously controlled the narrative.

Another factor in this break is the number of peculiar inaccuracies in Davis's account. The most obvious of these is that Pocahontas is described as being fourteen at the time of the Rescue in the winter of 1607–8 but only nineteen when she dies in 1617. In fact both of these ages are probably incorrect. The Simon van de Passe engraving, copies of which would have been available to Davis, makes it quite clear that she was twenty-one years old in 1616, so that by the time of her death in the following March she had possibly turned twenty-two. The earlier age for her demise is probably provided by Davis as an attempt to increase the tragedy and pathos of her death. More important, though, is his adjustment of the time of the narrative's crucial moment. At the time of the Rescue, according to Smith's description, Pocahontas would have been twelve or possibly thirteen, and although therefore probably old enough to have had a romantic (or even sexual) response to the handsome captain, she would not have been as nubile as Davis wished his readers to believe. He makes her fourteen to leave no doubt that a romantic attraction prompted her actions. Her love – for Smith, and later for Rolfe – was to be the primary feature of his version of the narrative, and so it was necessary for Davis's readers to see her as capable of mature emotions from the beginning.

Davis also makes his readers aware of his own antimonarchical feelings, which at times are quite similar to those expressed by Chastellux. In his introduction to the Pocahontas-Smith material, he describes a group of Indians whom he had seen at Occoquan, among whom were an old chief and a young woman. The latter obviously attracted his attention: "Of the women, the youngest was an interesting girl of seventeen; remarkably well shaped, and possessed of a profusion of hair, which in colour was raven black. She appeared such another object as the mind images *Pocahontas* to have been" (275). The chief had come to deliver a funeral oration for a fallen warrior, which, Davis tells us, was spoken with what had by then become the expected eloquence of the Indian speaker: "No orator of antiquity ever exceeded this savage chief in the force of his emphasis, and the propriety of his gesture" (278). His speech was followed by traditional dancing, but soon the reader is given a glimpse of the other, darker side of Indian life. "The dance took place by moonlight, and it was scarcely finished when the Chief produced a keg of whiskey, and having taken a draught, passed it around among his brethren" (279). The scene deteriorates into a violent brawl, the description of which ends with the pathetic old chief mourning over his empty jug, crying to bystanders, "*Scuttawawbah! Scuttawawbah!* More strong drink! More strong drink!" (279–80).

This passage is certainly meant to portray the corruption of the Indians by the Europeans, to the point where even a solemn occasion like the burial of a departed brave becomes a scene of savagery and decadence because of whiskey, which was often given to Indians by whites to gain their favor. But it also suggests that this type of corruption often begins at the top and spreads down through the rest of the tribe. The old chief is clearly in control of the available alcohol. And although he is still able to deliver a great oration, as it was believed his forefathers had been doing for centuries, at the same time he is leading his people, through his own weakness, to their eventual destruction. He is shown to have one foot in his noble past and one in a dissolute present, and to Davis there was no doubt as to which world he and his people, including the Pocahontas-like young woman, now belonged.

By way of contrast, we are told of the English hero of the Pocahontas narrative that when the colony's circumstances were most tenuous, "Captain *Smith* was elected Ruler by unanimous consent" and it was only because of "his judgment, courage, and industry" that the Jamestown settlement was able to survive (285). This is clearly the way a leader should be granted power; the people, given the chance, will select the person with the right skills for the job. The democratic prerogatives of the colonists are contrasted with the ruthless subjugation of the Indians under Powhatan, "a powerful king of *Pamunkey,* whose will was a law among his numerous subjects" (288). Davis makes his preference for the system of government of his adopted country, rather than that of his country of birth, quite clear.

When Davis describes the moment when Smith finally meets the emperor at Werowocomoco, there can again be no doubt as to the author's feelings about Powhatan's "savage state and magnificence" (295):

When Smith was brought into the presence of *Powhatan,* he was sitting upon a wooden throne resembling a bedstead, cloathed with a flowing robe of raccoon skins, and wearing on his head a coronet of feathers. He was about sixty years of age, somewhat hoary, and with a mien that impressed every beholder with awe. On each side of him sat a young *squaw,* who practiced every endearing softness of her sex, and contended for the caresses of her venerable Sovereign. It was ridiculous to behold the bald-headed letcher relax from his ferocity, and, waxing wanton, pinch the cheek of the damsel who most conciliated him. (295)

This is the way that the emperor of the Indians of Tidewater Virginia entertains himself, and a question is certainly raised as to whether there is any spirit left in the now-aged monarch. If he is to be perceived as the greatest man of his tribe, then it too must be seen as old, decaying, and far less powerful than in the days of its former virility.

King James also suffers at the pen of Davis, in a passage that reminds us of Chastellux's use of Beverley's text:

> It was on the 12th of June, 1616, that Mr. *Rolfe* arrived at *Plymouth* with *Pocahontas*. He immediately proceeded with her to *London*, where she was introduced at Court to *James I.* who, tenacious of his prerogative, was inflamed with indignation that one of his subjects should aspire to an alliance with royal blood. The haughty Monarch would not suffer *Rolfe* to be admitted to his presence; and when he received *Pocahontas,* his looks rebuked her for descending from the dignity of a King's daughter, to take up with a man of no title or family. (317–18)

Davis correctly predicted that early nineteenth-century Americans would appreciate this condemnation of the king for his prejudice, especially against this particular marriage. The United States was a nation that was proud to have done away with such titles. Also, during Jefferson's presidency it was home to a number of neo-humanitarian Anglo-Americans who were beginning to feel remorse for the destruction of many of the eastern Indian tribes, and, as we have noted, others who expressed sadness that the two races had not blended into one people from the beginning of the colonial enterprise. Davis does not say a great deal about Thomas Rolfe, although he does give him the usual credit as a progenitor of "two of the most respectable families now in *Virginia;* the *Randolphs* and *Bollings*" (321). However, Davis's apparently egalitarian sentiments did not keep him from cultivating members of these and other great families, and, when he could get it, he took pains to make their patronage of his works a matter of public knowledge.[24]

Davis does not overly emphasize the place of the Smith-Pocahontas relationship in any sort of mythohistoric chronicle of America within the actual text of the *Travels*. Only once, when he describes Smith's departure from Jamestown and the accompanying ruse perpetrated on Pocahontas, does the author look to the future greatness of the struggling colony. (Pocahontas is told here that Smith is dead, primarily so that she will not, as Davis's Smith fears, take revenge on the English colony for his having spurned her romantic advances.) "It was on Michaelmas day, 1609, that Captain *Smith* bade farewell to that shore on which he had founded a Colony, that was decreed

in the progress of time to become an independent empire, and con-
federating itself with other Colonies, to hold a distinguished rank
among the nations of the earth" (305–6). Rather, in the *Travels,*
and in his later versions of the Pocahontas narrative, Davis chooses
instead to frame his creations with evidences of their, and his own,
national importance. The *Travels* opens with a reproduction of a
letter Davis wrote to President Jefferson requesting permission to
dedicate his book to the Virginian chief executive. This is followed
by an affirmative response from Jefferson, in which he makes a slight-
ing reference to his own *Notes on the State of Virginia*: "Should you in
your journeyings have been led to remark on the same objects on
which I gave crude notes some years ago, I shall be happy to see
them confirmed or corrected by a more accurate observer" (3–4).
That he was given this authority by the president of the United States
(who also happened to have been one of the architects of the Revolution) was enough for Davis. He felt no need to call further attention to his text or to attempt explicitly to place parts of the narrative
into the continuum of American history. To do so, in fact, would
have cost him his persona as a genial traveler, which he clearly
wished to maintain. Instead, he let the presence of his esteemed
patron attest to the importance of his work and let his relation of
what was obviously a crucial moment in the foundation of the colony, and therefore of the country, speak for itself.

In 1805 Davis published the first admittedly fictional rendering of
the narrative in America, *Captain Smith and Princess Pocahontas, An
Indian Tale,* which he quickly followed with the first "Pocahontas
novel," *The First Settlers of Virginia, An Historical Novel.*[25] He begins
Captain Smith with a list of "Testimonials," one of which is not unexpected: "*Th: Jefferson presents his compliments to Mr. Davis, and has
subscribed with pleasure to his Indian Tale.* Washington, March 8,
1805."[26] At times one gets the feeling that Davis enjoyed saying the
name "Thomas Jefferson" as much as the narrator in "Bartleby the
Scrivener" enjoys repeating "John Jacob Astor."

The Pocahontas material in *Captain Smith* is somewhat expanded
but basically much the same as in the *Travels.* At the conclusion of
the book, however, Davis provides his readers with a lamentation on
the passing of the Indians. When he describes how "The race of
Indians has been destroyed by the inroads of the Whites," he is
clearly aware of the irony that the salvation of John Smith, and by
extension of the white race in America, was made possible by the
mediation of an Indian girl.[27] The references in the text to the un-
derlying "humanity" of Indian figures such as Powhatan and Pocahontas are meant to invite consideration of the contemporary
relations between the races and of what the continuing destruction
of the Indians will mean to the future of the United States.

Indeed, in each of Davis's reproductions of the Pocahontas material, the greatest emphasis is reserved for her humanity. As he puts it in the *Travels,* "the humanity of *Pocahontas* exacts emotions of tenderness; and the heart is interested in her history from the moment she suspends by her interposition the axe of the executioner, till she draws her last breath on the shore of a foreign country."[28] This humanity, however, unlike the less complicated compassion described by Marshall, is expressed in terms of her ability to feel the entire gamut of emotions, from love and compassion to anger, as well as by what would have appeared to be her rational choice to turn her back on savagery and join with the English. It was also important to portray her as a complete human being at this time when there was still some question about the place of the Indians in what had been traditionally called the "Great Chain of Being."

Barbara Ruf argues that Davis used the Pocahontas narrative in part to continue the work that Jefferson began in the *Notes:*

> In the *Travels* he [Davis] was using the story to support a thesis about the Indian which, in turn, would vindicate a philosophy about the American continent. Like his mentor Jefferson, Davis was refuting the theory proposed by Georges Buffon in *Histoire Naturelle* (1749–1804) to the effect that the western hemisphere was in an early and immature state of growth, that it was inferior in climate and environment to the rest of the world, that as a consequence the Indian was akin to the beasts and only slightly above them, and worst of all, that the environment of the hemisphere was intellectually and physically degenerating and debilitating to those who came here to live.[29]

Ruf is certainly correct in stressing this purpose, but there were other motivations as well. Davis quickly recognized the popularity of the Pocahontas-Smith section of Chastellux's *Travels,* and he wasted little time before attempting to exploit this discovery, as much for his own benefit as for that of America and its native inhabitants. Davis did not lack in self-esteem, and his early insistence on the importance of the narrative, and especially on its being reserved for his "pen alone," was partly impelled by his belief that if he could be remembered as the writer who had done the most to immortalize the hero and heroine of this most American of stories, then he too would ultimately be immortalized, if only on their coattails.

John Davis set out to make the Pocahontas narrative his own, and in many ways he was successful. And just as Chastellux had been his model, even his inspiration (perhaps in the same manner as Cooper was inspired to write *The Pilot* to correct what he saw as the inadequacies of earlier sea stories), so Davis became the model for many of those who told this romantic tale during the remainder of the nineteenth century, whether in literary or pictorial media. Davis won out because he realized and exploited the romantic potential in the narrative, and by doing so he initiated its removal from the exclusive preserve of historians and biographers. In the decades that followed, the Pocahontas story became more the purview of romancers, dramatists, and poets, who, because Davis had broken ground by creating a fictional context for her actions, were free to devise whatever kind of story they wished to around the Rescue. Finally, Davis was also one of the first to address not simply her actions but what her actions had come to mean. The narrative would still revolve around a singular act of individual heroism, but after the work of Davis and his contemporaries, including the dramatist James Nelson Barker, this compassionate moment would also come to occupy an important place in American cultural history.[30]

It was a rare occurrence during the first two decades of the nineteenth century when a reference to the colonial past was not made to fit into the tapestry of the national prehistory, especially when an event could easily be read as in some way preparatory to the founding of the nation. As William J. Free puts it, "Nationalistic fervor demanded that history be used to figure the political, social, and moral glory of the present."[31] The figure of Pocahontas and the events that made up her narrative certainly served this function and were duly used by writers of various genres, many of whom had a particular historical vision or agenda to express. One of the earliest and oddest uses of Pocahontas's name, if not her whole story, occurred in Joseph Croswell's 1802 drama, *A New World Planted*.[32] Here we have an Indian princess named "Pocahonte," but the play is set in Plymouth instead of Jamestown, and she is made a daughter of Massasoit, rather than Powhatan. Other than the fact that she is in love with the white colonist Hampden, and he with her, there is little about this play that reminds one of the circumstances of the founding of Virginia or the Pocahontas narrative. Rather, this is the first obvious use of her name as what today would be called a "hook." She could be immediately identified as a good Indian, and so her presence allows the audience to make some immediate assumptions about the relationship between the colonists and at least some of the other Indians, who must necessarily must be bad.

The central problem of the play is that a small band among the English colonists consider John Carver and his followers to be traitors for taking upon themselves the authority to sign a treaty with the Indians rather than wait for royal approval. These rebels against the colonial leadership, who are later revealed to be Catholics, and so would have found little sympathy from the New England audience, see themselves as simply being loyal to their king, James I.

Their actions, however, are presented as terrible crimes that endanger the fragile stability of the young colony. These conspirators are ultimately discovered, defeated, and, surely to the great joy of the audience, forced to return to England to live under the yoke of the king they love so well. Meanwhile, the Pilgrim Fathers sign their treaty with Massasoit, and the play ends with peaceful coexistence, both among the colonists and in their relations with the Indians. An epilogue then provides a vision of the colony that describes the "future destiny" of English America through the presidency of Washington and into the nineteenth century.[33]

Pocahonte is onstage only briefly, and the love subplot never really gets started, although there is time for Hampden to utter a handy, explanatory sentiment that is often repeated in later romantic versions of the Pocahontas narrative: "I know she's browner than European dames, / But whiter far, than other natives are."[34] There is, however, no obvious reason in the plot for Croswell to have chosen this name for his princess. One possible thematic explanation is that she is drawn to the good colonists, and perhaps her sympathy helps to sanction the sympathy of the audience for them and against those who would choose to be under the tight control of a distant king. There can be no doubt, however, that an American audience would have automatically favored this group. Her inclusion may also be seen as an attempt to reinforce the importance of the friendship of Indians like Pocahontas to those who wanted to free themselves from royal domination. Most likely, however, Croswell was simply using her name to provide a familiar image for his audience and perhaps, by word of mouth, lure a few more paying customers into theater seats.

William Free also points out that for those who were attempting to create a national history for the United States, "Classical literature was the inevitable model . . . ; an American *Aeneid,* the ideal."[35] Among the American poets involved in this project during the early national period were the Connecticut Wits. They believed that one of their most important tasks was to write an American epic in the spirit of the *Aeneid* which would both catalogue the events that, at the turn of the nineteenth century, were seen as important to the founding of America and identify the spirit behind those events. One of the last and most ambitious attempts at such a work was Joel Barlow's *Columbiad* (1807).[36] This poem, an expansion of his 1787 attempt, *The Vision of Columbus,* was eagerly awaited by a public that saw the completion of an American epic as another manifestation of their destined glorious nationhood.[37] (Indeed, Barlow's title change suggests the growing primacy of the *Aenied* model in the years between 1787 and 1807.)

The Columbiad opens with a description of the miserable condition

of the aged and imprisoned Christopher Columbus. Hesper, the
"guardian Genius" of the Americas, appears and provides Columbus
with a vision of the great future in store for the hemisphere he had
discovered. In Book IV Barlow describes, among other events, the
founding of Virginia, and compares the Pocahontas-Smith relationship to that of Medea and Jason.[38] This parallel, when one gets beyond the usual problem that Pocahontas did not marry Smith, works
quite well. The classical myth tells of the daughter of a barbarian
king who, against the will of her father, saves the life of a young
foreigner and ultimately turns against her people to join with him
and his. This reference reminded readers who were familiar with the
myth of both the great love of Medea for Jason and, perhaps as
important, of the injustices perpetrated by kings who wished to maintain their power. The Golden Fleece in the Pocahontas story, however, is Smith's life, which she restores to him so that he can return
to his people and become a great figure among them. (One could
point out that both Jason and Smith come to disappointing ends,
perhaps because each finally rejects the love of his princess.) Although *The Columbiad* was not a great popular success, this connection of the Pocahontas narrative to the well-known classical story
probably contributed in some small way to the continuing elevation
of the American couple to mythic status and thereby helped to fulfill
the poet's promise to Pocahontas: "For thine shall be his friends,
his heart, his name; / His camp shall shout, his nation boast thy
fame."[39]

As stated earlier, what holds such works together is the attempt to
find typologically the American present (and often, the American future) in the historical events of the past. By the end of the first decade
of the nineteenth century the Pocahontas narrative had become an
important part of this history, and when it was invoked it was usually
with an eye toward the republic that had so recently emerged. Her inclusion in this greater narrative helped to balance the far more numerous portrayals of the savagery of the Indians, and helped to
suggest that the history of America was in fact the history of the coming together of a single nation, in which individuals from both the Indian and white races had played necessary roles. Although not, for the
most part, an apt historical parallel, the model of Latium, where the
descendants of two peoples ultimately lived in peace and merged into
one, was often preferred to that of Canaan, where one people strove
to dispossess and destroy another. The *Aeneid* was also a useful model
in that it had the added feature of focusing on the marriage of a
leader of the invaders with a princess of the indigenous peoples,
which certainly would have seemed to be anticipatory of the Pocahontas narrative. And although Pocahontas does not marry John Smith as

Lavinia marries Aeneas, this did not stop Samuel Lorenzo Knapp, in his *Lectures on American Literature* (1829), from referring to the captain as the "Aeneas of the New World."[40]

There are other contemporary testaments to the idea that aspects of the Pocahontas narrative were reminiscent of Virgil's epic. John Davis himself, in the *Travels,* quotes from the scene in Book 6 of the *Aeneid* where Aeneas meets Dido in the underworld to describe the meeting of Smith and Pocahontas in England.[41] Another parallel was noted by C. K. Blanchard, who took part in the Grand National Festival and Jubilee held at Jamestown in May 1807 to celebrate the two hundredth anniversary of the founding of the first permanent Anglo-American settlement in the New World.[42] An article in the *American Gleaner and Virginia Magazine* for May 30, 1807 (preceded, perhaps coincidentally, by a "List and Character of Eminent Roman Writers," which of course included a section on Virgil) describes some of the events of the festival.[43] After Pocahontas had been "eulogized in an appropriate manner," Blanchard recited a short "Ode" he had written to honor the bicentennial. Ironically, his poem describes the Indians specifically as a people that needed to be conquered in order for the white race to succeed, so references to the Pocahontas story were necessarily omitted. In his closing comments, however, Blanchard issues this challenge: "The Verse writers for the next *'Virginiad,'* are requested to pay their respects to Princess POCAHONTAS, unavoidably neglected in this first Essay."[44] This proposed *Virginiad* would presumably have told the story of the peaceful coexistence between the races brought about by the saving of Smith and the marriage of Pocahontas to John Rolfe.

The fact of the matter, of course, was that many whites, as Davis and others had pointed out, were actively engaged in finding ways to do away with the Indians. The inclusion of Pocahontas and other "friendly" Indians in the romantic works created during the postwar period both helped to assuage any guilt that might have been felt at this process, in that these "good" Indians were often portrayed as complicitous in ensuring the success of the white race, and, conversely, promoted a belief in the fantasy of absorption, which Jefferson and many of his followers maintained was still a possibility. What tied the stories of these virtuous Indians together was that for such figures to be seen in this light they generally had to act against the best interests of their own people. These positively portrayed acts of rebellion, whether political or familial, were what gave such long-dead Indians as Pocahontas, Massasoit, Squanto, Samoset, and Hobomoc their celebrity and ultimately caused these figures, who were so important to the colonies' beginnings, to be raised to positions in the Anglo-American historical hierarchy equal to those of many of the early white settlers. Coupled with the romanticization of the passing of the Indian, this elevation saw the actual histories of these figures replaced by mythic narratives depicting the crucial moments when aid was given to the whites, such as the first Thanksgiving dinner in New England and the saving of John Smith.

It is ironic that Edmund Randolph, a direct descendant of Rolfe and Pocahontas, perhaps most succinctly articulated the post-Federalist separation of the flesh-and-blood woman who was his ancestor from the event that by his last years had taken on mythic status.

> Let the moralist and poet vie with each other in the description of this extraordinary reverse in the fate of this most extraordinary man. Let the Virginia patriot rather ascribe the preservation of Smith to that chain of grand events of which the settlement of Virginia was destined to be the foremost link, and which finally issued in the birth of our American Republic.[45]

In his introduction to the 1970 edition of Randolph's *History of Virginia*, which was written between 1809 and the author's death in 1813, Arthur H. Shaffer points out the impulse among historians of the post-Revolutionary period to define local history in terms of the "search for a national historical identity."[46] It was therefore logical for Randolph, like William Wirt a "Virginia patriot," to view Pocahontas's rescue of Smith in national terms. His presentation was another attempt to put the Virginia colonists on an equal footing with the New England founders. As Marshall had suggested earlier, the Rescue was chronologically (and, Randolph would have us believe, spiritually) one of the primary events in the series that culminated in the founding of the country. Those who took part in this dramatic incident needed to have their memories preserved and appreciated, no matter how they would ultimately come to be described by "moralists" and "poets."

Randolph's choice of "moralists" as a category is intriguing because it points to the fact that it is difficult to state with any confidence exactly what the moral of the Rescue would have been to an early nineteenth-century audience. A comparison with another story that gained its popularity during this period – a tale with an apparently more obvious meaning – may offer some useful clues.

In the early twentieth century the historian John Gould Fletcher compared the Rescue to another well-known moment in American mythology: "This incident has caused more ardent discussion and denial than anything in Smith's career, indeed than anything in American history except the famous cherry tree story of George Washington."[47] These two American foundation myths have a great deal more in common than the question of whether or not either was historically accurate. Both were added to already existing narratives and were meant to enhance previous characterizations by providing an additional, dramatic example of the strength of the central figure. (One could argue that in the case of the Rescue, this applies to Smith as well as Pocahontas.) Each portrays an incident from the youth of the protagonist that in some way foreshadows his or her adult actions. Each is a story of bravery in a moment of crisis. And, most importantly, at the heart of each is a defiance of patriarchal power, a fearlessness of the consequences of such defiance, and an appeal to a form of honesty, whether in response to a direct question or to the emotions engendered by an impending event, as the key to unlock an expression of paternal love.

As Jay Fliegelman points out in his discussion of Weem's *Life of Washington,* "In the ideal parent–child relationship of George and Augustine, honesty and not obedience is the organizing ethic."[48] After his having chopped at, if not down, the cherry tree, young George's decision not to attempt to deceive his father ("I can't tell a lie, Pa; you know I can't tell a lie. I did cut it with my hatchet."[49]) is portrayed as a brave act that only increases the parent's affection for his child. One might question whether or not young George was capable of telling a lie but reasoned that it would be better not to, or whether the fact that this was George Washington meant that by nature lies did not exist for him and therefore the truth was the only response he could have made. In either case, it was the young Washington's fidelity to the truth that brought him his reward, and it has long been his honesty that has been most widely praised when attempts are made to describe the moral of this incident.

In the Rescue, the crisis is apparently brought about by her having to choose whether or not to be true to her inherent, often mentioned humanity, which, whether because of romantic love or simple compassion, demanded that she intercede for the captain. In the end she had to act, and it was her disregard for herself, both in that she conceivably could have been killed by those aiming at Smith as well as that she was clearly going against the wishes of her father and king, which elicited Powhatan's display of love for his daughter and compassion for the prisoner. Readers have traditionally seen this moment as a powerful example of generosity and self-sacrifice. I would agree, but also point out that her action would also have been seen as a manifestation of her truth to the humanity that was constantly portrayed as one of the dominant attributes of Pocahontas. And while there are many possible lessons to be learned from Weems's anecdote, from "Honesty is the best policy" to an acknowledgment of the shrewd and generous parenting strategies of Augustine Washington, it would not have been lost on those who had rebelled against their king that in the cherry tree incident is depicted an act of bravery in the face of a patriarchal power, and that the Pocahontas narrative, which contains the first important event in the history of the Anglo-American settlements, turns on an act of rebellion against a father and king and reinforces the idea that such acts often have positive results.

When discussing the love of Virginians for their favorite Indian princess, Richard Beale Davis connects her story to the founding of the nation and the rise of Romanticism:

> The birth of the American nation and the beginnings of the triumph of Romanticism as an attitude toward art and life came almost simultaneously. Pride in liberty, nostalgic and sentimental glances at the past, and genuine antiquarianism existed side by side. Each state consciously and unconsciously was intent on finding at least some of its roots in an American rather than a European past. For Virginians, many of whom had known already that they bore blood of Pocahontas in their veins, the story of the rescue of Captain Smith, their symbolic English ancestor, was a tradition exactly suited to arousing pride and fancy and sentiment.[50]

He goes on to point out that many of those who produced versions of the Pocahontas narrative during this period were Virginians.[51] However, I do not believe that we can successfully isolate the story or consider it to have been only regionally popular. Its appearance in such works as Webster's *American Selection* and in periodicals such as the *Columbian Magazine, American Magazine,* and *Port Folio* point to its widespread circulation and popularity.[52] And its inclusion in American biographical dictionaries, whether under the name of "Smith," as in Belknap, or under her own name, as in William Allen's *American Biographical and Historical Dictionary* of 1809, make it clear that this was more than simply an interesting Indian tale.[53] By the early nineteenth century, Pocahontas had become an American historical personage, one who was in the ambiguous position of being both "other" – in that she was by birth a "savage" – and also (at least in spirit) an American – for her display of compassion that saved John Smith and with him the Jamestown colony. Indeed, to this day that act ties her to most Anglo-Americans far more strongly than her later adoption of the religion and culture of the English. The Rescue comes to be seen as part of a greater pattern of history which ultimately led to the Revolution and American nationhood.

In the era of the Indian romance, which was soon to begin its hey-day, the historical importance of Pocahontas's actions would continue to be expressed. The focus of the narrative, however, will move to the character of the princess herself. On the one hand, she will still be portrayed as a good Indian – an alternative to whorish squaws as well as to various other kinds of savages who would impede the apparent destiny of America. On the other, her persona as a lovely young prin-cess, who charms and is charmed by Smith, who impresses all good Europeans with her beauty and virtue, and who innocently captures the heart of John Rolfe, will be featured. Indeed, by placing greater emphasis on the relationship between Pocahontas and Smith rather than that with Rolfe, John Davis and his followers helped to remove the narrative from what could have become a troubling racial issue. Any romantic feelings that may have existed between the captain and the young princess were clearly not consummated. Therefore, if one concurrently deprioritizes her relationship with Rolfe, the problems of portraying miscegenation could be avoided. As we shall see, this proved to be a boon to those who created literary interpretations of the narrative later in the nineteenth century, when a portrayal of a happy interracial marriage, even that of Pocahontas and Rolfe, would not have been acceptable to their readers. (It is useful to compare the relatively passionate love scenes between Pocahontas and Rolfe in the works of Davis and Barker with the restrained courting depicted by the next generation of romancers and dramatists.)

This change of emphasis also marks another type of movement away from the historical bases of the narrative. The relationship of Pocahontas to Rolfe is specific to the beginnings of the Jamestown colony. It looks back to their marriage, their son, and the formation of the bloodlines of many of the great families of Virginia. Her re-lationship to Smith, on the other hand, looks ahead to the ultimate destiny of America. The question of why she acted to save him comes to have two interwoven answers. On the personal level, she may sim-ply been smitten by the sight of the brave captain. On a national level, however, it had become clear by the second decade of the nineteenth century that Pocahontas had rescued Smith, and by im-plication all Anglo-Americans, so that they might carry on the des-tined work of becoming a great nation – a task that was still in its early stages when Davis, Marshall, and Barker were invoking and expanding on that moment. Her contribution to this present and future process can therefore only be addressed with reference to Smith, and so it is not surprising that he assumes the role of the most important man in her life in the American historical conscious-ness. One could also argue that in the Englishman's stoic bravery and the Indian princess's inherent understanding of the natural world, Smith and Pocahontas embody two of the traits that would come to be seen as crucial for those who would face the continuing task of building a nation out of the wilderness.

The popularity of this moment, when her emotional appeal to her father had succeeded after all else, including Smith's brave acceptance of his fate, had failed, also marked a change from the era of the "Federalist stoicism" of Washington, Adams, and the Founding Fathers to a time when the power of Romantic sensibilities and the need to provoke an emotional response from the reader became the *Zeitgeist* of the American literary scene. In fact, stoicism, which had already been associated with particular Indians, becomes a standard trait of many of the Indians of later romances. Although they still have the potential for passionate actions, it is their antiquated, stoic acceptance of their individual fate and of the ultimate demise of their people that endeared these noble savages to white readers.

John Davis and the writers of his generation who used the Pocahontas material also initiated the process of incorporating the Indian as a potentially positive figure into American literary history. Prior to their work, the great majority of Indians – whether described as unwitting servants of God whose terrible actions had provided a way for fallen Christians to return to the fold, or as servants of the devil, to whom evil came naturally – were portrayed generically as not-yet-very-noble savages. There were a few notable exceptions, but for the most part the usual role of the native tribes was definable as that of the great adversary of the destined civilizing of the continent. The Rescue scene of the Pocahontas narrative, however, provided both a princess who not only was not evil, but who had acted to save the life of a great white leader and thereby ensure the survival of the first English colony, and her apparently loving, merciful father. It is Powhatan, after all, who actually makes the decision to spare Smith's life. Such figures complicated matters greatly, because they made clear that certain Indians, like certain blacks (of whom the great example was Phillis Wheatley), apparently had the potential for civilized behavior. Further, it also began to be posited at this time that something might be owed to the Indians who had supported (and might yet support) the Anglo-American cause. There is little doubt that the sympathetic depictions of good Indians during the first decade of the nineteenth century, by serving as a counterweight to the portrayals of savages, such as those who caused the demise of Colonel Crawford, John Vanderlyn's killers of Jane McCrea, and the Indians of Charles Brockden Brown's *Edgar Huntly*, played a role in the rise of the pro-Indian sentiments of the 1820s and 1830s.

The idea that Pocahontas was deserving of a monument did not die out in the post-Federalist era. Many of the authors who used the narrative later in the nineteenth century expressed their intentions in terms similar to those used by Mary Webster Mosby (Mrs. M. M. Webster), who tells her readers that her poem *Pocahontas: A Legend* is meant to "raise a shrine to Pocahontas's shade."[54] One of the more interesting examples of this phenomenon occured in a critique of Samuel Drake's *Biography and History of the Indians of North America* (1836), in the *North American Review* for April 1837.[55] In a chronological survey of the Indians discussed by Drake, the reviewer, after quoting at length passages about many little-known natives, pauses only briefly when he arrives at the Indians who made the first contact with the Jamestown colony. "We next meet with an account of Powhatan; the romantic and daring adventures of Captain John Smith; and the eventful history of the heroic and high-souled Pocahontas. But these are familiar themes. The universal sympathy of mankind has reared to the memory of Pocahontas a monument as enduring as the human heart's reverence for virtue."[56] To Davis and Marshall it was again the humanity of Pocahontas that had emerged to save John Smith. In this reviewer's opinion, "the universal sympathy of mankind" had by his time rewarded her with a monument constructed of materials far more permanent than any visual, tactile, or literary tribute. This is all that need be said about the Virginia Indians of her time. The themes are now familiar, because in the years between Davis and Drake many writers had reinterpreted the Pocahontas narrative, or, as we shall see, had borrowed incidents from this well-known source that would have been easily identifiable to their audiences.

Before we discuss the Romantic Indian texts written between 1820 and 1840, however, we must go back to the turn of the century and briefly examine the work of Chateaubriand. His extremely popular fiction was probably the most important model for many of the romancers who portrayed noble Indians during the first third of the nineteenth century. It was also he, as much as Davis and his American contemporaries, who transported notions of European Romanticism across the Atlantic by having his passion-filled fictions take place, and become immediate sensations, in the young nation. The bravery of his beautiful Atala would find a receptive audience among the readers of the early republic, perhaps because they were already accustomed to the idea that such behavior was not unusual among Indian princesses.

THE POCAHONTAS NARRATIVE IN THE ERA OF THE ROMANTIC INDIAN

"When I think of Pocahontas, I am ready to love Indians."[1]

In his far-reaching review of James Fenimore Cooper's *The Spy*, published in the July 1822 *North American Review*, W. H. Gardiner delineates the "three great epochs in American history, which are peculiarly well fitted for the historical romance; – the times just succeeding the first settlement – the aera of the Indian wars, which lie scattered along a considerable period – and the revolution."[2] As he looks back to the beginnings of the Anglo-American enterprise, he muses about the stouthearted New Englanders, who formed a colony "with the humble hope and firm resolve to expend their lives and their children's lives in the wilderness, for the sake of worshipping their God after the fashion of their own hearts."[3] Such honorable men "afford a singular contrast to those of Raleigh's successors in the south, headed by that man of adventure, who had challenged a whole Ottoman army in his youth, carrying off the heads of three Turkish champions at his saddle-bow, and who was now solacing his riper years . . . in the arms of the renowned Pocahontas."[4] The "man of adventure" is of course John Smith, whose link to Pocahontas had become even more pronounced in the twenty years since John Davis had first postulated that romantic feelings were at the root of her heroism.

In his extended preamble, Gardiner provides an early example of the sectionalist partisanship that in less than forty years would erupt in the Civil War. There can be no doubt about where his regional sympathies lay, and his New England allegiance was made even clearer by his subsequent discussion of the beginnings of slavery in Virginia. We also see here what had become a characteristic conflation of the Pocahontas narrative, which places Smith and his rescuer together romantically and thereby necessarily excludes John Rolfe from the picture. Gardiner's obvious attempt to ridicule Smith takes the dual forms of insinuating that the self-proclaimed deeds of his youth were inflated if not wholly untrue, and of showing him to be the "lover" of Pocahontas – not as a father loves a child, or in some vague or Platonic sense, but "in her arms." Smith therefore was not only a liar, but was also guilty of taking part in what by the early nineteenth century was again viewed as the despicable practice of interracial sex. Gardiner suggests ironically that Smith was therefore an appropriate founder of a southern culture whose economic success was based on the "contributions" of two races.

It is not as though such relationships had ever become generally acceptable to white Americans. By the 1820s, however, the fantasy of absorption that had been proffered by some enlightened Jeffersonians had for the most part faded, and the fear of miscegenation had again become obsessive.[5] Such heightened feelings presented a major challenge to those who would choose to reproduce the Pocahontas narrative during the antebellum period because in it one ultimately had to deal with her successful marriage to John Rolfe and the birth of their son Thomas. Literary artists had to find a way around this perceived problem, and various solutions were tried in their attempts to rescue the narrative from its culturally troublesome conclusion. In this chapter I first look briefly at an important and rarely discussed reason for the reemergence of these strong antimiscegenation feelings. I then examine the ways in which loving relationships between Indians and whites were presented in a variety of texts written during this period, and finally discuss how some purveyors of the Pocahontas narrative chose to deal with the difficulty that was presented by the denouement of this most popular of American stories.

Charles M. Lombard has discussed the popularity of Chateaubriand's *Atala* and *Génie du Christianisme* in the United States at the beginning of the nineteenth century and noted the possible influence of these texts on antebellum American representations of the noble savage.[6] In the introduction to the second volume of his series, *The Romantic Indian,* which contains two dramatic versions of the Pocahontas narrative (James Nelson Barker's 1808 *The Indian Princess* and Robert Dale Owen's 1837 *Pocahontas*), Lombard argues specifically for the importance of *Atala* to these interpreters of the Pocahontas material, and points out that "Pocahontas' successful effort to stop Smith's execution parallels Atala's rescue of Chactas."[7] Although traces of the latter scene can certainly be found in some of the nineteenth-century interpretations of the Pocahontas narrative, it is far more likely that excerpts from the life of Pocahontas were models for Chateaubriand, rather than the other way around. Smith's *Generall Historie* had been translated into French by the mid-eighteenth century, and so the version of the narrative that includes the Rescue would certainly have been available to Chateaubriand.[8] Indeed, by the time he was working on *Atala*, the Pocahontas story itself had appeared in Europe in translations of Smith's account and of other histories of the New World; in the novels of Unca Eliza Winkfield (1767) and Carl Friedrich Scheibler (1781); and in a drama by Johann Wilhelm Rose (1784). Also, tales with Pocahontas-like elements, such as the many versions of *Inkle and Yarico*, which portrayed the tragic love of an Indian woman for an Englishman whose life she had saved (an anonymous version in French was published in 1778), and dramas with similar elements, such as *La Sauvagesse* and *Les Mariages de Canada*, had met with varying degrees of success on the Continent.[9] Any or all of these texts could have been known to Chateaubriand as he was composing his own tale of a heroic but short-lived Indian princess who risked her own life and her father's love to save a prisoner, became a Christian, and ultimately died and was buried in "foreign soil."[10] Although the rescues portrayed in particular antebellum texts may at times closely approximate that of Chactas by Atala, it is likely that earlier versions of the Pocahontas narrative had served as the ultimate inspiration for both.

The writings of Chateaubriand understandably had an enormous influence on many of the later domestic portrayals of American Indians. Versions of his descriptions of the unspoiled beauty of the New World wilderness, as well as of his often noble native characters, can be found in the poetry of Bryant, the fiction of Cooper and Child, the paintings of Cole, and in the works of most nineteenth-century thinkers who took a sympathetic view toward the indigenous American cultures. What is also evident, however, particularly in "the burning twins," *Atala* and *René*, is that in Chateaubriand's fiction can be found an early expression of a motif that would come to dominate antebellum portrayals of Indian-white relations.

From his opening description of the Meschacebe (Mississippi) River in *Atala* – the western shore is a quiet savannah, as opposed to the murmuring and sometimes quite noisy forest on the eastern side of the river – to his contrasts of the Old World and the New, paganism and Christianity, and sexual passion and the power of religion, Chateaubriand presents his readers, and often his characters, with a number of apparently irreconcilable extremes.[11] There can be no middle ground, no compromise between these poles, and, as he often makes clear, attempts to bring these differing elements together can lead to disaster. This argument is expressed powerfully through examples of the destructive influence of the invading Caucasian peoples on the native population, and most strongly concerning the possibility of any actual mixing of the red and white races.

Although Chateaubriand is primarily concerned with asserting the primacy of the Catholic idea of eternal bliss over any type of earthly happiness, the misery that he inflicts on characters who result from interracial unions seems especially harsh. Atala herself, the daughter of a Spanish aristocrat and a converted Indian woman, is portrayed as something of an outsider in her tribe by virtue of both her biracial heritage and her chosen religion. Further, although she lives as an Indian, she is apparently no longer connected to the natural, sensual world around her. In part this is because of her paternal ancestry and her early exposure to white civilization, but another important factor is that Atala sees herself as bound by a promise that her mother had made to the "Queen of Angels" (the Virgin Mary) that her daughter would remain a virgin. This vow forces her to fight sensuality at all costs, and therefore she cannot allow herself to requite the love of the devoted Chactas. In the end she chooses suicide, which, though a suitably romantic solution, would in the Catholic tradition have damned her to an eternity in hell, over an earthly life of continuous physical and spiritual torment.

At the beginning of the tale that bears his name, René is adopted into the Natchez nation, but soon, because of his constant unhappiness and melancholy, will only communicate with Father Souël and Chactas, his "foster father." The reader learns that René had taken an Indian woman (Celuta) to be his wife in order to conform to tribal custom, but that "he did not live with her."[12] The problems that would have resulted from their sexual union are therefore apparently avoided, and this is implicitly confirmed when we are not told of any offspring from this relationship within *René* itself. Readers familiar with *Atala*, however, will remember the narrator's encounter with the granddaughter of René and Celuta as she hung the bones of her dead little son, the representative of the future of her people, to dry on the branches of a tree. This woman, her husband, and a small, tattered group of Indians were all that remained of the great Natchez nation. They were damned to a life of wandering in the wilderness, carrying the bones of their ancestors as the Trojans carried their household gods, in what the narrator makes clear was most probably a hopeless quest to find a new homeland. It is from this mixed-blood woman that the narrator learns of the deaths of René and Father Aubry, and is able to contemplate their bones, literally, as well as those of Chactas himself.

In fact, the deaths of Chactas, René, and Fathers Aubry and Souël all take place during interracial or racially inspired tribal warfare. One could argue that the miseries and/or deaths of all of the principal characters in both *Atala* and *René* are the inevitable results of such racial and cultural mixings, whether it be on the microcosmic level of miscegenation, or the macrocosmic level of the often violent, always tragic interrelations between the red and white races on the frontiers of the New World. Such cultural clashes were still taking place when the earliest American editions of "the burning twins" were published during the first decade of the nineteenth century and would continue for another ninety years. Chateaubriand almost certainly believed that all American Indians would ultimately suffer the same fate as his Natchez, either at the hands of the white race, or of fellow Indians in the employ of the Europeans, who themselves would eventually be destroyed. So, although attempting to show, as Richard Switzer puts it, that "Christianity as the true religion was far more capable of moving the reader than any representation of the pagan mysteries and religions," Chateaubriand also points out how the power of Christianity was invoked by these suffering people (and, by extension, could be invoked by any suffering people) to help them find the strength to endure their hardships.[13] This religion would allow them to understand that such trials can actually prepare people to receive the eternal joys of heaven. The great problem with this model, of course, is that to be saved eternally the Indians had to associate with the Europeans and thereby place themselves at risk of earthly destruction.

The catastrophic power of the mixing of the races as portrayed by Chateaubriand in these very popular texts was an important factor in the reemerging fear of "unnatural mixing" that took hold in the United States during the early nineteenth century. In presenting these stark oppositions in his portrayals of the New World, Chateaubriand leaves little opportunity for a modus vivendi in Indian-white relations. The process of the destruction of the native cultures would continue inexorably onward. Interrelations between the races would do nothing to stop it, and in fact would only ensure the destruction of all of the individuals concerned.

The reawakening of this fear of miscegenation was an important reason for the growing dominance of the Pocahontas-Smith elements of her narrative. Their relationship, though perhaps sexually charged, did not necessarily have to end in cohabitation, as did her marriage to Rolfe. Even the Pocahontas-Smith material, however, was problematic, as Leslie Fiedler points out in his discussion of Pocahontas's foiling of a conspiracy planned by her father, which he calls "her other [than the 'Rescue'] mythological exploit":[14]

> But there are troublesome ambiguities even here; for it was a *White* community which the Red Girl, Pocahontas, warned – just as it was a *White* man she married, and, before that, a *White* man she saved from death. Try, therefore as they will, the sentimental writers for women cannot make her story a myth of Richardsonian salvation alone. It remains also, what Smith had dreamed it,

a myth of reconciliation between the races by love and marriage. Any combination of sex and race raises for White Americans the bugaboo of miscegenation, so terrifyingly versified by Shakespeare, while Smith still trod the forests of Virginia in search of love.[15]

By the 1820s, the notion of a possible amalgamation of the red and white races to form a single American people had given way, and individuals of parentage similar to that of Thomas Rolfe, who once, at least in theory, had represented a step on the road to the dream of assimilation, had come to be most often seen as nightmarish beings, who were dismissed by most white Americans as repulsive and "unnatural," a term with which many seventeenth-century lawmakers would have agreed.

That "civilized" white people did not want to associate with such individuals is perhaps not surprising, but the aversion was not confined to social contact. There must have been tremendous pressure on American literary artists to keep their works free of interracial sex, or at least to ensure that when such unions were depicted the resulting children were portrayed in the appropriate fashion. In this view, because the circumstances that allowed for the production of "half-breed" or "mixed-breed" individuals must necessarily have been tragic, the lives of such characters, like that of Atala, had to be made to reflect their problematic incarnation.

Most writers simply chose to avoid presenting situations that would have allowed for such interracial entanglements. And even in texts where such a relationship seems possible, most often it was not allowed to take place. *The Last of the Mohicans* is the most obvious example of such a work, but this type of conspicuous nonconsummation confronts the reader in a number of other antebellum texts. In *Typee*, for instance, Melville allows his readers to believe in the apparently idyllic love of the white sailor Tommo and the beautiful Fayaway, but then resists the temptation to allow them to remain together in either the white or the Marquesan world. In the end, Tommo's need to return to his own culture, as well as his ever-present fear of the possibly cannibalistic intentions of his hosts, cause him to abandon this "paradise" and all its inducements, including the woman for whom he obviously has powerful feelings, and who, judging by her response to his escape, has similarly powerful feelings toward him.

While a study of the absence of such relations where they seem to be expected would be rewarding, I am more concerned with texts in which an interracial joining occurs. The resultant offspring were usually presented in one of two ways.[16] In some works this individual (one rarely meets two in the same text) is already an adult, and is an antagonist of the heroic white character. These figures, such as Ned Bloney (Goggle) in William Gilmore Simms's novels *The Partisan* and *Mellichampe,* or Boddo in Walt Whitman's novelette *The Half-Breed,* are often portrayed as violent, untrustworthy characters who live on the outskirts of society and take advantage of their freedom from its legal and cultural constraints. And while it is true that some adult mixed-bloods, such as Poe's Dirk Peters, are depicted in a somewhat more positive light, they too are generally made to embody many of these unattractive traits. Such characters are therefore unlike Cooper's trustworthy and prudent Natty Bumppo, who also lives on the outside but who, we are often reminded, is "white" through and through. Contemporary feelings about mixed-bloods are epitomized in Natty's comment in *The Prairie:* "the half-and-halfs that one meets in these distant districts are altogether more barbarous than the real savage."[17]

In other texts the relationship that leads to the sexual union is portrayed, and we meet the child shortly after its birth. (It should be mentioned that in many cases of literary intermarriage no offspring are produced, which in itself was a comment on the perceived incorrectness of such mixings.) The three works that I will examine briefly here – Eastburn and Sands's *Yamoyden,* Child's *Hobomok,* and Cooper's *The Wept of Wish-ton-Wish* – present temporal circumstances similar to those of Pocahontas and John Rolfe.[18] In each of these texts we see that when intermarriages are allowed to be consummated, the characters, particularly the Indian involved, have usually taken the first step on the road to disaster. At the conclusion of each text, the "father," as well as the native side of the family, must die or be displaced in order to ensure that the child will grow up among the Europeans. Also, in these works the children are all male and are therefore capable of taking possession of the land and passing it down to their progressively whiter descendants. The one great difference from the Pocahontas narrative in these texts – the fact that the Indian spouses are male and the whites are female – allows for the Indian involved to suffer the appropriate, often brutal consequences, which would have been more difficult for readers to accept if the Indian had been a woman, and more particularly, a lovely princess.

In their extremely popular poem of 1820, James W. Eastburn and Robert Sands take pains to convince their audience of the reciprocated love between the Indian man Yamoyden and the white woman Nora Fitzgerald. It is made clear that this is not the love of a captive for her captor. Rather, Yamoyden "wooed and won" the heart of Nora during his visits to the English settlements. They go off to the forest together and have a son, but their married life is soon over-whelmed by the events of King Philip's War. In the end, Yamoyden is killed as he rescues his white father-in-law from death, and Nora gives up her spirit in the arms of her dying husband. It is left to Nora's father to care for their child.

There is much prophecy in *Yamoyden*, especially concerning the passing of the Indian race, which is seen as part of a natural pro-gression. A "Prophet" describes the disappearances of the mam-moths, the race of giants, and of the human cultures that had preceded those of the Indians, and places the destruction of the tribes by the European invaders in this context. In fact, the nobility of Indians like Metacom (King Philip) and Yamoyden in the face of this unstoppable onslaught is one of the crucial themes of the work. Yamoyden seems to sense his destiny when, early in the poem, he looks ahead to the time after his death and hopes that his son will be the "Indian's friend."[19] There is no allowing for the possibility that his half-Indian son will be raised an Indian. If we look at this scene in terms of the greater theme of the poem, Yamoyden's rea-soning becomes clear; since his people are apparently fated to die out, his son will stand a much better chance for survival in the white world than in the Indian. All that Yamoyden can do is hope that the boy will not take an active part in the process that is destroying his father's people.

As Carolyn Karcher asserts, it was reading *Yamoyden* that inspired Lydia Maria Child to write *Hobomok*, a novel that tells the story of a positively portrayed Indian man who eventually becomes the hus-band of a white woman.[20] In this text, the title character is presented as a great friend of the English colony. After the supposed death of Charles Brown, the beloved of Mary Conant, Hobomok marries Mary and they have a son together. They are raising the boy outside of the white settlement when Charles suddenly reappears. Hobomok, somewhat surprisingly, gives up all rights to Mary and the child and leaves for the "West." All of the love and care that he has shown Mary are clearly not enough to counteract his perception of her need for Charles: "[T]he heart of Mary is not with the Indian. In her sleep she talks with the Great Spirit, and the name of the white man is on her lips. Hobomok will go far off among some red men in the west. They will dig him a grave, and Mary may sing the mar-riage song in the wigwam of the Englishman."[21] Hobomok must be made to suffer for his presumption, which has led to this doomed mismatch. And even though he survives, he is left with nothing but the memory of what this union has cost him, and a request to Charles concerning the well-being of his child: "For Mary's sake I have borne the hatred of the Yengees, the scorn of my tribe, and the insults of my enemy. And now, I will be buried among strangers, and none shall black their faces for the unknown chief. . . . Be kind to my boy.''[22]

Charles offers to take Mary and the son, Charles Hobomok Conant, back to England, but Mary refuses. " 'I cannot go to England,' she replied. 'My boy would disgrace me, and I never will leave him.' ''[23] Although John Rolfe was able to take his wife and child with him, the fact that this boy has his father's Indian blood in him changes his relationship to white society, which would be less prone to accept the son of a savage brave. We learn, however, that young Charles ultimately goes off to Cambridge (Harvard), finishes his studies in England, and that "by degrees his Indian appellation was silently omitted." Mary did not forget the love of the boy's biological father, and, Child tells us, "his [Hobomok's] faithful services to the 'Yengees' are still remembered with gratitude," but these niceties do not change the fact that Hobomok had to be sacrificed for the romance to have its requisite happy ending.[24]

Perhaps the most surprising antebellum comment about intermarriage is contained in the review of Cooper's *Last of the Mohicans* in the May 1826 issue of the *United States Literary Gazette*. This piece has become famous, or infamous, because of the sentiments expressed by the anonymous author concerning one of the subplots.

> We are in general disposed to have works of fiction terminate happily. We like a good wedding or two, to set all right. Still we know that this cannot always happen in real life, and that, for the sake of variety, as well as probability, the dark side must be sometimes turned toward us in fiction. But we had reason to believe that Cora and Uncas were preserved through so many dangers for some good end. Every event as we go along points to a favourable termination, when just at the winding up, the design seems to be capriciously reversed, and these two unfortunate persons are most summarily and unnecessarily disposed of.[25]

The wish for the triumph of love, which in this case translates to a wish for the successful culmination of the interracial relationship, as opposed to Cooper's choice, which was to kill off both of the young lovers, is startling. We learn, however, that there is an extenuating circumstance that would have allowed for this particular pairing.

> Uncas would have made a good match for Cora, particularly as she had a little of the blood of a darker race in her veins, – and still more, as this sort of arrangement is coming into fashion, in real life, as well as in fiction.[26]

Cora's own mixed racial heritage would have allowed what otherwise might have been a problematic relationship. As the product of such a joining it would have been less of a problem to see her as a participant in one. (This marriage would, of course, have also prevented the possibility of her becoming romantically involved with a white man.)

To be sure, particular couples, such as Sir William Johnson and Molly Brant, Sacajawea and Toussaint Charbonneau, Mr. and Mrs. Henry Schoolcraft, and, of course, Pocahontas and John Rolfe, had proven that mixed marriages could occasionally succeed. It was also true that on the frontier there was the occasional marriage between an Indian and a person of European descent – usually of a white trapper or pioneer to an Indian woman. But I am not aware of any evidence that such relationships were actually "coming into fashion, in real life." And in literature, as we have seen, the tendency was decidedly in the opposite direction.

Primarily because of the tragic conclusion of *The Last of the Mohicans,* readers have long felt that they understood Cooper's opinions about the portrayal of intermarriage in fiction. Robert Berkhofer reiterates the standard view:

> Not only did Cooper subscribe to the contemporary tension between progress and simple nature, savagery and civilization, he also obeyed the romantic conventions of the novel of the time in not allowing an Indian, no matter how noble, to marry a White, and therefore no Indian could be a true hero in his novels if it meant wedding the heroine.[27]

In fact, however, only three years after *The Last of the Mohicans* Cooper portrays the marriage of a heroic Indian chief to a white woman in *The Wept of Wish-Ton-Wish,* a novel that looks back to the seventeenth century, when the racial and cultural relationships of the period of the Leatherstocking Tales were just being established. Washington Irving had already romanticized the capture and death of Conanchet, chief of the Narragansetts, in "Philip of Pokanoket," and Cooper, perhaps feeling that he could immortalize Conanchet, as Eastburn and Sands, Irving, and a number of other writers were attempting to accomplish for Philip, weaves a complicated tale around this figure and the English Puritans with whom he comes in contact.[28]

In this romance, Ruth, the adolescent daughter of the Heathcote family, is taken captive by the Indians. She eventually suppresses her memories of the civilized world, is given the name "Narrah-mattah" (sometimes spelled "Narra-mattah" or "Narramattah"), and becomes the wife of Conanchet. Although it appears that she has become an Indian, in that she has changed in name, habits, and outlook during her captivity, the reader is constantly reminded throughout the second half of the novel of the indelibility of race. The descriptions of Narrah-mattah, first by Philip and then by Conanchet, emphasize that she is white, even though she may appear to be, and believe herself to be, an Indian. This sense of racial indelibility is reinforced by Whittal Ring, a white simpleton who comes to believe that he is an Indian warrior. Cooper uses Whittal not only as a symbol of the impossibility of "crossing" the two races, but also of the foolishness of the attempt. The most eloquent expression of this sentiment, however, comes in the dialogue between Conanchet, who had been captured by the English, and his innocent wife just before his death:

> "Thou hast seen the bright bow which shines in the skies, Narrah-mattah, and knowest how one colour is mixed with another, like paint on a warrior's face. The leaf of the hemlock is like the leaf of the sumach; the ash, the chestnut; the chestnut, the linden, and the linden, the broad-leaved tree which bears the red fruit in the clearing of the Yengees; but the tree of the red fruit is little like the hemlock! Conanchet is a tall and straight hemlock, and the father of Narra-mattah is a tree of the clearing, that bears the red fruit. The Great Spirit was angry when they grew together."[29]

Narra-mattah does not yet understand and attempts to resolve their problem. Her solution, though, is far from satisfactory.

> "The Great Spirit sees that the man and his wife are of different tribes," she at length ventured to rejoin. "He wishes them to become the same people. Let Conanchet quit the woods, and go into the clearings with the mother of his boy. Her white father will be glad, and the Mohican Uncas will not dare to follow."
>
> "Woman, I am a Sachem, and a warrior among my people!"
>
> There was a severe and cold displeasure in the voice of Conanchet, that his companion had never before heard. He spoke in the manner of a chief to his woman, rather than with that manly softness with which he had been accustomed to address the scion of the palefaces. The words came over her heart like a withering chill, and affliction kept her mute.[30]

Conanchet cannot become what he is not, nor would he do so if he could, if it would mean acting dishonorably or abandoning his people. It is significant that he is not "understood" and obeyed until he speaks as an Indian sachem would traditionally have spoken to his wife. The language of his fathers, and with it his spirit, has returned to him after all else has been lost.

His final words to Narrah-mattah also bear repeating, both as further evidence of his strength of character and as a clue to how this great chief had come to be in this predicament.

> "A woman of the palefaces; now let her see her tribe. Narrah-mattah, thy people speak strange traditions. They say that one just man died for all colours. I know not; Conanchet is a child among the cunning, and a man with the warriors. If this be true, he will look for his woman and boy in the happy hunting grounds, and they will come to him. There is no hunter of the Yengeese that can kill so many deer. Let Narra-mattah forget her chief till that time. . . . She will put a little flower of two colours before her eyes, and be happy in its growth. Now let her go. A Sagamore is about to die."[31]

Although Conanchet pretends to "know not" about Christianity, he alone, as opposed to the Reverend Meek Wolfe, had shown the Christian trait of mercy by not pressing an attack on the settlement when the conquest "seemed more than half achieved."[32] Cooper does not allow us to doubt that this seemingly positive attribute was acquired during his stay with the pious Mark Heathcote, and the reader at first commends this civilized behavior on the part of the Sachem. We begin to question it, however, when we see that this display of mercy costs both him, and ultimately Narrah-mattah, their lives and his son his heritage. His own brief captivity among the whites had somehow deprived Conanchet of the qualities needed to be a good Indian leader or, for that matter, a good Indian father, and his apparent failures as a chief and a parent must be taken into consideration even as we praise his mercy and native nobility.

Conanchet ceremoniously gives Narrah-mattah back to her people, and, following his death and her own emotional breakthrough, Ruth regains her memory as it was when she was first taken captive. The "record" of her years among the Indians, including her loving marriage to Conanchet, is literally erased during ths transformative ordeal. "The Wept" then dies, and the child of Conanchet and Narrah-mattah, much like that of Yamoyden and Nora, is taken in by his maternal (white) grandfather, never to be seen or heard about again in the course of the novel.

In all of these cases we see that, for the Indian involved, his intermarriage, while providing him with an opportunity to display bravery and "native" honor, also leads to his physical and/or spiritual demise. Miscegenation, even when it is based on true love or has grown out of the most noble of intentions, must be punished. And while Mary Conant is able to find and wed her white first love, Nora and Ruth are not so fortunate. These women see their Indian husbands, whom they love, die before their eyes, and soon they succumb as well. In *Yamoyden*, though we get a sense of the passing of the Indian, it is hard to include Nora's death in the process of their destruction. In *The Wept of Wish-Ton-Wish*, however, as in the Leatherstocking Tales, Cooper argues that sacrifices by both whites and Indians were essential to the future success of the Anglo-American settlements. This is a representative microcosm of the history of America that Cooper so often sought to portray. The hardships endured by the first white settlers of a territory, in combination with the regrettable but unavoidable destruction of the native population, allowed for the influx of followers and the civilizing of the area. For this reason the novel must close not only on the grave of "The Narragansett" but on that of "The Wept of Wish-Ton-Wish" as well.[33]

The children of these particular relationships, however, all survive, although their lives must be lived in the white world, far from the traditions of their paternal ancestors. What is crucial, especially to Cooper, is that no Indians are left to inherit the land, which ultimately becomes the possession of the Anglo-American colonists. Intermarriage, in literature if not in reality, was an apparently practical and effective method of land acquisition.

Little is learned about the child of Yamoyden and Nora, other than that Nora's father has taken custody of him. Charles Hobomok Conant, on the other hand, not only survives but prospers in the white world. The reader is told nothing about the son of Conanchet and Ruth, other than that he survives the death of his parents. We do not even learn his name, although even if we did it might not matter, since that name might have been lost over the generations, as we learn from the case of the Reverend Meek Lamb: "Though claiming a descent from him who ministered in the temple at the period of our tale [the Reverend Meek Wolfe], time and intermarriages have produced this change in the name, and happily some others in doctrinal interpretations of duty."[34]

One could argue, though, that Cooper did not wish to erase completely the effects of this intermarriage. His dedication, which appears in both the first English edition of the novel (*The Borderers: A Tale* [London, 1829]) and the first American edition (*The Wept of Wish Ton-Wish* [Philadelphia, 1829], suggests that *The Wept* was based on an actual historical situation, the effects of which could be traced in the contemporary world. Here Cooper reminds his readers that some descendants of such ancient Indian-white intermarriages have survived into their own day.

THE REV. J.R.C.

of

PENNSYLVANIA

The kind and disinterested manner in which you have furnished the materials of the following tale, merits a public acknowledgement. As your reluctance to appear before the world, however, imposes a restraint, you must receive such evidence of gratitude as your own prohibition will allow.

Notwithstanding there are so many striking and deeply interesting events in the early history of those from whom you derived your being, yet are there hundreds of other families in this country, whose traditions, though less accurately and minutely preserved than the little narrative you have submitted to my inspection, would supply the materials of many moving tales. You have every reason to exult in your descent, for, surely, if any man may claim to be a citizen and a proprietor in the Union, it is one, that, like yourself, can point to a line of ancestors, whose origin is lost in the obscurity of time. You are truly an American. In your eyes, we of a brief century or two must appear as little more than denizens quite recently admitted to the privilege of a residence. That you may continue to enjoy peace and happiness, in that land where your fathers so long flourished, is the sincere wish of your obliged friend.[35]

It was clearly difficult for Cooper to portray intermarriage, and he almost certainly shared his culture's fear of the contemporary "mixed-bloods" of the territories. But if we are to believe this dedication, he actually held those of mixed, if extremely diluted, Indian-white parentage in high esteem.

Cooper's source wished for and was granted anonymity, but it should not be thought that this was out of shame or embarrassment about the admixture of Indian blood in his family. It was most probably a gentleman's wish for privacy, like that desired by Scott, Cooper (as he did in the early editions of *The Wept of Wish-Ton-Wish*), and many other writers of the period who kept their names off the title pages of their works. Cooper kept the identity of "The Rev. J.R.C." confidential, but made his racial status clear. If, however, Cooper's readers needed corroboration concerning the existence of civilized offspring of interracial marriages, the numerous descendants of Pocahontas would have been by far the most visible examples.

It must be mentioned that this dedication subsequently disappears, as does a mention of Pocahontas and Powhatan that was included in the preface to the first English and American editions of

The Wept. Perhaps Cooper came to feel that it was inappropriate to emphasize the miscegenative aspect of the tale, and so he removed this opening passage which suggested that such relationships do not necessarily have to end in tragedy. It is interesting that he concurrently chose to do away with his invocation of the woman whom he describes as "the ill-requited Pocahontas."[36]

Because of the sentiment against the portraying of successful interracial unions during the antebellum period, it is not hard to imagine the dilemma faced by early nineteenth-century writers who wanted to use the already popular Pocahontas material. In a literary climate in which a rendering of a happy mixed marriage, even that of national heroine Pocahontas and John Rolfe, might be seen as inappropriate, what had to be discovered was a way to avoid the seemingly unfortunate turn that the narrative takes toward its conclusion. When we look at the attempts to do so, we see that two strategies emerged. One was to make adjustments to the narrative itself, so that while John Rolfe could be featured and the lovers' feelings toward each other alluded to or even specifically expressed, an explicit portrayal of their marriage or a mention of their son could be avoided. The other was to present episodes either directly adapted from, or very closely resembling, incidents from the life of Pocahontas in other texts. By presenting Pocahontas-like actions performed by other native women, authors could preserve and exploit the more exciting elements of the Pocahontas narrative while providing a resolution that steered clear of the problematic issue of miscegenation.

Among those who chose to make use of the Pocahontas material were a number of antebellum dramatists. Although the role of Rolfe in these texts ranged from primary, as in Charlotte Barnes's *The Forest Princess,* to nonexistent, as in the now-lost *Virginia, or Love and Bravery* by Albert M. Gilliam, most playwrights chose to include Rolfe and to make reference to the sympathy between him and Pocahontas but to avoid portraying their marriage.[37] The most important of these dramatists was George Washington Parke Custis, the grandson of Martha Washington, whose *Pocahontas, or The Settlers of Virginia* (1830) became one of the most popular theatrical presentations of the narrative.

Arthur Hobson Quinn, in his introduction to Custis's *Pocahontas,* points out the main problem with staging her story. "The trouble with the Pocahontas plays in general is that the most dramatic incident, the saving of Smith's life, comes too early in the play."[38] Custis solves this problem by adjusting the historical events so as to place the Rescue at the end and thereby make it the climactic moment of the drama. This also has the added effect of ending the play before the marriage of Pocahontas and Rolfe, who are clearly in love, can take place. Powhatan, who gets the last word, is, however, allowed to look to the future:

> And may the fruits of this union of virtue and honour be a long line of descendants, inheriting those principles, gifted with rare talents, and the most exalted patriotism. Now it only remains for us to say, that looking thro' a long vista of futurity, to the time when these wild regions shall become the ancient and honour'd part of a great and glorious American Empire, may we hope that when the tales of early days are told from the nursery, the library, or the stage, that kindly will be received the national story of POCAHONTAS, OR THE SETTLEMENT OF VIRGINIA.[39]

Once again, their descendants, like the products of the process of absorption posited by Jefferson, are made residents of the "American Empire" of the future and therefore need not be worried about in the present. This type of conceit may have served to reassure those viewers who would leave the theater with a positive feeling about the native tribes that the Indian Removal Act of 1830 was simply a temporary measure and that Indians, or at least their mixed-blood descendants, would play a role in the forthcoming empire.

As might have been predicted in view of the playwright's Revolutionary family connections, patriotism is one of the most important themes of *Pocahontas*. Custis makes it clear from the outset that the love of one's own country is important to both the English and the Indians. In the first scene, which is set before the arrival of the Jamestown colonists, we meet Barclay, an English castaway and the lone survivor of an unnamed earlier expedition, who has been living with the Indians for some time. He is told by the noble Prince Matacoran that English ships have been sighted, which initiates a conversation during which Matacoran questions Barclay's loyalty to his former country. His response tells the audience something about Barclay himself, and also about the Indian prince: "Surely, Prince Matacoran, the brave in war, the just in peace, the favourite of his king, the friend of his country, must admire that patriotic feeling in another, which he himself possesses in no ordinary degree."[40] Matacoran's love of his country wins the respect of the English, but also keeps him from participating in the peaceful resolution at the end of the play.

In an interesting twist, we are introduced to Barclay's Indian wife Mantea and told that they have children. This suggests that although Custis apparently felt the need to avoid involving his heroine in a biracial marriage during the course of the play, he had at least to

allow for such a mixing in order to avoid offending any of her powerful descendants, many of whom still wielded a great deal of power
and influence in his home state of Virginia. Mantea and Barclay gave
Custis the opportunity to present a happily married Indian-white
couple, and thereby to make the point that the crosscultural problems of such a relationship could be successfully overcome, without
the need of a wedding scene or the production of a Thomas Rolfe
before the final curtain.

In his 1837 *Pocahontas: A Historical Drama,* Robert Dale Owen, the
son of social reformer Robert Owen, purports to take a more historical approach to the Pocahontas material, although he does provide this disclaimer: "The characters introduced into the piece, with
two very trifling exceptions, are strictly historical; and every principal
event represented or alluded to, in the course of the Drama, occurred, if Smith's own history may be trusted, with very little varia-
tion as here set down."[41] In fact, Owen, although he does apparently
trust Smith for most of his factual information, strays more from
"recorded history" than he would like his readers to believe. For
instance, he creates a rather Shakespearean subplot that revolves
around a revolt against Smith's rightful leadership of the colony; he
contrives an interesting explanation for the changing of the princess's name from "Matokes" to "Pocahontas" (see pp. 91–2 below);
and he makes his heroine an early spokeswoman for women's
rights.[42] This Pocahontas believes that women should be equal to
men, and should "stand beside, / Not crouch behind" the men who
love them.[43] In fact, the best evidence for his self-proclaimed more
historical approach lies in his presentation of the Rescue early in
the drama.

Owen's solution to this troublesome chronology is to balance Pocahontas's bravery by providing a second rescue – in this case, of
Pocahontas by Smith – as his climactic moment. Owen's staging of
the traditional Rescue earlier in the play helps to emphasize the
importance of the political controversy within the Jamestown colony
that follows. Smith's dramatic saving of the princess from her white
kidnappers is then presented as something of a compensation for
her earlier actions. The captain leaves Pocahontas and Rolfe together for the final curtain, but that is as far as their relationship
goes. As in Custis's *Pocahontas* and James Nelson Barker's earlier *The
Indian Princess,* Owen makes the love of the princess and Rolfe clear.
In all of these works, however, it must remain unconsummated during the actual proceedings. No matter how much of what had gone
before was based on "facts," at this point a break from the historical
record had to be made.

John Brougham's highly successful 1855 comedy, *Po-ca-hon-tas, or*

The Gentle Savage, is the play that is generally thought to have ended the vogue for "Indian dramas" on the American stage.[44] He borrows a few events from her life, but for the most part uses what plot there is as a vehicle for wordplay. When Smith, rather than "Rolff" (here, a Dutch buffoon) tries to win the heart of the princess, Pocahontas points out a crucial problem, for which the captain has a ready reply.

> POCANONTAS: Stop! One doubt within my heart arises!
> A great historian before us stands,
> *Bancroft* himself, you know, forbids the *banns!*
> SMITH: *Bancroft* be *ban*ished from your memory's shelf,
> For spite of *fact,* I'll marry you myself.[45]

This is typical of Brougham's disregard for the historical basis of the narrative, and for historians like Bancroft who had provided the fodder for the serious Indian dramas that had prompted his satire. Even the Rescue scene is not exempt from his wit.

> *Pocahontas rushing in heroineically distressed and dishevelled, followed by sailors.*

> POCAHONTAS: Husband! for thee I *scream!*
> SMITH: *Lemon or Vanilla?*

> POCAHONTAS: Oh! *Fly* with me, and quit those vile dominions!
> SMITH: How *can* I fly, beloved, with these pinions?
> *Duet – Smith and Pocahontas*
> "Prima Donna Waltz"[46]

Brougham's Pocahontas is a wonderful parody of the archetypal Indian heroines of drama and romance, all of whom were ultimately based primarily on John Smith's representations of the original Powhatan princess.

Smith flirts with Pocahontas throughout the play and finally wins her hand in a game of cards. Powhatan, who is known here simply as "King," joins their hands "*patriarchally,*" and Smith, in response to a complaint by Rolff about the historical accuracy of this arrangement, describes the true nature of his own relationship with Pocahontas:

> SMITH: Old King of Clubs [Powhatan], you are a jolly trump!
> And don't you be so downcast, you Dutch pump;
> All future history will see you righted,
> With her, in name alone, I'll be united.[47]

As this John Smith correctly predicts, to this day Pocahontas is far
better known for her relationship with him than for that with her
husband. But what is most important here is that Brougham's comic,
ahistorical ending does away with the need to portray even the possibility of miscegenation. Pocahontas is left holding Smith's hand as
the cast asks for the audience's approval of their labors.

The second alternative available to those who wished to make use of
the Pocahontas narrative was to present elements from the life of
the princess in different contexts. As one would expect, the moment
most often borrowed was her intercession at the execution of John
Smith. These reworkings of the Rescue, however, often varied in
detail and emphasis. In some, such as the folk tale "The New England Pocahontas," or the story of "Malee – The Pocahontas of
Florida," the princess was invoked openly, so that there would be
no doubt about what the reader was getting.[48] These short works
provided the drama of a rescue scene without the problematic romantic material that should necessarily have followed.

A less obvious solution was to weave such rescues into longer,
more complex works, in which the elements borrowed from the Pocahontas narrative would be recognizable, even though they were
presented as moments in the lives of alternative characters. There
are many Pocahontas-like saviors in antebellum romances, but I shall
concentrate here on the rescue scenes that are crucial moments in
James Kirke Paulding's *Koningsmarke* (1823), Catharine Maria Sedgwick's *Hope Leslie* (1827), and William A. Caruthers's *The Cavaliers of
Virginia* (1834–5).[49]

Paulding, who had glorified Pocahontas in *Letters From the South*
and would again in his "Ode to Jamestown," parodies her most
famous endeavor in *Koningsmarke,* his satirical romance about the
short-lived colony of New Sweden. Although Sir Walter Scott and his
followers are Paulding's primary targets, the Rescue of John Smith
and its literary descendants take a hit as well. In this case the Pocahontas figure is Aonetti, or "Deer Eyes," who is described as "the
beauty of the [Indian] village."[50] She first saves the captive Christina
Piper by adopting her as a sister, and then, because of her love for
Christina and her clearly unrequitable feelings for the handsome
and heroic Koningsmarke, Aonetti springs into action when he and
Lob Dotterel are about to be executed.

> Arrived at the stake, they proceeded to strip the two victims . . .
> and to paint them black with charcoal and grease. They were
> then fastened to the stake, and, all being ready, the horrible
> ceremony was about to begin, when Aonetti came rushing fran-
> tically to the spot. . . .

As the Indian maid approached, she called upon them to stay a moment, ere they lighted the piles. The noise was hushed, by the command of some sages who were presiding at this solemn ceremony, for so it was reckoned by the Indians. Aonetti then urged every motive she could think of, to induce them to spare the two victims. She stated the rewards that would be given, if they carried them to the *Big Hats* [Quakers] at Coaquanock, and the terrible vengeance the white-men would take, when they heard of the sacrifice of their brothers.[51]

Aonetti is at first rebuffed in this more reasoned than passionate attempt at a rescue. However, higher powers soon intrude on the proceedings.

It was now one of those bright, clear, still afternoons, which are common in the month of September. There was not a breath of air to curl the river, or wave the leaves of the forest, nor a cloud to be seen in the sky. At this moment, when they were about to set the funeral pyre, a sudden burst of thunder, loud and sharp, arrested them. The eyes of all were turned upwards, with a sensation of awe and surprise.[52]

Aonetti interprets this apparent intervention by the Great Spirit as a warning against the carrying out of the execution. She is able to win a one-day reprieve for the captives, which allows for the timely arrival of a delegation of Quakers, who successfully barter for their release.

Paulding's inclusion of this parody of the Rescue suggests his sense that such scenes were as ridiculous and as widely circulated as the plot contrivances engineered by the "Great Unknown" (Scott), who is humorously accused of being "Mephostophilos," because of his amazing ability to write clever books as well as his success at remaining "invisible."[53] Paulding clearly felt that the saving of captives through the agency of an Indian maiden had by 1823 become a generic device that through repetition, if not through the unbelievability of the notion that Indian girls always immediately fall in love with the first young, Caucasian male that they see, had lost the evocative power that original rescue story may once have had. If his effort was a serious attempt to put an end to the proliferation of such heroic maidens, however, it had little success.

The introductory materials in Sedgwick's *Hope Leslie* and Caruthers's *The Cavaliers of Virginia* share a clever authenticating stratagem. At the end of the preface to *Hope Leslie,* Sedgwick provides a disclaimer for those who might have doubts about the possible existence of a character such as Magawisca, who, in part by performing a rescue, emerges as one of the heroines of the novel. "The writer is aware that it may be thought that the character of Magawisca has no prototype among the aborigines of this country. Without citing Pocohontas [*sic*], or any other individual, as authority, it may be sufficient to remark, that in such delineations, we are confined not to the actual, but the possible."[54] Sedgwick asserts herself as the creator of this story and warns readers against seeking real-life models for the behavior described in the book. Yet in the course of denying that Pocahontas is a model for her heroine, Sedgwick succeeds in connecting the two and putting the Pocahontas narrative into the minds of her readers as they begin her novel.

Caruthers begins the text of *The Cavaliers of Virginia* by invoking that moment in history that he deems best suited to the skills of the romancer. "The romance of history pertains to no human annals more strikingly than to the early settlement of Virginia. The mind of the reader at once reverts to the names of Raleigh, Smith, and Pocahontas. The traveller's memory pictures in a moment the ivy-mantled ruin of old Jamestown."[55] Caruthers makes the connection between his own novel and the famous figures of the founding of the Virginia colony, with the predictable exception of John Rolfe, whose name would kindle the memory of his marriage to Pocahontas. We are reminded of her relationship to Smith, however, which ensures that as his version of rescue scene unfolds the reader will make the appropriate connection.

Michael Davitt Bell asserts that the "Indian plot" of *Hope Leslie* has two sources. The first, upon which is based the attack at Bethel and the kidnapping and marriage of Faith Leslie, is a historical event, the Deerfield Massacre, as described in John Williams's *Redeemed Captive Returning to Zion*. The other is more easily identifiable: "The second source of the Indian plot is not so much historical as legendary (at least by 1827). It is clear that Magawisca's intervention to save Everell from her father is inspired by the story of John Smith and Pocahontas."[56] Magawisca, by far the most interesting figure in *Hope Leslie,* other than the freethinking title character, is a young Indian woman who is the childhood friend of Hope and Everell Fletcher (the young male lead); the sister of Oneco; and (not surprisingly) the daughter of the old Pequod chief Mononotto. In one of the early turning points of the novel, the captured Everell is about to be killed by her father in vengeance for the death of his son at the hands of the English:

> At this moment a sun-beam penetrated the trees that enclosed the area, and fell athwart his [Everell's] brow and hair, kindling it with an almost supernatural brightness. To the savages, this was a token that the victim was accepted, and they sent forth a

shout that rent the air. Everell bent forward, and pressed his forehead to the rock. The chief raised the deadly weapon, when Magawisca, springing from the precipitous side of the rock, screamed – "Forbear!" and interposed her arm. It was too late. The blow was levelled – force and direction given – the stroke aimed at Everell's neck, severed his defender's arm, and left him unharmed. The lopped quivering member dropped over the precipice. Mononotto staggered and fell senseless, and all the savages, uttering horrible yells, rushed toward the fatal spot.[57]

Magawisca's heroic action is based on her romantic love for Everell. It is made clear from the outset, however, that Everell, though certainly fond of Magawisca, does not love her. And while her selfless conduct saves Everell's life, her love for this white man causes her to be mutilated. Following this courageous action, the now maimed Magawisca has no future happiness to look forward to, either as an individual or as one of the few survivors of her decimated tribe. Everell, on the other hand, goes on to marry Hope and live happily ever after.

One unconventional aspect of *Hope Leslie* is Sedgwick's presentation of the loving relationship of the young Indian brave Oneco, the brother of Magawisca, and Faith Leslie, the younger sister of the title character. Faith, like Narrah-Mattah in *The Wept of Wish-Ton-Wish*, was taken captive by the Indians as a child. Although this marriage characteristically has yet to produce any offspring, the union of Faith and Oneco is similar to that of Cora and Uncas in *The Last of the Mohicans* in that, no matter what the social conventions may prescribe, the reader is convinced that they belong together. However, their relationship, like those of Yamoyden and Nora, Hobomok and Mary, and Conanchet and Ruth, can only exist away from the settlements. The white world, as described by Sedgwick, Cooper, and their contemporaries, was not yet ready to bear continual witness to such a joining.[58]

We also learn that Faith, like Atala, had become a Catholic. In general, rather than being seen as one possible way to eternal salvation, Catholicism, with its belief in "superstition," was often described in nineteenth-century America as being closer to an Indian religion than to Protestantism, particularly to the austere Puritanism of the early New Englanders. The successful joining of Indian and Catholic is therefore not very surprising. However, although Faith is a member of what was believed to be the most undesirable sect of Christianity, she cannot be described as a "heathen," or, worse still, a "devil worshiper," as Indians traditionally were. Indeed, Faith's Catholicism provides her sister with some solace: " 'Thank God!'

exclaimed Hope fervently, for she thought that any christian faith was better than none."[59] Thus, Faith's Christianity helps to allow for Hope's final acceptance of her life with Oneco, in that, whatever her sins, Faith will be in a position to ask the Christian God for absolution.

Caruthers sets *The Cavaliers of Virginia* approximately two generations after the founding of Jamestown. In England, the days of the Protectorate are over, and Charles II has been restored to the throne. The hero of *The Cavaliers of Virginia* is loosely based on the historical Nathaniel Bacon, the future leader of the rebellion that bears his name. He is portrayed as a suitably attractive, passionate young firebrand. This passion, when galvanized by the apparent impossibility of his love for Virginia Fairfax, causes Bacon to flee the civilized world of the English settlement and ride wildly off into the forest. He is captured, made a prisoner by the Chickahominies, and subjected to the traditional tortures of the white captive. After a respite, Bacon is again tied to the stake and his torments are about to be resumed, when "an Indian female of exquisite proportions rushed to the scene of the butchery, and threw herself between the half immolated victim and his bloodthirsty tormentors."[60] This young woman is Wyanokee, the former friend *cum* servant of Virginia Fairfax, who had returned to her people and assumed her rightful, royal place among them. "She placed herself before the captive, and elevating her person to its utmost height, and extending her hands before him as a protection, she cried, 'Strike your tomahawks here, into the daughter of your chief, of him who led you on to battles and to victory, but harm not the defenceless stranger.'"[61] Wyanokee actually offers to marry Bacon, but it is clear, as in the relationship between Magawisca and Everell in *Hope Leslie,* that such a ceremony will never come to pass: "When this was proclaimed, Wyanokee slowly and doubtfully turned her eyes upon Bacon to see whether the proposition met a willing response in his breast. A single glance sufficed to convince her that it did not."[62] As Curtis Carroll Davis puts it, in his brief comparison of *The Cavaliers of Virginia* to the Pocahontas narrative, "Wyanokee, like the original Pocahontas, is the daughter of a chieftain. Like the original Pocahontas, too (and like John Davis' subsequent treatment), she is quite good-looking. Unlike the original, who finally married a white man, Wyanokee does not succeed in bringing home her Bacon."[63] In this humorously phrased passage, Davis makes the point that Caruthers gave Wyanokee rank and beauty, which were the traditional trappings of an Indian heroine, but could not provide the ultimate joining with a white man that he presents Wyanokee as desiring. And while I would agree that this tradition goes back to Pocahontas, it is more to the Pocahontas whose salvation of Smith was thought to have been based on her amorous feelings toward him than to the more mature young woman who fell in love with and married John Rolfe. Both Pocahontas and Wyanokee are denied the love of the men whose lives they save.

Although it is Bacon's true, and ultimately requited, love for Virginia Fairfax that keeps him from taking advantage of Wyanokee's proposal, the Indian princess had just saved his life, and there was no guarantee that he would continue to survive if he did not marry her. What seems clear is that the revulsion against interracial marriage was so strong that Caruthers could not have his young hero survive in this manner, since his readers would not have accepted it, nor would they have enjoyed being robbed of the mating of Bacon and Virginia, who were obviously meant for each other. Indeed, it was probably the fondness for Bacon among Virginians that allowed Caruthers to take this firm stance against an intermarriage without the fear of offending the numerous, Virginia-based descendants of Pocahontas.

I have no doubt that the nineteenth-century audiences of *Hope Leslie* and *The Cavaliers of Virginia* would have made the connection between the heroism of Magawisca and Wyanokee and the bravery traditionally identified with Pocahontas even without the aid of the prefatory clues provided by Sedgwick and Caruthers. That these authors chose to emphasize the connection points to their sense of the historical importance of the Pocahontas story. On the one hand, the authority of the Pocahontas narrative provided something of a thematic, if not a factual, basis for each of these romances, whose audiences may well have been convinced that such noble actions by Indians were possible, or at least had been in the seventeenth century. More significant, however, was the symbolism of Rescue of Captain John Smith as a decisive event in the Anglo-American conquest of the New World. Both of these authors, who saw themselves as writing in the tradition of Scott, hoped that the particular events that they described would also be seen as crucial, if less well-known, links in the chain of American history.

It is worthwhile here to look briefly at one more text that pulls together some of the themes we have been considering.[64] In 1851, a dramatic adaptation of Cooper's *The Wept of Wish-ton-Wish* opened on Broadway.[65] This two-act play, which remained popular for the next decade, uses some of the incidents provided by Cooper as a skeleton, but then adds a number of exciting moments to spice up the action. The playwright also seems to have been familiar with Sedgwick's novel, for here it is Hope Heathcote, the twin sister of Faith and sister-in-law of Content, who is captured by the Indians,

transformed into Narramattah, and has a son with Conanchet. In
this quite short play Narramattah effects no fewer than four separate
rescues. She saves a traitorous white man, Satisfaction Skunk, from
the wrath of her husband; her husband from the first attempt by
Uncas to execute him; her father, Major Gough, from conspirators;
and finally, her husband from Uncas a second time. At this climactic
moment, however, Conanchet pushes her away and bravely accepts
his fate. She, not surprisingly, falls on his body and gives up her own
spirit, leaving their child in the arms of her sister. In the end, as
usual, the parents who took part in the interracial union must die,
and the child must be raised among the white settlers. In this play,
though, to ensure against any wandering of the minds of those in
the audience, we also have strategically placed rescue scenes to re-
focus their attention.

Diana Reep, in her discussion of Mrs. E. D. E. N. Southworth's
The Three Beauties, or Shannondale, makes the obvious point about why
rescues were frequently included in antebellum texts.

> It is a mark of how appealing the Pocahontas legend must have
> been that Southworth, finding no practical way to get an Indian
> into her plot, inserted an episode in which an old priest tells
> the legend of Lover's Leap. . . . The only reason Southworth
> could have had to include this story was that the tale of an
> Indian maiden rescuing a white man was so popular that in-
> cluding it automatically enhanced the novel's appeal whether
> or not it enhanced the novel's coherent structure.[66]

Whether the rescue scene played an integral role in the development
of the plot or simply provided an exciting episode in what would
otherwise have been a dull chapter, such scenes, which without a
doubt would have conjured up the image of Pocahontas and Smith,
became one of the standard conventions of nineteenth-century writers.[67] Romancers could not miss with a rescue – its inherent drama
would add to the enjoyment of the text, while providing Anglo-
Americans with a fond recollection of a crucial moment from their
mythohistoric past.

Such incidents are representative of the uses made of the most easily
adaptable aspect of the Pocahontas narrative. However, less dramatic
expressions of Pocahontas-like behavior can also be found in other
antebellum works. One instance occurs in perhaps the most distinguished and popular historical text of the period.

In William Hickling Prescott's *History of the Conquest of Mexico* we
are introduced to Doña Marina, a captured Indian woman who becomes the interpreter for, and ultimately, the lover of Cortez.[68] She

is portrayed as an attractive young woman of noble birth, who had been sold into slavery through the machinations of her unscrupulous mother. Although her characterization by Prescott is not generally reminiscent of Pocahontas, Doña Marina consistently acts in the best interests of Cortez and the conquistadors, and therefore against most of the indigenous population. Doña Marina is not given the chance to enact a dramatic rescue of Cortez in the style of Pocahontas, but she does resemble the Virginia princess in her response to a different type of threat against the lives of Cortez and his followers, in an incident that may have its roots in the second rescue of Smith by Pocahontas, her warning him about the "dinner conspiracy."

In Chapter 8 of the third book of the *Generall Historie of Virginia*, Smith, in his usual self-promoting manner, tells his readers about another of the fiendish plots of Powhatan against the English colonists. (This is the "conspiracy" to which Leslie Fiedler refers.)

> Powhatan and his Dutch-men brusting [bursting] with desire to have the head of Captaine Smith, for if they could but kill him, they thought all was theirs, neglected not any opportunity to effect his purpose. The Indians with all the merry sports they could devise, spent the time till night: then they all returned to Powhatan, who all this time was making ready his forces to surprise the house and him [Smith] at supper. Notwithstanding the eternall all-seeing God did prevent him, and by a strange meanes. For Pocahontas his dearest jewell and daughter, in that darke night came through the irksome woods, and told our Captaine great cheare should be sent us by and by: but Powhatan and all the power he could make, would after come kill us all, if they that brought it could not kill us with our owne weapons when we were at supper. Therefore if we would live shee wished us presently to bee gone.[69]

The word "strange" here means "unexpected" rather than "peculiar" because, if we are to believe Smith's earlier testimony, Pocahontas had already saved his life from the wrath of Powhatan. This foiling of the dinner conspiracy was yet another instance of her placing the lives of the English settlers above the wishes of her father and the apparent best interests of her people.

In the *History of the Conquest of Mexico*, we learn that one of the greatest threats to the expedition of Cortez prior to its arrival at the Aztec capital was the conspiracy of the Cholulans. Prescott briefly describes the suspicions of Cortez, which were based, among other things, on changes in the behavior of his Cholulan hosts. He then informs us of how the plan was finally defeated through the agency of "Marina, the good angel of the expedition."[70]

The amiable manners of the Indian girl had won her the regard of the wife of one of the [Cholulan] caciques, who repeatedly urged Marina to visit her house, darkly intimating that in this way she would escape the fate that awaited the Spaniards. The interpreter, seeing the importance of obtaining further intelligence at once, pretended to be pleased with the proposal, and affected, at the same time, great discontent with the white men, by whom she was detained in captivity. Thus throwing the credulous Cholulan off her guard, Marina gradually insinuated herself into her confidence, so far as to draw from her a full account of the conspiracy. . . . [71]

While this conversation was going on, Marina occupied herself with putting up such articles of value and wearing-apparel as she [the Cholulan woman] proposed to take with her in the evening, when she could escape unnoticed from the Spanish quarters to the house of her Cholulan friend, who assisted her in the operation. Leaving her visitor thus employed, Marina found an opportunity to steal away for a few moments, and, going to the general's apartment, disclosed to him her discoveries. He immediately caused the cacique's wife to be seized, and, on examination, she fully confirmed the statement of his Indian mistress.[72]

Both of these native women foil conspiracies that would have caused the deaths of a number of the invaders, including the leader of each expedition. And while one could argue that Prescott here is simply relating embroidered historical facts about the actual conquest of Mexico, he may have placed such emphasis on this particular incident, and on the contributions of Doña Marina throughout the entire expedition, because he knew that success based on the aid of a native woman would have resonance for the citizens of the United States. As they read about the beginnings of the Spanish conquest, the Anglo-American conquest would have come to mind, and the aid provided by Marina would have recalled that provided by her Virginian counterpart.

In this century, Walter O'Meara has made an interesting point about Doña Marina's intriguing exploits.

[I]n purely objective terms, Doña Marina was a traitor who betrayed her own people and, perhaps more than any other single person in Cortés' expedition, brought them to their knees. And here we happen on a phenomenon that, in William Christie MacLeod's words, is both surprising and abundant: "the constant betrayal of their own people by Indian women," usually to white lovers. Catherine, the Chippewa mistress of Major

Henry Gladwin, foiled Pontiac's surprise attack on Detroit. A
native woman's treachery upset the Natchez' plan for wiping out
the French at Fort Rosalie. Garcilaso reports the betrayal of
their own people by Indian women as far back as DeSoto's time.
Weetamo, "the Queen of Pocasset," went over to the English
side when things became too hot for her in King Philip's camp.
And, apart from overt treachery, we have numerous instances
of young Indian girls conniving in the escape of white captives.
Such conduct, it has been noted, is not marked among any
other people, and it is especially surprising to find it in women
whose sense of loyalty was otherwise so strong. It has been suggested that matters sexual may be at the bottom of it.[73]

I would argue, however, that whenever the heroine is a young native
woman who in one way or another acts as a protector of the male
leader of the white race, it is fair to say that Pocahontas, the best-
known Indian woman who responded to an invader's peril in this
manner, would have been called to mind. O'Meara's failure to mention her here is most probably based on the reputedly chaste relations between the princess and Captain Smith.

Such Anglo-American interpretations of the actions of indigenous
American women point to the popularity of a particular white male
fantasy. The Indians are defeated not solely by the superior arms of
the Europeans, but also by the irresistible sexual attractiveness of
their charismatic leaders.[74] What also becomes apparent is that each
of the women listed by O'Meara, as well as Pocahontas, can therefore
be depicted as a convenient scapegoat for the subjugation or destruction of her culture. These exemplary native women, who were for
one reason or another drawn to the colonists, were often presented
as being complicitous in the process of political and/or cultural gen-
ocide that resulted from the continuing European colonization of
the New World. The Indians could therefore be usefully portrayed
as having had a hand in their own demise.

I am not the first to make a connection between Pocahontas and
Doña Marina. In fact, a reference to the best-known paramour of
Cortez set the stage for one of the most important early "defenses"
of Pocahontas and her narrative. Waddy Thompson, who describes
himself as the "Late Envoy and Minister Plentipontentiary of the
United States at Mexico," was convinced by his friends to publish
the memoirs of his life among "that unique, and, in a great degree
primitive people."[75] In his *Recollections of Mexico* (1846), Thompson
also recalls the ancient city of Cholula and the important event that
took place there, which in his opinion might well have changed the
course of Mexican history. "The Cholulans had received him [Cor-

tez] with every demonstration of friendship into their city, and had afterwards concerted a plan to destroy all the Spaniards; this plot was discovered through the address and sagacity of that miracle of a woman Doña Marina, the Indian interpreter of Cortez, whose great qualities throw into the shade our own Pocahontas."[76] This comment drew a strong reaction from James Chamberlayne Pickett, who rose to uphold the honor of the great heroine of the South. In a pamphlet explicitly entitled *The Memory of Pocahontas Vindicated Against the Erroneous Judgment of the Hon. Waddy Thompson,* by "A Kentuckian" (1847), Pickett first defends Pocahontas against this apparent insult, and then takes the opportunity to vent his spleen on a number of other subjects related to Mexico.[77] One can sum up the feelings for Pocahontas that are expressed throughout this article in Pickett's own words: "In all history and in all romance it would be difficult to find a more perfect character than Pocahontas; and taking her as she has come down to us, it appears to me to be impossible to say wherein it could have been improved."[78] This is followed by a fifteen-page appendix that consists of quotations from various texts in various languages, all of which supposedly substantiate his opinion about the princess.[79] William W. Jenkins notes that Thompson's disparaging remark "is the earliest piece on record to make any negative comparison of the Indian maiden with any other historical figure," and goes on to point out that such comments, and refutations such as Pickett's, would ultimately become commonplace.[80]

The sexual relationship between Doña Marina and Cortez differs greatly from the Platonic love of Pocahontas and Smith. Their liaison, however, as well as the arranged intermarriages between other Aztec women and Spanish conquistadors as described by Prescott, could have been understood, if not condoned, by the majority of his audience because of the conquistadors' Catholicism. As we have seen in the cases of Atala and Faith Leslie, to American Protestants the supposedly superstition-based nature of this oldest form of Christianity seemed to allow that Indians and Catholics would on some level be able to understand each other; therefore, interracial relations between them should not be greatly surprising. The military and sexual conquests of the Spanish explorers portrayed by Prescott and other mid-nineteenth-century literary and visual artists (such as Emanuel Leutze, whose painting of *The Storming of the Teocalli by Cortez and His Troops* [1848] was based on Prescott's text), as well as of French adventurers and fur trappers on the northern and western borders of the United States, were thought to be part of an earlier, essential stage in the development of the New World, during which the inevitable march of the Europeans was launched, but in which problems were clearly evident.[81] It would take the Anglo-American, Protestant domination of the continent to fulfill the ultimate destiny of the New World.

This view of the actions of Doña Marina as part of a yet-to-be-perfected process mirrors the sentiments of many antebellum New Englanders toward the Virginia founding. Individuals ranging from W. H. Gardiner, whose lightly veiled ridicule of Smith and Virginia opened this chapter, to northern sympathizers like Daniel Webster and Rufus Choate, who simply favored the New England founding, to historians like John Gorham Palfrey, Charles Deane, Henry Adams, and Edward Neill, who actually attacked Smith and through him the Pocahontas narrative, all generally believed that the largely commercial endeavor that was the Virginia planting was necessary, if only for the maps drawn by Captain Smith, but that the Anglo-American colonial enterprise was perfected by the coming of the Puritans to New England. Indeed, it could be argued that a crucial problem with both the Mexican and Virginian conquests was their dependence on the help of native women, without whom these ventures would certainly have failed. This suggests that figures like Doña Marina and Pocahontas, who represented women and Indians – two groups whose roles in the success of the New England colonies had to that point been traditionally downplayed – were perceived by some nineteenth-century Americans as signifying the problematic nature of the colonies that men like Cortez and Smith had helped to found.

Finally, Prescott's description of the foiling of the Cholulan conspiracy, although not as exciting as a Rescue, may actually have been more meaningful to the average American reader of the antebellum period. While very few white Americans would find themselves in the captive position of a John Smith or of the Everells and Bacons of fiction, anyone, at any level of society, could be the victim of a conspiracy by his or her enemies. As Robert Levine has pointed out, conspiracy fears were common in antebellum America, and the "impulse toward romance . . . was a form of countersubversion."[82] The popularity of figures like Pocahontas and Doña Marina might therefore also be explained by the countersubversive nature of their actions. These native women, and the heroines of romance modeled on them, were often portrayed as thwarting the attempted conspiracies of other Indians in their apparent realization of the rightful and inevitable domination of the continent by the European invaders.

The epigraph of this chapter is from Melville's *The Confidence Man*.[83] Our protagonist is in conversation with Charles Noble Arnold, and

his litany of apparently good Indians is of course meant to induce
Charlie to tell the story of Colonel John Moredock, the Indian-hater,
and thereby to provide descriptions of the real-life Indians one meets
on the frontier. Such individuals apparently differ greatly from
"Massasoit, and Philip of Mount Hope, and Tecumseh, and Red-
Jacket, and Logan," and, of course, "Pocahontas," who apparently
inspires this fond sentiment in the heart of the cosmopolitan.[84]

This passage reasserts the idea that Pocahontas had long been
identified as one of a small number of exceptional Indians, all of
whom possessed qualities that were respected by whites. That she is
the only woman on this list is itself significant. Her primary action,
as seen by white nineteenth-century Americans, was on one level a
male exploit, in that the virtues of activity and fearlessness exemplified in it were traditionally thought of as the purview of men. Her
great moment occurs when she, whether out of love for life, love for
Smith, or trust in the love of her father, breaks free of the passive,
woman's place and energetically asserts herself. No matter what her
motivation, however, this attractive, courageous young woman was
by far the most popular persona of Pocahontas throughout the nineteenth century and would continue to be so, despite the efforts of
Charles Deane, Henry Adams, and the other doubters of John Smith.

In fact, in a September 1888 letter to Thomas Janvier, the anthropologist and ethnographer Adolphe Bandelier complained that
a particular view of Native Americans had continued to thrive into
his own day, much to his annoyance:

> We have, Mr. [Lewis Henry] Morgan, and I under his directions,
> unsettled the Romantic School in Science; now the same thing
> must be done in literature on the American aborigine. Pres-
> cott's Aztec is a myth, it remains to show that Fenimore Coop-
> er's Indian is a fraud. Understand me: I have nothing personal
> in view. Cooper has no more sincere admirer than I am, but
> the cigar-store man, and the statuesque Pocahontas of the
> "vuelta abajo" trade as they are paraded in literature and thus
> pervert the public conceptions about Indians – these I want to
> destroy first if possible.[85]

In this indictment of the creators of the literary Indians that inhabited the popular literature of the nineteenth century, Bandelier
makes what by this time had become an obvious connection. The
era of the Romantic Indian had still not ended by 1888 because
Indians such as Cooper's braves and exotic Princess Pocahontases
continued to be encountered in popular romances and were the
crucial elements in the unscientific and therefore misleading opinions that most white Americans had about Indians. Bandelier be-

lieved that these romantic images were thought by many of his contemporaries to represent reality, whereas the work of researchers like Morgan and himself, which he believed went far toward determining truths about the native cultures, went unaccepted. Stereotypical Pocahontases and other noble savages therefore needed to be exposed as "frauds," if not "destroyed." What is somewhat ironic is that while Pocahontas was certainly the archetypal Indian princess, and therefore necessarily beautiful and sexually attractive, the section of the narrative that described her reality-based captivation of Englishman John Rolfe had been tenaciously suppressed in favor of the more traditionally "masculine" activity depicted by the rescue of John Smith, in the great majority of nineteenth-century formulations.

Despite the enormous popularity of the narrative, Leslie Fiedler observes that "The Pocahontas legend . . . is one which left untouched the imagination of our classic writers."[86] However, although it admittedly was never the explicit subject of Cooper or the other major antebellum romancers, many of the structures of the Pocahontas narrative had by the mid-nineteenth century become important elements of the Romantic Indian tradition. The question of why her story did not become a subject for the major writers of the period, though, has yet to be adequately addressed.

The most obvious answer is that these artists did not produce romances based on the lives of any of the great figures of the American past. Although Washington makes a brief appearance in Cooper's *The Spy,* important figures from the American Revolution, including John Paul Jones and Benjamin Franklin, appear in Melville's *Israel Potter,* and Hawthorne invokes the Puritan Fathers in *The Scarlet Letter* and his historical short fiction, none of the great national literary figures of the antebellum era chose to expand the life of Bradford, Winthrop, Franklin, Washington, or Jefferson into a full-fledged romance. (Such texts as Irving's *Life of Washington* and Simms's *Life of Captain John Smith,* which without a doubt contain romantic elements, still deserve to be categorized as biographies.) The lives of what might be called these American "world-historical" figures were far too well-known for them to be useful protagonists.[87] The life of Pocahontas, given the widespread knowledge about and extreme importance of the crucial events, would certainly have fit under this rubric. It was therefore in histories of Virginia or of the United States, in studies of important Indian figures, and in the works of lesser artists that she assumed her historically imposing role in the founding of America.[88]

While it might seem as though her life would have been a good kernel for a romance because of the great gaps that exist in the historical narrative, in fact the few bits of extant information had already been so overused by the mid-nineteenth century that there was little that could be said about Pocahontas that had not been rehashed in the many renderings of her own story or the countless other tales of brave, beautiful Indian maidens. Her paradigm had so penetrated the world of the romance that there was little to be gained in the attempt to construct a serious, full-length novel around this material.

In addition, if we agree with the reviewer of Cooper's *Gleanings in Europe*, which appeared in the *North American Review* for January 1838, in a novelistic portrayal of Pocahontas an author almost certainly would have had to present a protagonist whom we might call "too good to be true." This commentator points out one of the greatest difficulties of novel writing:

> Novels are pictures of life; and the characters presented in them must have that diversity and even contrariety of feeling, motive, and conduct, . . . which we daily witness among our friends, or we do not acknowledge the fidelity of the imitation. . . . It is only with such imperfect beings that we can sympathize, or take any interest in their concerns. . . . The most inhuman person has yet some touch of our common nature; the most perfect is not stainless from the universal infirmity. And it is precisely on these spots of sunshine or shade, that we fasten with an interest proportioned to the contrast they afford with the other traits of character.[89]

Although we should not assume that all contemporary writers saw this description as a fair representation of the necessary attributes of the romance protagonist, the call for completeness of character did have its adherents, especially among the admirers of Scott. Using such a formula, it would indeed have been difficult to center a romance on Pocahontas. There were no obvious negative traits available to balance her heroism, and so readers might well have doubted the "fidelity of the imitation." (We might argue that if one were to formulate the narrative from an Indian perspective, Pocahontas would have to be presented as an extremely problematic character. However, such a reading clearly would not have appealed to Anglo-American purveyors of the narrative during the antebellum period.)

Finally, in a book-length study it would have been impossible to avoid portraying her marriage and the birth of Thomas Rolfe. The marriage would necessarily have had to be presented as a boon, both to the lovers and to the Jamestown colony's chances for survival, and the birth, even more problematically, would have needed to be presented as a blessed event. Such a positive portrayal of interracial marriage would not have been tolerable to the reading public of the period, who as we have seen were more likely to invest in a work in which some sort of retribution was handed down to the guilty parties. Pocahontas's own early death from a European disease, as well as the possibly violent death of her husband at the hands of her uncle only five years later, might easily have sufficed as a suitably tragic conclusion. However, to the majority of the literary artists of the period it must have seemed far simpler just to avoid entirely the necessarily problematic subject of her later life.

The discussion of the true Indian name of the princess put forward by Owen in his *Pocahontas* examines one of the most consistently troubling questions about her youth.

NOMONY:	Pocahontas –
POCAHONTAS:	Why call me by that uncouth name? It sounds From your lips, dearest, still so cold and strange. Call me Matokes, as you used to.
NOMONY:	What! Cross our father's will, his strict command?
POCAHONTAS:	It seems like parting from a friend, to lose The old, familiar name that you, Nomony, My father, brother, all have called me by, Ever since I remember. And besides, I cannot see the use of such a change.
NOMONY:	Not see the use of it! Now, dearest sister, Have you forgotten what our Powhas said Of dangers threatening your life?
POCAHONTAS:	They said The Yengeese were magicians.
NOMONY:	Well?
POCAHONTAS:	They said, That with their wicked spells, these strange white men Strike whom they will, provided they discover The victim's real name.[90]

Owen provides a surprising solution to the problem of the apparent subversion her of "true" name. It is for her own protection that the Indians changed her name, because they believed, as many white cultures long believed about those whom they perceived to be "servants of the devil," that if your enemy finds out your actual name, he or she will immediately gain power over you.

This question about her name is in some ways still with us. When viewers first see a copy of the Simon Van de Passe engraving or the *Booton Hall Portrait* in the National Portrait Gallery in Washington, D.C., they are often surprised that on neither is the name "Pocahontas" mentioned. She is "Matoaka als Rebecka" in each of the renderings, and "Matoaks als Rebecka" in the subscript of each picture.[91] The latter is her "Christian" name, under which she was married to Rolfe and brought to England. It is thanks to Smith, who inseparably linked "Pocahontas" to her most valiant exploit, that her apparent nickname, which has been translated as everything from "playful one," to "little tomboy," to "little wanton," has become the name by which history remembers her and her deeds.

The event that signified the change from Matoaka to Rebecka had been a rarely discussed incident in her narrative, but toward the end of the era of the Indian romance, perhaps because it was thought to signify most clearly the change in her cultural allegiance, this moment was chosen as the scene from her life best suited to fill a panel in the Rotunda of the nation's Capitol. In my next chapter, I examine the circumstances of this choice, which was made by John Gadsby Chapman, a now little-known artist, who saw this prestigious commission as his breakthrough into the highest echelons of American painting.

4

JOHN GADSBY CHAPMAN'S BAPTISM OF POCAHONTAS

===============

4

"The first Christian ever of her nation"[1]

In an anticipation of the nineteenth-century debate about the suitability of American subjects for literary and visual artists, the anonymous author of a letter printed in the June 17–24, 1734 edition of the *Boston Gazette* argues for their usefulness, and goes on to provide an example of how one particular subject might be interpreted.

> YOUR *New England* POETRY gives me a great deal of Pleasure, as it discovers (besides a Beauty in the Composition) a tender and affectionate Mind in the Author. . . . If your Poets will indulge their Muse, there's no want of Subjects in that part of the Globe. What a glorious Figure wou'd the Princess Pocahontas make, Painted by a fine hand? How charmingly wou'd she shine interceeding with her Rigid Father for the Life of the *English* Captain, and when that wou'd not prevail, throwing her own Neck upon his, and by that means intercepting the Fatal Blow.
>
> How beautiful wou'd she appear afterwards a Captive in the hands of the Countrymen of him that she had saved? The Treachery of the *Indian King* that betray'd her, and the steady behavior of her Father, who wou'd not comply with terms to the disadvantage of the Country, even for the sake of a beloved Daughter, whom he doated on with utmost tenderness wou'd be incidents as great in their kinds as any the *Greeks* and *Romans* wrote of. Then her Marriage with an English Gentleman, her graceful and majestick Behaviour at the Court of K.J.1st [King James I], and her Sickness and Death at *Gravesend,* wou'd be ample Field to shew all that can be lovely or great in a Female Character, and all that can be lamented in the loss of such a one.[2]

The editor would have his readers believe that this is a letter to a New Englander from a friend in Great Britain, written as a positive response to certain poems that had been produced in the colony and sent across the Atlantic. However, we might well question the

4

93

existence of such poems, for two reasons. First, no specific authors or titles are mentioned. Second, in the columns immediately following this letter are excerpts from Robert Beverley's *History and Present State of Virginia,* which contained one of the few renderings of the Pocahontas narrative then available in the colonies.[3] The proximity of the letter and these excerpts suggests that this is in fact a pseudoepistolary advertisement for her story, which was strategically placed to sell copies of Beverley's work. In any case, Lawrence W. Towner is correct when he calls this 1734 letter "the first proposal published in America urging the elevation of Pocahontas to the status of American folk heroine."[4]

Although this correspondent was the first to call for a "painting," if only a poetic one, of the rescue of Captain John Smith, Virginia historian John Burk was the first to elaborate on the visual possibilities of such a production:

> The spectacle of Pocahontas in an attitude of entreaty, with her hair loose, and her eyes streaming with tears, supplicating her enraged father for the life of captain Smith, when he was about to crush the head of his prostrate victim with a club; is a situation equal to the genius of Raphael: And when the royal savage directs his ferocious glance for a moment, from his victim, to reprove his weeping daughter; when softened by her distress, his eye loses it[s] fierceness, and he gives his captive to her tears, the painter will discover a new occasion for exercising his talents.[5]

Burk was writing his *History of Virginia* in the opening years of the nineteenth century, and, like his contemporary John Davis, was attracted by the romantic potential of a successful rendering of this dramatic moment. Indeed, the Rescue quickly became the best-known visual image of Pocahontas, and, not surprisingly, there were a number of attempts to portray its emotional power in antebellum America.

The full-scale historical painting, however, was not the genre of choice. Those paintings that were attempted were generally conceived and executed as models for engravings (Figures 1, 2, 3 and 4). As Ann Uhry Abrams points out, "Smith's rescue by a scantily clad Pocahontas became a favorite topic for a number of popular prints that flooded the market from the 1830s well into the 1870s."[6] Such depictions, which were frequently included in the popular histories of the period, often portrayed the princess as a beautiful, well-endowed child of the forest, who, recalling the line from Joseph Croswell's *New World Planted,* was also generally "whiter far, than other natives are."[7]

Another important early national representation of this moment is

Figure 1. Frontispiece from John Davis, *Captain Smith and Pocahontas*. Engraving by "H.A." (Philadelphia: Benjamin Warner, 1817). Beinecke Rare Book and Manuscript Library, Yale University.

the 1825 relief by Antonio Capellano, which is located over the west door of the Rotunda of the Capitol in Washington D.C. (Figure 5) This piece, one of four such reliefs that depict various Indian-white interactions, shows the principal figures slightly after the moment of truth: the half-naked Pocahontas is still shielding the helpless captain, but the hand of Powhatan has been raised to stay the execution. Its inclusion in the Capitol at this early date makes clear that the rescue of Smith by Pocahontas had long been perceived as a crucial generative moment in the history of the United States.[8]

The opportunity would arise during the 1830s for another national rendering of this important event. Of the eight panels inside the Rotunda that were to contain historical paintings portraying seminal moments in the birth and coming-of-age of the new nation, four

Settlement of Jamestown, Virg.

Virginia

Pocahontas and Capt. Smith

Figure 2. This version of the Rescue is included in John Warner Barber, *Interesting Events in the History of the United States* (New Haven: J. W. Barber, 1829). United States History, Local History and Geneology Division, The New York Public Library, Astor, Lenox and Tilden Foundations.

had been filled by 1824. These works, all by John Trumbull, included two that dealt with the most important American military victories of the Revolutionary War, the *Surrender of General Burgoyne*, and the *Surrender of Lord Cornwallis*, and a third that portrayed the last action in arms by the great American commander, *George Washington Resigning his Commission*. Such subjects would serve to remind future generations of Americans of the importance of the War for Independence and of the monumental efforts that had been necessary to bring about their freedom. The significance of the event portrayed in Trumbull's fourth painting, the *Signing of the Declaration of Independence*, would be obvious to visitors to the political heart of the nation (Figure 6).

A painting portraying an event from the life of Pocahontas would become one of the four works that completed this collection, but its subject would not be another rendering of the Rescue as might have been expected. John Gadsby Chapman, the young Virginia artist who was awarded one of the commissions, chose instead to portray the baptism of Pocahontas, the moment when the princess became Rebecca, and symbolically abandoned her native culture in favor of that offered by the English (Figure 7). This chapter explores the implications of that decision. I first examine how Chapman gained his commission from Congress and prepared for this important assignment. I then look at the contemporary response to the painting and suggest possible interpretations of the *Baptism*, both in relation to the Rescue, the best-known event in the life of Pocahontas, and the works of other mid-nineteenth-century artists who were using Native American individuals and themes as subjects.

The topic of filling the four remaining panels in the Rotunda was raised only occasionally during the 1820s, but after the turn of the decade the matter began to get more serious attention. On December 15, 1834, Congress again took up the debate about which artists should be granted commissions to produce these important works. Although it had previously been resolved that four "native" artists be chosen, the additional discussion of this resolution allowed former president and now congressman John Quincy Adams to give his opinion about the soundness of the proposition. "Mr. J. Q. ADAMS expressed a doubt whether four native artists could be found who were fully competent to the execution of the task to be assigned to them."[9] This brought an emotional response from several members, including Henry Alexander Wise, a young congressman from Virginia, who took great offense at this apparent affront to the talents of American painters.

> The gentleman from Massachusetts says that he doubts whether four American artists can be found competent to execute these paintings. Sir, I am proud to say and believe that this country – the great masters dead – is richer now in native talents in the fine arts than any country on the globe. Without meaning to be invidious in the naming of our artists, as an American, I will boast that Allston is the finest historical painter, Sully the finest portrait painter, and Greenough is the finest sculptor in the world. And to these I could add the names of twice the number four. One – Chapman – I know to have slept upon his easel during a stay of three years in Italy, before the works of the old masters in the Vatican, and to have had an historical painting engraved by the academy of fine arts at Rome. The country is rich in artists. Though the fine arts are not encouraged here, they are indigenous to the country.[10]

Adams, as he later explained in his memoirs, was only trying to ensure that each of these paintings would be a masterpiece and feared that if four different artists *had* to be chosen, one or more of the works might prove to be less than satisfactory and therefore not be worthy of a place in the Capitol Rotunda.[11]

The former president apparently believed that the paintings by Trumbull possessed the requisite genius. Wise took this opportunity to express his opinion on this matter.

Figure 3. Edward Corbould, *Pocahontas Rescues Captain John Smith.* Engraving by T. Knight, 1850–60. This is one of the strangest antebellum renditions of the Rescue. The Indians portrayed represent both Eastern and horse culture (Plains) Indians, the flora is reminiscent of the landscapes of Church, and the falls would remind viewers of Niagara. These changes emphasize the American, rather than Virginian, nature of this scene. One could argue that this image is an early example of the process that would make the Plains Indians into the generic representations of all native cultures. (Private Collection.)

> The evil of a monopoly is now to be seen in the Rotundo [*sic*]. The precedent of Trumbull's paintings, instead of being quoted for the selection of one artist, should be cited for the selection of four. Does the gentleman from Massachusetts not know that the piece of the Signing of the Declaration of Independence was dubbed, by a former representative of Virginia, (Mr. Randolph), the "shin piece?" It may be seen by any who will look at them, that the faces in one are the faces of all four, and that all the faces in the same piece have all the same characteristics.[12]

Although it must be admitted that there are a number of shins on display in Trumbull's depiction of the *Signing*, it seems clear that "shin" is used here in the sense of to borrow. Wise would have his colleagues believe that Trumbull borrowed the faces from one work to use in the others, and that a similar embarrassment could occur unless four different painters were chosen.[13]

The final name dropped by Wise in his listing of the great artists of America – that of the painter who presumably did not get a great

Figure 4. Engraving after Alonzo Chappell, *Pocahontas Saving the Life of Capt. John Smith.* From J.A. Spencer, *History of the United States, Earliest Period to the Administration of President Johnson.* Vol. 1. (New York: Johnson, Fry & Company, 1866). The "halo" of light around the head of Pocahontas is an interesting addition. United States History, Local and Geneology Division, The New York Public Library, Astor, Lenox and Tilden Foundations.

deal of sleep during his sojourn in Europe – belonged to a young man who since his return to America had begun to get some attention for his portrayals of the people and places of Wise's home state. Indeed, John Gadsby Chapman was, not surprisingly, another native son of the Old Dominion. He was born on August 11, 1808, in Alexandria to businessman Charles T. Chapman and Sarah Margaret Chapman, the daughter of the well-known tavern keeper and hotel owner John Gadsby, proprietor of Gadsby's Tavern, Alexandria, and later of Gadsby's Hotel, on Pennsylvania Avenue in Washington City.[14] Among the young Chapman's aristocratic schoolmates in Alexandria was Lorenzo Lewis, son of Nelly Parke Custis Lewis, the granddaughter of Martha Washington, and this connection later turned out to be quite useful to the young painter.

Figure 5. Antonio Capellano, *Preservation of Captain Smith by Pocahontas*. 1825. Courtesy of the Architect of the Capitol, United States Capitol Art Collection, Washington, D.C.

Figure 6. John Trumbull, *Signing of the Declaration of Independence*. 1824. Courtesy of the Architect of the Capitol, United States Capitol Art Collection, Washington, D.C.

In 1827 Chapman left Alexandria and moved to Winchester, Virginia, with the hope of beginning his chosen life as a serious artist. It was here that he met and for a time was the roommate of one Henry A. Wise, then a young law student but later a Confederate general and governor of Virginia, who, as we have seen, began his political career as a congressman with a great deal to say about the four vacant panels in the Rotunda. During this period Chapman

Figure 7. John Gadsby Chapman, *The Baptism of Pocahontas*. 1840. Courtesy of the Architect of the Capitol, United States Capitol Art Collection, Washington, D.C.

honed his technical skills, and was able to make the acquaintance of a number of important figures in the American artistic community. This led to his going off on the requisite trip to Italy in 1829, where he studied briefly at one of the academies in Rome, went on at least two sketching trips with Samuel F. B. Morse, and spent most of his time copying the works of the old masters. On this journey he also completed his first important painting, *Hagar and Ishmael Fainting in the Wilderness,* which earned him a positive notice from Frances Trollope (Figure 8).[15]

Chapman returned from Europe in 1831 and began traveling around Virginia and painting just about anything that crossed his path. His special interest, however, was Mount Vernon, and his friendship with the Lee and Custis families allowed the young artist to paint many members of that distinguished clan, including the beautiful Hannah Lee Washington and Mrs. John A. Washington, whom he painted with her children on the porch at Mount Vernon. Chapman completed a number of works in the environs of Washington's home and of other Virginia locales connected with the life of the first president. Nelly Lewis's brother, the playwright George Washington Parke Custis, whose 1830 *Pocahontas* we have examined in Chapter 3, also permitted Chapman to copy some of the paintings owned by Washington, including the Charles Willson Peale portrait. As his fame grew, Chapman was able to paint such celebrities as the great folk hero of the moment, Congressman Davy Crockett of Tennessee, and another former president from Virginia, the elderly James Madison. On April 11, 1834, he had his first exhibition, a well-received showing of his copies of the old masters and paintings of Virginia at his studio on Pennsylvania Avenue, which was strategically located opposite his grandfather's hotel, as well as Jesse Brown's Indian Queen Hotel, where in the preceding decade many Indian delegations had been entertained after passing under the "fanciful and beautiful" painting of Pocahontas on the sign above the door.[16]

By this time Chapman was already well into a campaign toward obtaining one of the Capitol Rotunda commissions. On March 10, 1832, he wrote an apparently self-effacing but also quite self-congratulatory letter to Judge Josiah Stoddard Johnston, congressman from Louisiana, in which he requested Johnston's advice about a project he suggests he had been thinking about for some time.

> I have for the last two years engaged my thoughts upon a subject that has interested me the more as I reflected upon it, as one of National interest and pictorial grandeur, one connected with our history, . . . whose mention must rouse our warmest feelings

Figure 8. John Gadsby Chapman, *Hagar Fainting in the Wilderness.* 1853. This is a later rendering of *Hagar and Ishmael Fainting in the Wilderness,* the painting that Chapman had executed during his visit to Europe. The earlier effort is the work that received the positive mention from Frances Trollope, and to which Henry A. Wise refers when he states that one of Chapman's works had been "engraved by the academy of fine arts at Rome." Courtesy of the Alexandria Association and Alexandria Library, Lloyd House, Alexandria, VA.

of patriotism and we should ever cultivate with intense interest
its recollection as the first dawning of that gallant spirit that has
since spread so glorious a hallo around our navy. It is the Capture of the *Serapis* on 23 Sep. 1779 by John Paul Jones.[17]

This famous naval engagement was Chapman's original idea for a
suitable national subject, and after painting a word picture of the
event for Judge Johnston, he admits that, had he been more successful as a portrait painter, he would have been able to absorb the
expenses that such a work would entail. He then, finally, gets to the
point.

> I have now only to ask of you candidly if in your opinion there
> is any probability I should receive any aid from Congress in
> undertaking such a picture, if in the event of the vacancies in
> the Rotunda being filled I may dare hope any thing from my
> humble pretensions and what means I should adopt to such an
> object?[18]

From this letter it seems clear that Chapman already had a fairly
good idea about what type of means to employ to gain the end he
sought.

Henry Wise took his seat in Congress in December 1833, and as
we have seen he went prepared to help his young friend. The 1834
resolution was eventually passed, and so the search was on for four
American artists worthy of this prestigious assignment. On June 29,
1836, Chapman wrote to Wise to ask him to keep the pressure on
his southern peers on Chapman's behalf, but to forget the John Paul
Jones idea because "I confess honestly I don't like it upon maturer
reflection / There are others that have every requisite for a great
National work. . . . There are some subjects of thrilling incident connected with our history untouched, as far as I know unmentioned."[19]
In the end, the influence of Wise, James Kirke Paulding, Richard
Henry Wilde, possibly Senator Powhattan Ellis of Mississippi, and
other members of the Virginia and southern delegations was enough
to have Chapman's name placed near the top of the list, and after
Washington Allston had refused to accept a commission, and Samuel
F. B. Morse, who was suspected of authoring an article critical of
former President J. Q. Adams, had been all but disqualified, Chapman, in early February 1837, received the good news that he had
been chosen to execute one of the paintings.[20] His mandate was
simply to select a subject that served "to illustrate the discovery of
America, the settlement of the United States, the history of the revolution, or the adoption of the constitution."[21] There had been
some debate about limiting the subject matter to an event that had

occurred before the end of the Revolutionary War, but such language does not appear in the congressional report.

The public announcement of the commissions – a strangely disparaging article that focused on other unnamed "artists of superiour genius, who are now neglected" rather than on the four artists who had been chosen – was made in the March 4, 1837, edition of the *New-York Mirror*.[22] By this time Chapman had chosen an alternative to his John Paul Jones project and was clearly anxious to begin work. It was probably not a surprise to his contemporaries that he finally decided upon an incident from the life of Pocahontas, the heroine of the first permanent Anglo-American settlement and one of the great figures in the history of his home state. Indeed, Chapman had already painted a number of scenes concerning the founding of Jamestown, including *The First Ship, The Landing at Jamestown, The Crowning of Powhatan, The Warning of Pocahontas* (about the dinner conspiracy), and, of course, his own version of the Rescue, *Pocahontas Saving the Life of Captain John Smith*.[23] His subject for the Rotunda, however, would be *The Baptism of Pocahontas*, which he had not attempted to portray before and which certainly qualified as a previously "untouched" and unmentioned" incident.[24]

As soon as the commission was gained, Chapman packed his bags for England. As Georgia Stamm Chamberlain has pointed out, he was interested in ascertaining what types of costumes would have been worn by men such as Governor Thomas Dale and the Reverend Alexander Whitaker, who would necessarily be principals in his painting; in investigating what would have been the appropriate furniture for this period; and in finding a church that he could use as a model for the one at Jamestown.[25] Most importantly, however, he was hoping to see some portraits of his main characters – Dale, Whitaker, John Rolfe, and especially Pocahontas herself.[26] Unfortunately he was unable to find such likenesses in England, and so he returned to America with the hope of tracking them down in Virginia.

A number of models for Pocahontas would have been available to Chapman. As Abrams suggests, these were dominated by either the young, often half-naked girl of romantic rescue scenes, or images of a somewhat Anglicized Pocahontas in her court costume.[27] However, the *Booton Hall Portrait* – the eighteenth-century painting of Pocahontas in English court finery that was originally believed to have been painted during her lifetime, and which now hangs in the National Portrait Gallery in Washington, D.C. – would not have been one of them (Figure 9) Although Robert Dale Owen claims to have seen an oil painting of Pocahontas in "stiff, European dress" in New York in the late 1830s, there does not seem to be any corroboration that he saw this painting. In fact, as we shall see, the evidence sug-

Figure 9. Unidentified artist, *Matoaks als Rebecka* – The "Booton Hall Portrait." Mid-to-late eighteenth century. Courtesy of the National Portrait Gallery, Smithsonian Institution, Washington, D.C.

gests that what he saw was Robert M. Sully's copy of another painting, the *Turkey Island Portrait*.[28] It is now known that the *Booton Hall Portrait* was in private hands in England throughout the nineteenth century and was apparently unknown in America until its "discovery" in 1875.[29]

Copies of the 1616 Simon Van de Passe engraving and perhaps of the 1793, less "Indian" version, would have been available, but, although these engravings were possibly the truest to Pocahontas's

Figure 10. Simon Van de Passe, *Matoaks als Rebecka*. Engraving, 1616. Courtesy of the National Portrait Gallery, Smithsonian Institution, Washington, D.C.

actual appearance, neither of these portrayals of a rather (by Anglo-American standards) unattractive young woman conformed to the mid-nineteenth-century notion of what an Indian princess – and especially this particular Indian princess – should look like (Figures 10 and 11). The *Sedgeford Hall Portrait,* an eighteenth-century painting of a young Indian woman with a possibly biracial child that was believed by some people to be of Pocahontas and Thomas Rolfe, could possibly have been seen by Chapman, but again the young woman in question does not meet the romantic standard (Figure 12). There were other representations of Pocahontas, such as Mary Woodbury's mid-eighteenth-century portrait, which today would probably be classified as folk art, but such works, which were often loosely based on the Van de Passe engraving, would not have provided any useful information for Chapman (Figure 13). And finally, there were the countless popular renderings of Pocahontas and various other romantic Indian maidens upon which he could draw. Many of these young women came closest to the ideal that Chapman was seeking, but there would be the danger of making his Pocahontas either too generic or too sexually attractive for the somber religious ceremony that he wanted to portray.

Chapman's dissatisfaction with these choices is evidenced by his writing a series of letters to Colonel William Bolling, then of Goochland, Virginia, in late 1837 and early 1838. Colonel Bolling was the son of Thomas Bolling, the grandson of Colonel John Bolling of Cobbs and a direct descendant of Pocahontas and John Rolfe. The letters concerned two portraits of the colonel's remote ancestors that had hung at Cobbs during William Bolling's youth.[30] The painting of Pocahontas, now lost, has come to be known as the *Turkey Island Portrait.* It apparently had inspired a great deal of intrafamily debate concerning its authenticity, since it depicted, in William Bolling's words, "a female of sallow complexion with a head of thick, curled hair."[31] Neither Colonel Bolling nor, according to him, his father, believed that this was actually a likeness of the princess of Virginia, although Thomas Bolling seems to have believed that the companion portrait of Rolfe may have been authentic.[32]

The *Turkey Island Portrait,* which apparently portrayed a rather round-faced, full-figured young woman, disintegrated sometime during the early 1840s. It had been copied, however, by Robert Matthew Sully, the nephew of portraitist Thomas Sully, and in this manner a reproduction of it found its way into *The History of the Indian Tribes of North America,* by Thomas McKenney and James Hall (Figure 14).[33] McKenney had been superintendent of Indian trade under Madison, Monroe, John Quincy Adams, and Jackson, and Hall was a well-known expert on frontier life. (A passage from Hall's *Sketches of His-*

Figure 11. Unidentified artist, after Simon Van de Passe, *Matoaks als Rebecka.* Engraving, 1793. Courtesy of the National Portrait Gallery, Smithsonian Institution, Washington, D.C.

tory, Life, and Manners, in the West ultimately became the source of the "Indian-hating" section of Melville's *Confidence Man.*)[34] The authority of McKenney and Hall's *History* established the reputation of the copies of the *Turkey Island Portrait* as the truest likenesses of Pocahontas, although it must be mentioned that these too evolved over

Figure 12. Unidentified artist, The "Sedgeford Hall Portrait." Late eighteenth century. Reproduction permission courtesy of the Borough Council of King's Lynn and West Norfolk, King's Lynn, England. William Sturtevant has suggested that this painting may represent an "18th-century Iroquois woman and child." See Barbour, *Pocahontas and Her World*, 235.

the years. The later portraits diverged steadily from their predecessors, to the point where these representations bore little resemblance to the first Robert M. Sully copy, and probably even less to the Pocahontas of the *Turkey Island Portrait* (Figures 15, 16, and 17).[35]

Although Bolling was not able to provide Chapman with any sub-

Figure 13. Mary Woodbury, *Pocahontas.* c. 1738. Courtesy of the Massachusetts Historical Society, Boston, MA. This painting was apparently completed by Woodbury when she was at school. It is certainly the first original depiction of Pocahontas produced in the New World, and almost surely the first done by a woman. The Van de Passe engraving may have provided a thematic model for this work, as Pocahontas is in European attire, but it is in no way an attempt to copy the earlier portrait.

stantial help in terms of models, he did free him from one particular responsibility, for which the artist was grateful. In January 1838, in the letter mentioned earlier, Chapman wrote to the colonel, "I have also seen since the receipt of your letter Mr. Sully's copy of the portrait of Pocahontas – it is now in this city [New York] – and I most cordially thank you for absolving me from the obligation of following it as the authentic representation of the heroine of my picture."[36] In the end, Chapman, as Chamberlain suggests, may have used as his model a painting by his friend Charles Bird King of another Indian woman, Hayne Hudjihini ("Eagle's Delight" or "Eagle of Delight"), the young wife of the Oto chief Shaumonehusse (Figure 18). Others have speculated that he based some of the features of his princess on those of a "Miss Gardiner," daughter of Colonel C. K. Gardiner, or on the daughter of friend and fellow artist George Cooke.[37] Most likely, however, Chapman decided to trust his own conception of what Pocahontas should look like, but then, perhaps because of the lack of a suitable, authentic likeness, suffered a crisis of confidence. What is most surprising when one first views *The Baptism of Pocahontas* is that the artist does not take this great opportunity to extend himself in his depiction of her appearance. The viewer is barely allowed to see her face, which is almost in profile, with eyes closed and head bowed, and would be hard pressed to provide more than a general description of Pocahontas using Chapman's work as a model.

It is perhaps instructive here to look briefly at Chapman's version of the Rescue, *Pocahontas Saving the Life of Captain John Smith* (Figure 19). In this painting a very well-covered princess is nearly facing away from the viewer. Chapman turns her head so that she is looking toward Powhatan, thus allowing us to see one side of her face, but again, it would be quite difficult to describe Pocahontas from this portrayal. Such a depiction is peculiar when we compare it to the majority of the popular renderings of the Rescue, in which Smith's savior is clearly the featured performer.[38] (It should be noted that Chapman's conservative approach ultimately became conventional. A number of the later purveyors of the rescue scene, including Alonzo Chappell, also placed Pocahontas with her back to the audience. (See Figure 4 for example.)

While in both cases Chapman is quite clever in finding ways to avoid having to present Pocahontas full-face to his audience, what is more important is that in these paintings he chooses to subordinate his princess to the event being portrayed. In the *Baptism*, other characters, including Sir Thomas Dale, on the viewer's left, and the Indian relatives of the princess on the right, dominate the foreground. Pocahontas, who kneels before the Reverend Alexander Whitaker in the center middleground of the painting, is presented, in accordance with nineteenth-century popular iconography, as a fairly generic Indian girl, with long, dark hair. She is clothed, however, in a full-length, white, clearly European dress. The whiteness of her costume emphasizes her innocence, while its magenta trim

PO-CA-HON-TAS.

Figure 14. *Pocahontas*. Engraving after Robert Matthew Sully's copy of the "Turkey Island Portrait," as it appears in Thomas McKenney and James Hall, *A History of the Indian Tribes of North America*, 1844.

acknowledges that the English colonists were conscious of her royal heritage.

The color of her dress also directs the viewer's attention to the fact that Pocahontas is lighter in skin tone than the other Indians in the painting. This is immediately obvious, even though she is slightly in the shadow cast by Reverend Whitaker, on whom the light is most directly focused. This conventional depiction allows Chapman to suggest that a blanching of any distinctively Indian racial features has occurred through this Christianization process. Her momentarily neutral status – no longer an Indian, when contrasted with her relatives, but not yet fully assimilated into the white society

Figure 15. Thomas Sully, *Pocahontas*. 1852. Courtesy of the Virginia His-torical Society, Richmond, VA.

around her – perhaps temporarily frees Pocahontas from the con-straints and prejudices of both worlds, but there can be no doubt that her allegiance will ultimately lie with her newly adopted culture.

Her pose actually most resembles that of the kneeling Virgin Mary of Nativity scenes, with her hands clasped in prayer and her eyes lowered as if she were looking down into the manger.[39] In this pos-ture Pocahontas has her back turned to the other, traditionally dressed, Indians – including the partially unclothed young woman

Figure 16. Robert Matthew Sully, *Pocahontas*. 1855. Courtesy of the Virginia Historical Society, Richmond, VA.

whom Chapman identifies as her sister – who serve as obvious figures of comparison. This positioning emphasizes her decision to abandon her native culture in favor of that offered by the English. However, Chapman makes no attempt to portray any of Pocahontas's emotions or characteristics other than her serenity and innocence.

Dale and Rolfe are presented in strict profile. This may in part have been due to the lack of models for them, but more importantly, while they frame both Pocahontas and Reverend Whitaker, they are

Figure 17. Robert M. Sully, *Pocahontas*. 1855. Courtesy of the State Historical Society of Wisconsin (wHi (x32) 14660).

clearly looking at the princess as she undergoes her "conversion" and so direct the attention of the viewer to her as well. The Anglo-American nature of this ritual is thus emphasized by both the composition as a whole and the particular rendering of Pocahontas, who is being absorbed into the English society that surrounds her.

The Baptism of Pocahontas was opened to public view in its niche in the Rotunda on November 30, 1840, to generally positive reviews. On December 3, the Washington City correspondent of the *New York Herald* tells his readers, "The beautiful painting of the baptism of Pocahontas, by Chapman, was displayed this morning in the rotunda of the Capitol, where it fills one of the long vacant pannels."[40] There

Figure 18. Charles Bird King, *Hayne Hudjihini (Eagle of Delight)*. c. 1822. Courtesy of The White House Historical Association, The White House Collection, Washington, D.C.

follows a brief discussion of the selection process, including a copy of Allston's letter of refusal, before we return to a description of the painting that includes some bizarre errors. (For instance, the correspondent calls the Reverend Whitaker "Nitaker," and John Rolfe "John Wolfe.") The column ends in praise of both the artist and his work. "Mr. Chapman is an artist of great celebrity, and this last production is well worthy of its prominent place."[41]

The December 1 edition of the *Daily National Intelligencer* mentions the unveiling, and while not actually reviewing the painting, the cor-

Figure 19. John Gadsby Chapman, *Pocahontas Saving the Life of Captain John Smith.* c. 1836–1840. Courtesy of the New York Historical Society, New York, NY.

respondent reports that "it certainly left on our mind a vivid impression of its beauty as a work of art."[42] The *Intelligencer* then provides a copy of the first part of the informational pamphlet that was written by Chapman and issued at the time of the unveiling. (Such a pamphlet would have been expected for a major work such as the *Baptism.*) This text, entitled *The Picture of the Baptism of Pocahontas,* was divided into two sections: the first, "The Subject of the Picture," deals with Chapman's choice of the baptism as proper for a national painting; the second, "Historical Sketch, and Extracts From Contemporary Writers, Relating to the Subject of the Picture," provides a series of quotations from seventeenth-century sources about her baptism and eventual marriage to John Rolfe.[43]

In "The Subject of the Picture," Chapman first talks in general terms about Pocahontas and her various contributions to the Jamestown colony (although, as I shall discuss later, he omits one crucial event). In language that would remind Americans of another great Virginian and his role in the founding of the nation, Chapman asserts that it is these benefactions, which were crucial to the "course of human events," that make an incident from the life of Pocahontas suitable for inclusion in the Capitol.

> Though a simple Indian maid, her life and actions are closely associated with events, which, in their consequences, have assumed a magnitude that fully entitles her to be placed among those who exercised an extensive influence in the destinies of states and the course of human events. She was, therefore, deemed a fit subject for a National Picture, painted by order of Congress, to commemorate the history and actions of our ancestors.[44]

He then attempts to convince his readers that the little-known moment of her baptism is a subject worthy of national interest.

> But she has another claim, not less venerable and touching, to the remembrance of posterity, and which addresses itself to all Christian people and Christian churches. She stands foremost in the train of those wandering children of the forest who have at different times – few, indeed, and far between – been snatched from the fangs of a barbarous idolatry, to become lambs in the fold of the Divine Shepherd. She therefore appeals to our religious as well as our patriotic sympathies, and is equally associated with the rise and progress of the Christian church, as with the political destinies of the United States.[45]

Abrams argues that Chapman seems intent on making Pocahontas an "American Joan of Arc" whose actions had both religious and political overtones.[46] In this passage we can also discern his ideological preoccupation with Pocahontas as a former barbarian, who appeals to "*our* religious as well as *our* patriotic sympathies" [emphasis added]. Her baptism is portrayed as the most important step on the road to her becoming one of "us," a member of white, Christian society. One can surmise, therefore, that this representation would have seemed quite sensible to the majority of the primarily white, Christian viewers of the painting.

Chapman thus uses his pamphlet to justify his choice of subject. He argues for the national importance of her baptism and studiously avoids emphasizing any of the other important events of her life. However, because the crucial character is Pocahontas, and viewers would certainly have been aware of her role in the saving of John Smith and the Jamestown settlement, there remains the issue of why he did not choose to place a rendering of the Rescue in this prominent space. The simple answer might be that while he had already painted most of the other important events of her life, Chapman had not yet attempted to portray her baptism. This therefore would have provided him with the greatest challenge. Also, while there were many versions of the Rescue in circulation (as well as the Capellano relief, already in place in the Rotunda), no one else had attempted to paint a *Baptism*. Chapman therefore would not have needed to fear a negative comparison with another artist's efforts.

We must remember too that at the time of this commission Chapman was still young and ambitious, and there is no reason to believe that he saw this painting as the crowning event of his career. A well-received rendering of Pocahontas's baptism would not only have bolstered his position as one of the leading artists in America. It would also have established Chapman as a reinterpreter of American history to be reckoned with. The *Baptism* generated an alternative persona for the great heroine of the Virginia founding, and if he was successful in revising the way Americans viewed such a well-known figure as Pocahontas, the door would be open for him to provide revisionist portrayals of other persons or historical events. There was no dominant historical painter in mid-nineteenth-century America, and Chapman almost certainly saw himself as the most likely candidate to become the Benjamin West of his era.

By rendering this less dramatic turning point in her life, Chapman may also have wished to enhance the image of Pocahontas in the consciousness of the American public. Like John Davis thirty-five years earlier, Chapman had a vested interest in the perceived importance of his subject, because her increased stature would serve to enhance his own reputation. As her bravery and selflessness were already well known, he decided to remind the majority of his audience that Pocahontas had ultimately become "one of them," and had been granted the gift of eternal life. Finally, as we shall see, his removal of Pocahontas from the potentially savage moment of the Rescue was an attempt to free her from both the standard versions of her own narrative and from what had become the standard portrayals of "her people," who, even in the most well-intentioned pieces, were usually depicted as a primitive and dying race.

Another noteworthy commentary on Chapman's effort was provided by a reviewer in the December 16, 1840, issue of the Washington, D.C., *Daily National Intelligencer*. This critic, identified only as "W.," makes some positive comments about the *Baptism* but also has two criticisms, beginning with the portrayal of the princess. "Her hair flows negligently over her neck and back, and her features and complexion are those of the Indian, though her face is not so beautiful as it is represented to have been in life."[47] W. makes the same point again a bit later, although he or she seems to have had a change of heart about what race Pocahontas favors. "Her features are neither beautiful nor exactly Indian; nor does her bust possess that elegance and gracefulness of outline which characterizes female beauty."[48] Again, we get a sense of the neutral status of this delineation. Here, as well as being not quite Indian, Pocahontas is also seen as not quite beautiful. The question of whether she was losing her beauty with her loss of Indianness, or whether she was in the process of becoming more beautiful through her conversion, might have challenged Chapman's audience, although one can probably predict what would have been the majority opinion.

The second problem addressed by this critic concerns the scene Chapman chose to present: "The subject appears to me to have been an unfortunate one for an historical painting, being more local and individual than national."[49] In W.'s opinion, her baptism, though important to the biography of Pocahontas and the local history of Virginia, did not have the national implications that, for example, would have been implicit in a portrayal of the Rescue. This critic either had not seen or was unconvinced by the arguments made by Chapman in his pamphlet.

Such comments brought an almost immediate response. Five days later, in the *Intelligencer* for December 21, a correspondent calling himself "Landscape" energetically refutes W.'s comments about the subject of Chapman's effort.

[W]hen out of the swarthy hordes of arrow-sending barbarians there budded forth the flower of the desert, when the rose sprang up beneath the everlasting forests, and Christianity blew upon and expanded its leaves, there was a sublimity in the incident that certainly must have touched the hearts of those bold settlers, and thrilled through Europe. But when that rose was Pocahontas, she who had saved the colony more than once from butchery – who had resigned her own to save the life of Captain Smith, the sentiment became more elevated, and Christianity itself was ennobled by her neophyte. . . . It is an incident full of the solemn, the beautiful, and the grand, and Chapman has shown a high and noble sense of right in selecting it. . . . I am far from being a religious man; but my nature is bowed down when that consecrated scene is presented to me.[50]

The fact that Landscape defends the subject of Chapman's painting but does not refute W.'s comments about the delineation of Pocahontas herself suggests that the problematic nature of Chapman's presentation of the princess was generally recognized. In any case, his resounding blast at W. makes clear that Landscape shares the opinion about her formerly barbarian nature put forward by Chapman in his pamphlet. However, although Landscape does comment briefly on the painting itself, in terms of the use of color and light, his column is much more a defense of the historical importance of Pocahontas and her decision to become a Christian than it is a defense of Chapman's painting.

This response is typical of what one might call "defense literature." From this point through the remainder of the nineteenth century, whenever the figure of Pocahontas or some event from her life is attacked or doubted – whether in an insignificant slight, such as Waddy Thompson's comment about her being thrown into the shade by Cortez's Doña Marina (discussed in Chapter 3), or, as we shall see, in the serious attack on the veracity of the rescue story made by northern historians just prior to the outbreak of the Civil War – a strong reply, often by a southerner, is usually not long in coming. It is fitting that the remarks of Landscape, which constitute one of the first straightforward defenses of the princess, have to do with the *Baptism* because this painting, in its own way, is also a defense. Chapman here attempts to remove Pocahontas forever from the ranks of savages in the national memory, just as her actual baptism and eventual abandoning of Virginia for England had apparently removed the young Powhatan woman from those aspects of her native culture that would have been considered morally questionable by an Anglo-American audience.

There were a number of notices of *The Baptism of Pocahontas* in the months that followed its unveiling, and it was occasionally mentioned by critics in succeeding years, but Chapman's effort never captured the imagination of either the public or the American artistic community. The most revealing commentary on the theme of the painting was not written until almost five years after it was unveiled. In a piece pointedly entitled "Pocahontas: A Subject For The Historical Painter," William Gilmore Simms, a leading southern literary figure of the antebellum period, discusses the suitability of the events of Virginia history, and especially the story of Pocahontas, "with which every native [read "Anglo-American born in the United States"] is familiar," for the poet and painter.[51] He first talks in general terms about the process of choosing the precise moment in any scene which, if properly presented, will have the greatest effect on the viewer, and then becomes more specific:

It is the judgment which he exhibits in this particular – in thus choosing his moment – in the sensibility and the imagination which prompt him to catch the vivid emotion and the hungry passion, ere they subside into the repose which follows from natural exhaustion – that he establishes his pretensions as the poet of his art. . . . That moment, in the history of Pocahontas, is when Smith is rescued by her interposition from the stroke of the executioner."[52]

Simms asserts that American "artists" (a term he does not use loosely) have for the most part not made an earnest attempt to portray this striking incident, and that it had yet to be tried by an artist "with any of the necessary attributes of genius, taste and imagination."[53] He thereby dismisses the many popular renderings of the Rescue as something less than serious art. And although he is careful not to criticize either Chapman's craftsmanship or the painting itself, Simms does find fault with his choice of this incident as a national subject and with so-called artists who will not respond to the greater challenge.

> Mr. Chapman, a southern artist, whose large and peculiar merits it gives us great pleasure to acknowledge and assert, has given us a lovely picture of the reception of the Indian princess into the bosom of the Mother Church; but it is to the reproach of this gentleman that he has avoided the nobler event which first brought us to the knowledge of her character. Certainly, it is one of singular difficulty, demanding the highest powers of art, and an imagination equally warm and courageous, to say nothing of the inevitable requisites of the exquisite colorist and draughtsman; but it is this very difficulty, and the danger which attends it, which commend the subject to the affections, and stimulates the ambition of the proper genius.[54]

In his dual role as art critic and spokesman for the South, Simms takes exception to Chapman's failure to paint the Rescue because this was Pocahontas's critical contribution to the founding of the American republic, and would therefore have been the most appropriate choice for a painting to be placed in the Capitol. Simms also felt that this subject would have both provided a greater challenge to the artist and, if properly rendered, affected the audience with a more powerful emotional experience than even the most successful portrayal of her baptism possibly could. Finally, the Rescue would have recalled for every American the importance of the Jamestown colony, the young woman who with a wondrous display of courage ensured its survival, and the brave captain without whose sagacity the entire British colonial enterprise might well have failed.

Curiously enough, in 1845 Simms himself was working on his own version of the Pocahontas narrative, which would be incorporated into his 1846 biography of John Smith.[55] A portrayal of Smith's rescue would necessarily be a crucial scene in this text, whereas the baptism

Figure 20. Robert W. Weir, *Embarkation of the Pilgrims.* 1843. Courtesy of the Architect of the Capitol, United States Capitol Art Collection, Washington, D.C.

would not be, since the captain had returned to England long before her internment and conversion. This fact may not make Simms's arguments about the painting less valid, but the timing of his essay might make one suspect that this piece was, at least in part, something of an early advertisement for his soon-to-be-published biography.

It is possible to read *The Baptism of Pocahontas* as an attempt to further the political ends of the South. Abrams suggests that the painting is "a kind of Virginia manifesto to represent southern interests in the entrance hall of the federal legislature."[56] She quotes Mrs. M. M. Webster's often-cited lines concerning this incident, "The bright girl knelt, bathed in repentant tears – / Connecting link between two hemispheres," and notes that Chapman's choice of subject "linked Europe to America a full decade before the Pilgrim's arrival," and thus provided "a southern counterpart to Robert Walter Weir's *Embarkation of the Pilgrims*"[57] (Figure 20). What is ironic, however, is that while this may in some sense be true, the focus on her baptism rather than the Rescue or the founding of Jamestown actually deflects the attention of the viewer away from her southern origins. The crucial role that she played in the founding of the Virginia colony, of which the great majority of the viewers of this painting would have been aware, is made subordinate to a moment that signifies both her break with her native past and the beginning of her final break with Virginia. Less than three years after her baptism Pocahontas would be married to John Rolfe, the mother of Thomas, and preparing for her departure for England – a trip from which she would never return. One could argue that Chapman breaks her connection to the South by simultaneously breaking her connection to the Powhatan people, who were the original inhabitants – and in the case of her family, the original aristocracy – of Virginia, and to Smith, the English hero of the Virginia founding.

Chapman wrote to Bolling in 1838, "I regret very much that I cannot with propriety . . . introduce Capt. Smith into my picture."[58] It seems clear, however, that this omission was an important part of his overall strategy. Not only is Smith necessarily absent from the painting, but both he and the Rescue are conspicuous by their almost complete absence from Chapman's pamphlet, even when the artist takes a moment to recap the heroic deeds of the Pocahontas. At one point, when it seems as if he is about to discuss her most famous exploit, Chapman surprisingly changes direction, but not without mentioning the qualities that made the Rescue possible:

> The name of *Pocahontas* has descended to posterity as the great benefactress, the tutelary genius of the first successful Colony planted within the limits of the United States; who, when famine raged or conspiracy menaced it with swift destruction, ever interposed her benign and gentle influence to supply their wants and ward off their dangers. From all that history and tradition have preserved, as well as from the testimonials of the objects of her kindness and protection; from the particulars of her life that have come down to us, and from every authentic memorial now extant, she appears to have been, both in mind and person, one of the choicest models the hand of nature ever formed. With the purest simplicity she united the kindest heart, and to the timidity of a spotless virgin she joined a sagacity of mind, a firmness of spirit, and an adventurous daring, which more than once, when the existence of the Colony was at stake, prompted her to traverse the midnight forest alone, and brave the indignation of her kindred, to give advice and warning.[59]

It is the rare viewer who would not have been aware of the most famous instance of her interposing "her benign and gentle influence" to "ward off" a very specific "danger" and thereby "brave the indignation of her kindred," but Chapman refuses to mention the saving of Smith explicitly. Indeed, Smith's name is mentioned only once in "The Subject of the Picture," and that is merely in order to use his description of Nantequaus, the brother of Pocahontas.[60] Otherwise, there is no sense here that the captain and the princess ever had much to do with one another. And in what is certainly another effort to distract attention from the more famous rescue, Pocahontas and Smith are mentioned together briefly in the opening of Chapman's "Historical Sketch," and Smith's "preservation" is alluded to, but when Chapman gets specific he refers, surprisingly, to a different rescue, using Richard Potts's description of Pocahontas coming through the forest at night to warn Smith of a potential ambush.[61] It seems clearly to have been of the utmost importance to Chapman to do all that he could to subordinate the Rescue and thereby focus greater attention on her baptism, the event that he would have his viewers believe was actually primary.

Chapman emphasizes Pocahontas's courage not in terms of her heroism as a rescuer, but rather in her choice to place herself in the position of a "repentant" recipient, to use Mrs. Webster's word. The issue that then must be considered, however, is just what she is repenting. Is it her original sin, or perhaps the supposed "wantonness" or "playfulness" of her previous life?[62] The latter might be logical if the painting was of some generic Indian girl, but this is Pocahontas, and viewers would have been aware of her bravery and her willingness to sacrifice her life to save that of a foreign captive – an act that risked both that life and the love of her father, and symbolically, as many white nineteenth-century Americans would have understood it, ultimately allowed for the ongoing destruction of her own people. By placing Pocahontas in the role of recipient, Chapman reminds his audience that she was, ironically, a heathen at the moment of her most Christian act (the Rescue) and puts forward the idea that her baptism can be seen as a type of reward for, or a tangible acknowledgment of, her well-known heroism.

In this sense, the *Baptism* can be viewed as a contribution to a debate that had existed in the Anglo-American New World from the time of the earliest settlements, and would continue to be addressed, far more eloquently, as the nineteenth century proceeded. When Hester Prynne tells Dimmesdale in the forest that "What we did had a consecration of its own," Hawthorne raises the question of whether there are some actions that have an inherent "consecration" and are therefore far more powerful and binding than civil or religious ceremonies.[63] Is being true to one's own heart sufficient, or will there always be the need for an official ceremony, a sacrament, or a memorial, to impart a ritualistic blessing on an action, a person, or even a place?

President Lincoln made his belief on this subject quite clear. "But, in a larger sense, we can not dedicate – we can not consecrate this ground – we can not hallow – this ground. The brave men, living and dead, who struggled here, have consecrated it, far above our poor power to add or detract."[64] Seen in this way, the formal dedication of the cemetery at Gettysburg was simply an acknowledgment of the consecration that had taken place during the three hellish days of battle. The ceremony is important primarily as a public recognition of the earlier, bloody sanctification.

A viewer who was aware of Pocahontas's earlier actions might ask whether Chapman's *Baptism* simply portrayed an official acknowledgment of the conversion experience that had occurred seconds before the intended execution of John Smith. Did not the resulting, apparently quite Christian, self-sacrificial action of Pocahontas consecrate her far beyond the power of any minister? If one believes Christianity to be action-based, can her accomplishments up to the moment of her official baptism be explained by her having been at heart a Christian already? If, on the other hand, Christianity is believed to be institution-based, then her saving of Smith, though certainly an example of her bravery and her faith in her father's love, cannot provide a moral exemplar because at the time Pocahontas had not yet been initiated into God's chosen people. Chapman's painting, then, because of the power of her other, better-known persona, is able to ask its viewers to reconsider what they believe to be the fundamental tenet of their religion by raising the inevitable question of what was the most important event in the life of Pocahontas. (This issue is also raised by Joseph Mozier's 1859 marble *Pocahontas* [Figure 21]). This popular piece, which depicts a clearly prebaptism princess holding a cross as if she understood that this sacrament was in her future, was thought to have been less than successful by Hawthorne, who commented in *The French and Italian Notebooks* on Mozier's failed attempts at "higher ideality," in his description of a visit he paid to the sculptor's studio. See also, the *Flag of the Powhatan Guards* [Figure 31].[65]

Does her rescue of Smith pale in comparison with the moment of her baptism, during which her eternal salvation was made possible? Chapman would almost certainly have said yes. As has been mentioned, he saw this work, which was based, if loosely, on a factual rather than what had become by the mid-nineteenth century an almost mythological moment, as an elevation of the princess. Pocahontas's Christianity gave her something in common with the majority of the artist's American contemporaries, and so he might conceivably have been able to convince them that her baptism was an even more significant rescue than her intervention at Smith's execution. While acknowledging many of her contributions to the success of the Virginia colony in his pamphlet, Chapman largely avoids mentioning what she did for Smith because his ultimate emphasis is on what the English had bestowed on her. In effect, the sacrament of baptism evened the colonists' score with Pocahontas; indeed, it put her in the debt of Christian Anglo-Americans for the gift of possible eternal salvation that they had chosen to share. Chapman's painting also reinforced the comforting notion that the benefits of white culture were available to good Indians if they chose to take advantage of them, and served to alienate whites further from bad Indians, who would not allow themselves to be converted to European modes of thought. We need only look at the male Indians in the painting, who are portrayed in almost forestlike shadows, to perceive Chapman's opinion of their cultural distance from the Anglo-Americans at the ceremony, as well as from the convert.

When we examine the few memorable moments in the Pocahontas narrative from which an artist had to choose, we see that from the point of view of most white, mid-nineteenth-century Americans, the *Baptism* portrayed the least politically sensitive incident in her life. A traditional portrayal of the Rescue, for instance, would have had to depict acts of compassion by both the Indian princess and, even more problematically, her father, an apparently savage Indian chief. Even in the America of 1840, when Romantic sentiments about Indians were not yet completely out of vogue, such an idea would not have been appropriate for a national history painting. Indeed, a depiction of the Rescue would have recalled to contemporary viewers the missed possibility for an alternative, far less bloody history of the Anglo-American domination of the continent that might have followed had the white race acted with Pocahontas-like generosity toward the Indians. This might have caused visitors to leave the Capitol grounds with a less than absolute belief in the rightness of Anglo-American policies toward the native peoples. Such a response would not have been appreciated by many progress-minded representatives, including those interested in continuing the war against the Seminoles, who had not, as had been predicted, given up the fight after the suspicious death of their great leader, Osceola.[66]

Another possible subject would have been the presentation of the American princess to James I and Queen Anne. This meeting of royalty could have symbolized the joining of the Old and New Worlds, but such a choice would have had the unfortunate effect of putting a scene depicting the English court at the seat of the American government. It would also have had the added drawback of the need to include Smith. His letter "introduced" the princess to Queen Anne, and he was probably present, if not prominent, during many of the festivities attended by Pocahontas. His inclusion would

Figure 21. Joseph Mozier, *Pocahontas*. 1859. Courtesy of The Chrysler Museum, Norfolk, VA.

have automatically recalled the role of the princess in the Rescue, and thereby made this image doubly problematic to an antebellum audience.

The only other incident from the life of Pocahontas that might have qualified for portrayal in the Capitol would have been her marriage to John Rolfe, but this too, as we have seen, is fraught with obvious problems. Although this scene would have been the most optimistic, if not realistic, subject in terms of the romantic possibility for racial harmony, or even racial unity, at some point in the nation's future, it would not have sat well in a country where the fear of any such mixture was still overwhelming. Prints of *The Marriage of Pocahontas,* such as John McRae's engraving of Henry Brueckner's painting, became popular later in the nineteenth century, but only after any possibility for intermarriage between whites and Indians had virtually disappeared and any exemplary aspects of this scene had thereby been negated.

Chapman therefore chose to portray her baptism, the moment when Pocahontas freely abandoned her Indian beliefs and accepted an alternative cultural identity.[67] This conversion, which is portrayed as clearly the correct choice, can be usefully opposed to those undergone by other, less fortunate Indian subjects. For example, in George Catlin's earlier study, *Pigeon's Egg Head (The Light) going to and returning from Washington* (1831–2), we see that the removal of the traditional Indian costume (which was itself a representation of the way most Anglo-Americans wanted their Indians to look) makes the subject seem foolish, while it also reveals the degenerative effects of certain aspects of the civilizing process (Figure 22). Chapman would have the viewers of his work see that with an appropriate subject, such as Pocahontas, this process brings honor to both the convert and her adopted culture.

Chapman's choice of subject also took away any need to portray the activity and heroism for which Pocahontas was known, in favor of an image of a passive, submissive recipient. In terms of traditional mid-nineteenth-century gender roles, this subdued princess would have been far more acceptable to the painting's male viewers than would a depiction of a young, active woman with the fortitude to challenge her father, who was also the figurative father of her nation. Also, when we now view the *Baptism* in the context of the other historical paintings in the Rotunda, it quickly becomes clear that not only is she the only Indian featured; she is also the only woman featured in any of these works. Some scenes contain no women at all, while in others they are background or ancillary figures, such as those in the crowd as Washington resigns his commission, the praying Pilgrim women aboard the *Speedwell,* or the beautiful, half-naked Indian women fearfully watching the advance of De Soto (Figure 23). In her more passive persona, Chapman's Pocahontas clearly qualifies for inclusion into this extraordinarily male-dominated collection.

Pocahontas's new, "Christian" name, Rebecca, was conveniently loaded with symbolism appropriate to nineteenth-century perceptions of her historical importance. Perhaps the best-known Rebecca of Chapman's day was the dark Jewish heroine of Sir Walter Scott's *Ivanhoe*. Although, as the reader is often told, she is of a "different race," Scott's Rebecca uses her medical knowledge to save the life of the young Saxon nobleman. Whether she acts out of romantic love, which, because of nineteenth-century sensibilities could never be requited, or out of compassion for Ivanhoe, there can be no doubt as to the nobility of her actions and her nature.

As Pocahontas had saved the foreigner John Smith, the Rebecca of Genesis had made her worthiness to marry Isaac known at the well through her kindness to a foreigner, the servant of Abraham. Rebecca was the literal mother of two nations through her sons, Jacob and Esau.[68] The latter, in a prefiguration of the Indians selling their land for a few dollars or trading it for whiskey, had given up his birthright for a bowl of soup, while the former was the father of the twelve tribes and an ancestor of David and ultimately of Jesus. To antebellum Virginians who could claim direct lineage from the converted Powhatan princess, this sense of Rebecca as a matriarch might have implied that their line would be among the "chosen people" of their era.

As she is invoked in Romans 9, her only mention in the New Testament, Paul uses Rebecca and her children as symbols of the power of God to ignore traditional human hierarchies and thereby allow for the preeminence of the younger son over the elder. By implication, this interpretation would have supported the dominance of the younger, more vigorous Anglo-American invaders over the older, apparently declining, Indian cultures. Such a reading would have been especially useful at a time when ethnologists were expending a great deal of energy trying to deduce the age and origins of the native tribes. These studies had become particularly important after the founding of white settlements in Ohio and on the Mississippi, which brought Anglo-Americans into more frequent contact with the works of the Mound Builders.

Whether one believed that the ancestors of the Indians had built the mounds or that they were constructed by an ancient, now extinct race, it was generally acknowledged that these strange monuments were of great antiquity, and they therefore raised the question of whether the Indians were in fact an "older" as well as a more primi-

Figure 22. George Catlin, *Pigeon's Egg Head (The Light) going to and returning from Washington.* 1831–32. Courtesy of the National Museum of American Art, Smithsonian Institution, Washington, D.C.

tive people than the whites. Although the dominant belief was that the Native Americans were clearly in an earlier stage of development, and therefore "younger," there was also a competing idea that civilizations represent stages in a larger, cyclical pattern. If we consider, for instance, Thomas Cole's series, *The Course of Empire*, we see that the stage represented by figures who clearly appear to be Indians seems to be earlier than that of the civilized, white empire builders. (The intriguing issue of whether the Indians would one day evolve

Figure 23. William H. Powell, *Discovery of the Mississippi River.* 1855. Courtesy of the Architect of the Capitol, United States Capitol Art Collection, Washington, D.C.

into whites is thus raised.) The discovery of the mounds and the other vestiges of ancient American civilizations, however, allowed for the idea that the Indians might in fact be in a later, postempire stage of development, and therefore older than the Anglo-Americans who at that point were only in the process of assuming their sovereignty. Much of this debate, and many of the arguments concerning the ultimate fate of the native cultures, centered on the apparent inability of the Native Americans to progress (or return) from their savage state to a more civilized condition.[69]

This issue has recently been discussed by Matthew Baigell, who argues that many of the nineteenth-century painters who portrayed Native Americans in scenes of the frontier or of white westward expansion were engaging in a discourse that actively sought to display the correctness of what by mid-century had come to be known as America's Manifest Destiny – the ultimate, rightful domination of the continent, from Alaska to Mexico, by the Anglo-Americans of the United States.[70] Baigell sees this policy, which both prophesied and encouraged the destruction of the Indian civilizations, reflected in the works of some of the most important visual artists of this period, who "used the idea of progress to eliminate native Americans.[71] Whether the Indians are portrayed as taking part in explicitly savage acts or are in some less threatening way depicted as simply being in the way of white expansion, the clear message is that the backward, barbarous native cultures will eventually have to give way before the advance of Anglo-American civilization.

This concern is expressed in even the most seemingly sentimental or nostalgic representations of the native cultures. Indians were almost always presented in a natural, or, as white nineteenth-century Americans would have seen it, a savage context. Every portrayal of Indian life, from depictions of battles or buffalo hunts to those of tranquil village scenes, fits under this rubric. In this way, although those Indians pictured may not be committing any overtly violent actions against whites, they are shown to be part of an outdated natural world, that, as it passes away, should be remembered, and perhaps even mourned, but certainly not resurrected or preserved on lands needed by white settlers. In none of these paintings is there a call for contemporary Americans to attempt a return to an uncivilized state, or for that matter to return any land to the Indians. Indeed, as Baigell points out, the acquiring of more land was what many of these paintings were about. In their primitive, timeless world the Indian way of life was appropriate, but in the face of a forward-moving, progressive, time-conscious, and providentially favored civilization like that of the Anglo-Americans, the native cultures were seemingly doomed.[72] What, if anything, should be mourned is the white viewer's inability to experience the simplicity of this timeless world, rather than the outdated and virtually extinct, or, as it was believed, about to become extinct, occupiers of it.

Even the portraits of Indians by such artists as George Catlin and Charles Bird King, both of whom felt the need to "preserve" the native cultures, if only on canvas, fit into this category. While the fixed and formal poses in these paintings remove the subjects from Indian activities that white viewers might see as explicitly threatening, these portraits often needed the traditional trappings of each subject's native existence – headdresses, beads, feathers, and/or paint – to satisfy the white audience that presumably would be interested in seeing and perhaps buying them. Therefore, such works still served to give Anglo-American viewers a sense of the potential threat posed by these anachronistic beings, and thereby reinforced the idea that even the most noble of these savages, and their outmoded way of life, must pass away.

This hypothesis provides another way of looking at Chapman's decision to paint a *Baptism* rather than a *Rescue*. A portrayal of the saving of Smith, while expressing the bravery of Pocahontas and the compassionate response of Powhatan, would necessarily have been bound to a savage context in terms of the action, the costumes of the Indians, and the location. Chapman instead removes Pocahontas from a scene of savage violence like an execution, from the stereotypical costume of her people, and from nature itself, the traditional home of all Indians. The baptism takes place indoors, in a European building inside of a European settlement, far from the natural world that will ultimately have to be either controlled or exterminated. Her European costume, and her "turning her back" on the other Indians in the painting, all of whom are in traditional native attire, can be seen as representing a turning away from the latent savagism of all Indians – not just her obviously untrustworthy uncle Opechancanough, but even her noble brother Nantequaus, her sister, who personifies what Pocahontas would have become if she had not been converted, and the future generations of her people, who are represented by the Indian baby at the ceremony.[73] And just as the still savage, although apparently unarmed, Indians are crammed into the lower, right-hand corner of the painting and are greatly outnumbered by the armed Englishmen around them, so those natives who will not convert to a white way of thinking will be forcibly constrained and eventually pushed off the American canvas. Also, by depicting not a momentary, possibly anomalous instance of her turning against her people, such as the rescue of Smith, in favor of her final abandoning of her cultural heritage, Chapman effectively removes his rather generic Pocahontas (and other lesser-known Indians who would make this same choice) from the ranks of those natives who in traditional Manifest Destiny terms would inevitably have to be destroyed. This is the theme that most clearly connects his unusual portrayal of Pocahontas with the cultural concerns of the painting as a whole.

In Baigell's brief discussion of the *Baptism* he focuses on the painting as a portrayal of the white belief that Christianity "represents civilization, and that native Americans become acceptable only by becoming Christian and accepting white values and customs."[74] He goes on to point out, however, that "the subject of Chapman's painting was already anachronistic in 1840, for it was predicated on the discredited belief that native Americans could be incorporated into white society."[75] I do not believe, however, that Chapman intended primarily for his painting to be an inspiration toward red-white assimilation or for his Pocahontas to be a model for other Indians to follow. His most important concern was to redirect and enhance the traditional perception of Pocahontas by providing a peaceful, religious moment, rather than the normal "action shot," for his viewers to contemplate. It is true that when we study Chapman's work in the context of nineteenth-century westward expansionism, the *Baptism* can be interpreted as purveying standard Manifest Destiny sentiments. However, rather than their being expressed only by the overt subject of the painting, they are also presented in a second, more subtle manner. My reading can be clarified by a brief explication of a work by one of the most popular American poets of Chapman's day.

In his 1834 poem "The Prairies," William Cullen Bryant presents a fairly standard expansionist argument about the passing of races and the replacement of established cultures by invading, militarily superior peoples. His focus is on the Mound Builders, whom he describes as "a disciplined and populous race / [who] Heaped, with long toil, the earth, while yet the Greek / Was hewing the Pentelicus to forms / Of symmetry, and rearing on its rock / The glittering Parthenon."[76] The Mound Builders cultivated the land, domesticated animals, and presumably lived a peaceful, orderly existence, and therefore would have been viewed as having more in common with contemporary Anglo-Americans than with the surviving Indian cultures. Their destruction is described in one sentence: "The red man came – / The roaming hunter tribes, warlike and fierce, / And the mound-builders vanished from the earth."[77]

We learn, however, that a single Mound Builder may have escaped the fate of his people.

> Haply some solitary fugitive,
> Lurking in marsh and forest, till the sense
> Of desolation and of fear became
> Bitterer than death, yielded himself to die.
> Man's better nature triumphed then. Kind words
> Welcomed and soothed him; the rude conquerors
> Seated the captive with their chiefs; he chose
> A bride among the maidens, and at length
> Seemed to forget – yet ne'er forgot – the wife
> Of his first love, and her sweet little ones,
> Butchered, amid their shrieks, with all his race.[78]

As usual, the reader is not told explicitly that any children resulted from this interracial union. There can be no doubt, however, that this individual became a member, and perhaps even a dignitary, of the conquerors who had slaughtered the rest of his people.

As Julie Schimmel has pointed out, the "doomed Indian" motif was extremely popular during the second and third quarters of the nineteenth century.[79] Cooper, through *The Last of the Mohicans* and the many solitary Indian figures in his other novels, became the primary literary purveyor of this idea, but as Schimmel suggests, Bryant, in such poems as "An Indian at the Burial-Place of His Fathers," "Indian Girl's Lament" (which was interpreted in marble by Mozier – see Figure 24), and "The Disinterred Warrior" was also an important contributor to the furthering of the belief that the Indians' days were numbered.[80] Visual representations such as Tompkins H. Matteson's 1847 painting *The Last of the Race* (Figure 25) and Hiram Powers's 1867 marble *The Last of the Tribes*, in which the "last" is a very Pocahontas-like young woman, also portray what the white viewer was to see as the last survivors of an apparently homogeneous indigenous culture.[81]

In an interesting adaptation of this idea, Bryant presents the "last" Mound Builder, but rather than have his poem imply that the final, tragic end of this race was imminent, he portrays the lone survivor as being absorbed into the conquering, and surprisingly compassionate, Indian culture. More importantly, although he cannot forget his first wife and children, the last Mound Builder, perhaps resigned to the "Manifest Destiny" of the Indians, apparently comes to forgive the invaders for what they did to his people. Bryant would have his readers believe that something of this ancient race survived through this single, mythic absorption of the last Mound Builder into the triumphant Indian community. And since the white race was then apparently destroying the Indians as the Indians had presumably destroyed the Mound Builders, this type of absorption must have seemed an attractive notion. Such a theoretical assimilation, which can be seen as an aspect of the preservationist impulse that was felt by many white mid-nineteenth-century Americans, was based in great part on the need to assuage any lingering guilt over the destruction of so many of the native cultures of the eastern forests. Such theories, when coupled with the idea that the Indians could be "preserved," either on canvas or, as Catlin also suggested, in a park where whites could come and see them, helped many of their conquerors to get past any remorse they might have felt over the fate of their victims.[82]

I believe that Chapman is presenting not so much the old idea of an actual absorption, which I would agree had ceased to be viewed as a practicable solution to the Indian question by the end of the Jeffersonian era, but rather this type of mythic absorption. The primordial assimilation of Pocahontas into the Anglo-American community can be interpreted as allowing for the destruction of all other Indians because their race, through her unique absorption, had been granted a kind of perpetual survival.[83] Therefore, although *The Baptism of Pocahontas* did on one level present the possibility that other Indians might be so absorbed, it also served to mitigate the guilt that contemporary white audiences might have felt about the impending destruction of uncooperative native cultures because the survival of the Indians had been symbolically assured.

Pocahontas is particularly useful to such a strategy because two levels of absorption are present in her narrative. If it became necessary

Figure 24. Joseph Mozier, *Indian Girl's Lament*. 1858. Courtesy of the Eugene P. Watson Memorial Library, Northwestern State University of Louisiana, Natchitoches, LA. This figure has often been mistakenly identified as Pocahontas.

for contemporary Anglo-Americans to do away with all of the remaining Indians, or if the native cultures simply "passed" before the march of white civilization, their race would live on, both through the flesh-and-blood descendants of Pocahontas and John Rolfe and, perhaps more importantly, through the mythic adoption portrayed in her baptism. Further, the Christian audience of this painting would have realized that this ceremony, which theoretically allowed for her survival, also, ironically, portrayed the moment when this representative Indian became prepared for martyrdom. Her death, and the deaths of other such converts, because these Indians had been given the chance for eternal salvation, would not have to be mourned at all.

Although Chapman was chiefly concerned with elevating Poca-

Figure 25. Tompkins H. Matteson, *The Last of the Race*. 1847. Courtesy of the New York Historical Society, New York, NY.

hontas above the half-naked girl of generic Rescue scenes, and himself above the other young artists of his day, the Manifest Destiny implications of his painting for the Capitol Rotunda would have been obvious, both to him and to his audience. The Christianizing of the West was, ideally, a crucial part of the territorial conquest, and although the *Baptism* did suggest an option that would allow for the survival of some Indians (if not *as* Indians), it also allowed for the continuation of the process of westward expansion by reminding its viewers that this courageous young Indian woman, who was the progenitrix of a thriving and often aristocratic lineage who were proud to claim her blood in their veins, had been welcomed into the race that in Chapman's day was carrying out a seemingly unstoppable campaign against those of her people who would refuse to be so absorbed. It is ironic, however, that many of the East Coast Indians, including those who, like Pocahontas, had chosen to convert to Christianity, had by the mid-nineteenth century either passed out of existence or, at the very least, been uprooted from ancestral homelands. Their conversions – the abandoning of their traditional belief systems – had removed these Native Americans from the path of white expansionism as effectively as any rifle.

In the column adjacent to the mention of *The Baptism of Pocahontas* in the December 1, 1840 *Daily National Intelligencer* is a continuation of this newspaper's report of the results of the recent presidential election.[84] The somewhat surprising outcome of this campaign was that although the popular vote was close, the incumbent, Democrat Martin Van Buren, was soundly defeated in the electoral college by the Whig candidate, General William Henry Harrison, who, although he had served as both a representative and a senator, was best known as a soldier, and especially for his exploits as an Indian fighter.[85] His most famous campaign slogan, "Tippecanoe and Tyler too," has survived as a cultural artifact, although few nonspecialists understand its meaning. Some contemporary readers might recognize Tyler as the name of John Tyler, the vice-presidential candidate, who took over the presidency when Harrison died of pneumonia a month after his inauguration. "Tippecanoe" is more trouble for twentieth-century Americans, but their antebellum ancestors would have been quite familiar with this turning point in the conquering of the West.

Although his name is most often associated with the great Shawnee chief Tecumseh, General Harrison's most famous engagement against the Indians, the Battle of Tippecanoe, was actually fought primarily against the followers of Tecumseh's brother, Tenskwatawa, the "Open Door," who came to be known simply as the "Prophet" (Figure 26). As R. David Edmunds has shown, the Prophet, a one-eyed, reformed alcoholic and ne'er-do-well, who one day began to have visions of the "Master of Life," was in many ways the leader of the rebellious western Indians during the late eighteenth and early nineteenth centuries.[86] Indeed, for a time he was more feared by white Americans than his brother, not because of his ability to fight, but because of his ability to preach.

The Prophet told his Indian audiences that they had to stop all contact with those offspring of the devil who had invaded their lands, and that they must give up the great majority of the vestiges of "civilization" that had come to them through their contact with the Anglo-Americans. This was especially true of alcohol, the great evil that the white race had inflicted upon the Indians. He also told them that if they purified themselves and followed his instructions, the Master of Life would "overturn the land, so that all white people will be covered and you alone shall inherit the land."[87] In teachings that recalled the New England Puritan view that the evils that people suffered were brought about by their own backsliding, the Prophet saw the advance of the evil white race as a punishment to the Indians for having lost their spiritual focus, and promised that the invaders, whom he saw in a vision as a giant crab, would

Figure 26. Engraving after Charles Bird King, *Tenskwatawa*. As he appears in Thomas McKenny and James Hall, *A History of the Indian Tribes of North America*, 1844.

be destroyed if all Indians would unite and be guided by his in-spired doctrines.

This notion of an alternative history of America – a history where the white race's early successes could be explained but in which the day of reckoning was about to dawn – caught the imaginations of many western Indians, who traveled to Ohio to follow the Prophet, and many eastern whites, who fearfully read of the massing of Indians on the western frontiers under the military leadership of the great Tecumseh and the spiritual leadership of his revered brother. Ironically, and fortunately for the white American forces, the decisive battle of this period was fought while Tecumseh was away in the South attempting to attract more tribes into their union. On November 7, 1811, Harrison's forces engaged and defeated the followers of the Prophet in the Battle of Tippecanoe, and for all intents and purposes destroyed any chance for a union of the western tribes, not because this victory was so devastating, but because the "medicine" of the Prophet, who had guaranteed victory and had told his followers that the white men's bullets could not harm them, had failed.

General Harrison had done more than simply win a battle. He had restored the confidence of white Americans in the power of their armed forces, the rightness of their pushing back the frontiers, and the correctness of their historical vision during this crucial early stage of the westward migration. In the presidential campaign of 1840, it was proven that "Tippecanoe" was still synonymous with the military defeat of Indian forces, but by this time it had also come to be associated with the Anglo-American sense of the providential nature of the westward expansion. The statistics of Harrison's defeat of Van Buren, which can be seen as a mandate for continued expansionism as well as against Jacksonianism, were therefore logically placed in the column next to the mention of Chapman's painting. Both the campaign and election of "Old Tippecanoe" and *The Baptism of Pocahontas* served to remind white Americans of the defeat of Indian belief systems, one by superior arms, and the other, as powerfully, by the revealed truth of Christianity. Each in its way served to reaffirm for its Anglo-American readers that God was truly with the white race in the great endeavor of civilizing the West, as well as to remind them of the eventual, inevitable end of those Indians who would choose to believe differently.

Although *The Baptism of Pocahontas* was seen by thousands of visitors to the nation's capital each year, it never became what one would call popular, and soon the painting, while remaining prominently displayed, began to slip into obscurity.[88] An anonymous writer in the January 1856 issue of the *Crayon: A Journal Devoted to the Graphic Arts, and the Literature Related to Them*, while attempting to praise the *Baptism*, unwittingly makes this clear. In a piece that calls for more and better paintings of Indians, primarily because the native cultures were quickly disappearing and future generations of white Americans will be curious about what they looked like, the writer takes a moment to single out what he or she considers to have been successful previous renderings: "We have had some remarkable pictures of the red man already painted, but few of them of sufficient pretension to be considered by posterity as authority. A few years since, Chapman's *marriage* of Pocahontas, in the Rotunda at Washington,

– [is] the most ambitious attempt we now remember" [emphasis added].[89] Even this critic, who presumably was an art scholar committed to the task of studying "The Indians in American Art," could not correctly recall the true subject of Chapman's work.

This writer goes on to talk at some length about the suitability of American scenes, especially scenes of Indians in their primitive state, for the historical painter. This argument, as exemplified by the 1734 *Boston Gazette* letter and the comments of Burk and Simms, had often been made, but at mid-century, when the native cultures really did appear to be "passing," it had taken on a new urgency. The history and mythology of the precontact Indian past, the era of the first confrontations between Indians and Europeans, and the continuing clash of cultures that was currently taking place on the western frontiers had come to be seen as untapped sources of material from which great visual and literary historical narratives could be constructed.

Such comments often had a single, concrete suggestion in common. Although all stressed that the native American heritage of the nation should be exploited, as, indeed, the Native Americans had been, these writers often made their point by invoking specific incidents from the life of Pocahontas. Her romantic narrative, which called to mind the image of the lovely Indian girl leaping between Captain Smith and his executioners, would challenge the talents of romancers and historians of all genres.

We must acknowledge Chapman's attempt to free Pocahontas from her popular persona as the savior of Smith, but if this was in fact his goal, we must question his decision to deemphasize the figure of Pocahontas in favor of the more politically evocative narrative portrayed in the scene as a whole. Images of the dynamic princess of Rescue scenes were simply too powerful to be overcome by Chapman's relatively small, kneeling convert. Visual representations of the Pocahontas narrative maintained their popularity during the period leading up to the Civil War, but this fame continued to be based primarily on the Rescue and enhanced by artists' often risqué pictorial renderings of that moment. And as the *Baptism* could not compete successfully with these more popular images, so Chapman, who had thought of himself as the rising young star of the American artistic community, was unable to compete with Church, Bierstadt, and the new generation of landscape painters who would come to dominate American art through and beyond the mid-nineteenth century.

In April 1859, a "pleasant pilgrimage" was made "to the ancient site of Jamestown."[90] Among those in attendance was the great New

England orator Edward Everett, who, in response to his being cer-
emonially welcomed, rose to say a few words to the assembled party.
Although "all sectional questions were ignored on the excursion,"
Everett made a point of mentioning the "Pilgrim fathers at Plymouth," who were the next after the Jamestown settlers to plant a
successful English colony in the New World.[91] He then returned to
the business at hand.

> What memories come back to the mind, as we stand on the spot,
> where two hundred and fifty-two years ago, those thrilling scenes
> of our early history began to be acted out! What solemn and
> tender images crowd upon us, as the shadowy forms of the chiv-
> alrous Smith, the friendly Powhatan, the gentle and compas-
> sionate Pocahontas, (whose name, truly Christian before she was
> baptized, figures on the little steamer that has just glanced over
> these shining waters) present themselves to the mind's eye.[92]

Indeed, "as if by a happy coincidence," the steamer *Pocahontas* had
just passed the group on its run up the James River.[93]

Everett suggests that through her actions the princess had become
a Christian before she was formally baptized, and that "Pocahontas,"
rather than "Rebecca," is her truly "Christian" name. Had Chapman been fortunate, this sort of comment might have reminded
people of his Capitol Rotunda painting and perhaps even attracted
some new attention to his work. The importance of Pocahontas as
the first Christian among her people never threatened her role as
the savior of John Smith, however, and as the sectional conflict grew
closer, her persona as a convert also became increasingly less important than her identity as a southerner. Her Virginia heritage,
coupled with her well-established national identity, would come to
make her a target of, and ironically at times a weapon for, northern
interests in the years prior to, during, and immediately after the Civil
War. Also, as we shall see, her royal heritage and her well-established
role as a mediator between two disparate races would lead to the use
of the name "Pocahontas," if not her narrative, in some of the more
interesting abolitionist literature of the prewar period.

THE FIGURE OF POCAHONTAS IN SECTIONALIST PROPAGANDA

―――――

"Tom, Dick and Harry! d'ye hear? Tell your mistress that Miss Pocahontas is in the parlor. And half a dozen bare, black feet hied away."[1]

[Confidential.]   NAVY DEPARTMENT, *April 5, 1861.*
    SIR: You will proceed to sea with the *Pocahontas* and on the morning
of the 11th instant appear off Charleston bar, 10 miles distant from
and due east of the light-house, where you will report to Captain Samuel Mercer of the *Powhatan,* for special service. Should he not be there,
you will await his arrival.
    I am, respectfully, your obedient servant,

                              GIDEON WELLES, *Secretary Navy*
              Commander J. P. Gillis, *Commanding U.S.S. Pocahontas,*
                                              Norfolk, Va.[2]

The "special service" referred to here by the Secretary of the Navy
was the proposed relief of Fort Sumter. The armada arrived too late
to assist Major Anderson and his men, however, and so the first
engagement of the Civil War was an easy, promising victory for the
southern forces under General Beauregard.
    The ship that was to have led this effort under the command of
Captain Mercer was arguably the nation's most important military
vessel. Since its launching in February 1850, the *Powhatan* had been
used to signify the power of the United States Navy on a number of
different missions.[3] She had patrolled the seas off Mexico, and then
was ordered to accompany Commodore Matthew C. Perry on his two
trips to Japan. The *Powhatan* was Perry's flagship on March 31, 1854
when the Treaty of Kanagawa, the first agreement between Japan
and the United States, was signed.[4] After this assignment the *Powhatan* engaged in successful raids against Chinese pirates. She was
Flag Officer Pendergrast's flagship at Vera Cruz, Mexico, in late
1860, but was ordered to return to the east coast when the outbreak
of sectionalist hostilities began to seem imminent. Although the *Powhatan* and her task force arrived too late to relieve Fort Sumter, she
did aid in the relief of Fort Pickens later in April 1861, and went

on to serve the Union navy valiantly throughout the remainder of the war.

The practice of naming ships for individual Indians or Indian tribes was already long established by the outbreak of the Civil War. There had been a number of other *Powhatans* before this vessel, as well as many ships that bore the name of his famous daughter. There are records of six merchant ships named the *Pocahontas* afloat at various times during the antebellum era, as well as at least three whalers, one of which was stove in by a whale off Brazil in December of 1850. (Reports of this incident reached the United States in March, 1851, while Melville was completing *Moby-Dick*.[5]) This total does not include various types of passenger vessels, barges, small transports, or crafts like the "handsome rowboat" named *Pocahontas* owned by former president John Tyler, and so I suspect that there were probably many ships and boats afloat bearing the name *Pocahontas* during the first century of American nationhood.[6]

The United States Navy apparently had an inclination toward Indian names for its vessels. In fact, the only ships of the American (Union) fleet in Atlantic waters that were "in commission" at the outbreak of the Civil War were the *Powhatan*, the *Pocahontas*, and the *Pawnee*. The *Mohawk* and the *Wyandotte* would also serve in the war, and among the ships christened or renamed between 1859 and 1865 were the *King Philip* (formerly a non-navy ship named *Powhatan*), the *Wampanoag*, the *Narragansett*, the *Seminole*, the *Nansemond*, the *Mohican*, the *Osage*, the *Osceola*, and the *Pequot*.[7] One could interpret this phenomenon as a display of trophies of previous wars, but it seems to me to have been more a way of honoring both recently conquered chiefs and peoples, as well as those Indians who, as Melville put it concerning the derivation of his *Pequod*, were by his time as "extinct as the ancient Medes."[8] Such names recognized that the Indian, or at least those Indians who no longer constituted a threat, had been important to the Anglo-American history of the nation, and perhaps even that they personified certain attributes that whites could by the mid-nineteenth century afford to find attractive. Rayna Green asserts that Indians used as figureheads were meant "to represent strength, power, dignity, pride, the ability to cope with nature, and a willingness to fight" (Figure 27).[9] An Indian name on a ship could also help to broadcast this message, and perhaps to suggest that the primarily white crews on these ships had acquired noble, native traits through an absorption of the tribes into the greater whole of America.[10] It is not surprising that the only woman's name identifying an American Naval vessel of this era is that of Pocahontas, whose image combined the valor necessary for fighting with a reminder of the peaceful relationship that might be possible through cooperation.

Figure 27. Figurehead of Pocahontas, attributed to William Rush, c. 1825. Courtesy of the Kendall Whaling Museum, Sharon, MA. There is some question concerning which ship this figurehead first adorned, and about who is portrayed in the cameo that Pocahontas holds. Is it George Washington or the Philadelphia merchant Stephan Girard who may have commissioned the figurehead?

Such names, however, especially in cases like that of the *Powhatan* in Yedo (Tokyo) harbor, with its guns facing – if not aimed at – the Japanese contingent on shore, do provide an ironic commentary on American imperialist tendencies. These ships of conquest, without whose guns many commercial agreements would not have been reached, were named after the previous victims of the Anglo-American thirst for economic and territorial expansion. And while certainly showing a measure of respect for the conquered native peoples, the point was perhaps being made to prospective or potential enemies that this same fate might await them should they decide against American wishes. The prevalence of such names being given to Union navy ships during the war suggests that there may have been a conscious attempt to send a message to secessionists about the futility of challenging the power of the American armed forces.

In the early part of the Civil War there were in fact two *Pocahontases* in the Union navy's fleet. One was the steamer seen by Edward Everett and his party, which had been chartered to the War Department as a troop and cargo transport.[11] This craft was ultimately caught in a gale off Cape Hatteras and run aground on January 18, 1862. (All 60 men on board survived. However, all but 19 of the 108 horses were killed.) The *Pocahontas* of the failed relief of Fort Sumter, after a change in commander, was involved in one of the many incidents that illustrated the fratricidal nature of the sectionalist controversy. Robert Selph Henry describes an early military engagement off the South Carolina coast.

> In command ashore in this first close battle between the [northern] fleet and the forts was Brigadier-General Thomas F. Drayton, of the Confederate States Army; afloat, in command of the *Pocahontas,* one of the ships in the attacking line, was his brother, Captain Percival Drayton, of the United States Navy – South Carolinians both. On the island for which they fought was the home where they were reared.[12]

It is of course ironic that ships designated *Pocahontas* and *Powhatan,* which were named after the ancestors of many prominent southerners, were called upon to use their guns against the Confederate forces. This, however, was not the first instance in which the name "Pocahontas" was used by northerners to attack southern interests, especially the institution of slavery, during the antebellum period. For instance, "Pocahontas" was used as a pseudonym by the authors of two abolitionist texts which, although written more than thirty years apart, expressed similar sentiments against the way of life that had become the foundation of the southern planter economy.

Moreover, the initial attacks by Northern historians on the veracity of the rescue story, and therefore on the word and character of John Smith and the importance of Pocahontas in the Anglo-American colonial enterprise, were made in the years immediately preceding the outbreak of hostilities in order to discredit the South's effort to formulate a history of its own. The Pocahontas narrative could be construed as a recollection of the founding moment of a particularly southern culture (as opposed to that of the United States as a whole), and so it became crucial to many southerners who were seeking to create an alternate history, and especially so to those who based their need to establish a separate, Confederate nation on the racial differences they perceived between themselves and citizens of the "Union." Northern writers could do little about the genealogical aspect of the Pocahontas narrative, since her descendants were indeed conspicuous members of southern society. However, the Rescue, her best-known accomplishment, became a target for their preemptive assaults. The flexibility of the narrative was again manifested during this period, in that both northern and southern writers were able to use it for their differing and often antagonistic purposes.

In 1820 Pocahontas was invoked in a satirical antislavery pamphlet entitled *Pocahontas; A Proclamation: With Plates*.[13] The author identifies himself, but then informs his readers of how he would like to be addressed in future: "Written by William Hillhouse Esqr. of New Haven, Conn. In consequence of writing this, he now goes by the nick name of 'Old Pocahontas' " (1). There is no further explanation of his choice of pseudonym and so the reader is left to sort it out, which is especially peculiar because of our being informed that the author is a man.

Hillhouse takes on the persona of a Virginian, and his parodic work is ostensibly written in praise of the South as a whole and the Old Dominion in particular, as well as of the institution of slavery. He begins by elucidating what will be his central point.

> THE welfare and happiness of the body politic, depends on the subordination of the inferior members to the head. This is most happily illustrated by the subjection of the slave to his master, in our system of domestic slavery, which places under our absolute, and individual control, in many instances, hundreds of human beings, thereby impressing on our minds, and on the minds of our children, correct ideas of freedom and republican principles. This is manifested by a dignified air, arising from a sense of superiority, and by an unabashed adherence, at all hazards, to whatever may tend to our own gratification and interest. (3)

This ideology is satirized in both the discussions of the mechanics of slavery and of the ultimate domination of the populace of the non-slaveholding states by the "majestic and lordly lions of the South"

Figure 28. "The Noble Virginians Going To Battle" (above) and "The Noble Virginians In The Heat Of Battle" (opposite page) as they appear in William Hillhouse, *Pocahontas; A Proclamation: With Plates,* (New Haven: J. Clyme, 1820). General Research Division, The New York Public Library, Astor, Lenox and Tilden Foundations.

(12). To ensure an attentive audience, Hillhouse makes use of the authority of the maternal progenitor of the Virginia aristocracy: "We are the descendants of Pocahontas, which entitles us to royal consideration" (3). The name of the princess, rather than his own, is signed at the end of the pamphlet, because it is in her name that the author supposedly speaks. In fact, it quickly becomes clear that this Pocahontas is being ironic about the gentry of her home state.

The plates mentioned in the title are a pair of engravings that satirize the heroism of Virginians in combat (Figure 28). In the first, entitled "The Noble Virginians Going To Battle" (Figure 28A), we see the mounted Virginia planters advancing *behind* a wall of slaves, with whips rather than swords raised. The second, "The Noble Virginians In The Heat Of Battle" (Figure 28B), shows the Virginians fleeing from the advancing enemy, while their slaves die in an attempt to save their cowardly masters. The subcaption here reads, "They who have 'wit to run away. / May live to fight another day.' " Hillhouse presents such tactics as the logical manner in which Virginians would conduct a battle, and thereby portrays both the cowardice of the supposedly chivalric southerners and their truly "Cavalier" treatment of those on whom they depend to maintain their debased existence.

The author mentions the recently passed Missouri Compromise

THE NOBLE VIRGINIANS IN THE HEAT OF BATTLE.
They who have "wit to run away.
May live to fight another day

on a number of occasions, usually to point out the problems brought about by wrong-thinking northern politicians. The feelings of this "Pocahontas" concerning the ultimate fate of such compromises is made clear in "her" long, pseudoprophetic summation, which describes the wonderful days that will come to pass after the establishment of the Order of the Opossum. (I quote this passage at length because when it is read as a whole the true agenda of the writer becomes quite clear.)

And in those days shall the majestic and lordly lions of the South lead forth the meek and silly lambs of the North; and we will send some of our royal race to take the rule, and to have dominion over them. Then every neck shall bow, and every knee shall bend, in token of their submission. The laws prohibiting the importation of slaves shall be repealed. All restriction on the domestic slave trade, and slavery, those birth-rights of the South, shall be removed. Slave ships shall arrive, with rich cargoes of despair, but of profit, from the Calabars, from the Islands, and from beyond the Plate. California, the Mexicos, and the adjoining dominions shall disgorge into the bosom of our new and western world, continued streams of black or slave population, till all the regions from the Gulph to the Pacific, and to the mouth of the Yellow-stone, and of the Missouri, shall assume a sable aspect.

Our manufactures or slave-breeding establishments shall flourish. Slave dealers, kidnappers, and negro drivers shall run to and fro through the land, and greatly multiply. . . . Then shall the eyes of the people of the slave holding states be constantly gratified with the sight of children torn from their parents, and parents from their children, and wives and husbands from each other, and driven by fifties, by hundreds, and by thousands, under the scourge, chained together, and galled to the bone with hand-cuffs, and with shackles, from the Atlantic to the rocky mountains, and to the borders of the *"further Ocean:"* which sights, by habit, and their constant repetition, are become necessary to their gratification and happiness, even as the sight of the tortures inflicted on captives, who were to be sacrificed at their council fires, and at their dances of death, were necessary for the savage gratification of the subjects of our red progenitor, and of his contemporaries, and predecessors.

When slavery shall thus arrive to its *"maximum"* of increase, and extent, then, and not till then, shall the lords and people of the slave-holding states, arrive to their *maximum* of enjoyment and earthly happiness!

Given at our imperial City of Richmond, the first year of the crusade for unlimited slavery: — In testimony whereof we have caused to be hereunto affixed the royal name of

POCAHONTAS

(12–13)

The reference to "our red progenitor" is clearly to Powhatan, the father of Pocahontas, and therefore an ancestor of many of the Virginia gentry. Their "gratification and happiness" at the tortures suffered by their own "captives" should thus be seen to be consistent with their "savage" inheritance, a part of the moral legacy left to southerners by those from whom many Virginians so proudly claimed descent. The great irony of an aristocracy of "mixed-bloods" in a society based on racial separation is also made obvious.

This pamphlet also raises another interesting issue. We now tend to remember the Missouri Compromise only in terms of its original intent, the dividing of the Louisiana Purchase and the maintaining of the balance between free and slave states during the first third of the nineteenth century. As Colin McEvedy points out, however, mid-century southerners saw it as having far more force. "Admittedly the Missouri Compromise only referred to the Louisiana Purchase but the extension of the 36° 30' line westward was the very least that the south expected when the territories acquired from Mexico came up for discussion."[14] David M. Potter notes that historians have, for the most part, failed to discuss this issue adequately. "To a surprising degree, historians have overlooked the strength of the movement to extend the Missouri Compromise line, and it has become, in a sense, the forgotten alternative of the sectional controversy."[15]

"Old Pocahontas," writing in 1820, was obviously aware of the possible ramifications of such an extension and points out what could one day come of such attempts to keep the nation equally divided. The idea that slavery should be extended to the Pacific was clearly under consideration even at this early date, and Hillhouse paints a sarcastically humorous and terrifying picture of what could be the ultimate result. Speaking with an arrogance and bravado that by 1820 was perhaps already the stereotypical northern impression of southern rhetoric, Hillhouse pretends to champion a way of life that he portrays as inhumane for the slaves and, in fact, disastrous for both slaves and masters.

Hillhouse used the name "Pocahontas" against Virginia and the South in part because her name in his title would have attracted some attention to the pamphlet, but primarily because she was the literal and/or figurative progenitrix of the Virginia gentry. This pseudonym helps him to express the foolishness of having a mixed-blood aristocracy in a society where racial separation is mandatory, and where the great majority of both whites and blacks must necessarily be reduced to positions of poverty and servitude. He is thereby able to question ironically the essential distinctions upon which the southern planter ideology was based.

A second significant use of the nom de plume Pocahontas was by Emily Clemens Pearson, author of the 1852 abolitionist novel *Cousin Franck's Household, or Scenes In The Old Dominion*.[16] Pearson is almost certainly also the "Emily Catharine Pierson" who had previously authored *Jamie Parker, The Fugitive*, another novel about the problems inherent in the slavery system.[17] This earlier work, which featured the escape of a group of "servants" from a Virginia plantation, was also the first in which Pearson invoked the name of the famous Indian princess. Two of the minor characters in *Jamie Parker* are the daughters of the aristocratic Chadwick household, Pocahontas and Virginia, the former of whom, even without her black "servant" who had escaped to Canada, is predicted to be the belle of the upcoming Saratoga social season. In this novel the given name "Pocahontas" is presented without comment, as if readers who were familiar with the archaic life of a southern plantation would not be surprised that a daughter of the house was given this exotic appellation. It also suggests that the Chadwicks are direct descendants of the royal family of Virginia. The fact that this Pocahontas is a beautiful young woman makes the obvious connection to the heroine of Jamestown even stronger.

Jamie Parker apparently had few readers in its day, however, and perhaps Pearson felt that she needed some way to attract the attention of the reading public to her next effort. The pseudonym "Pocahontas," combined with a title that suggested her book's thematic similarity to the most popular novel in America, Stowe's *Uncle Tom's Cabin*, were her chosen methods. This strategy, as well as the fact that her writing had improved a great deal since the composition of *Jamie Parker*, made her second book somewhat more successful. *Cousin Franck's Household* was into its fourth edition by 1853.

Sterling Brown begins his brief discussion of *Cousin Franck's Household* by referring to it as "*Swallow Barn* in reverse," and it is worth taking a moment to look briefly at John Pendleton Kennedy's extremely popular novel of 1832, which had been reissued in a revised edition in 1851.[18] The narrative voice in *Swallow Barn* is that of Mark Littleton, Esq., of New York. He is challenged by a letter from his southern cousin, Ned Hazard, who believes that his northern relative has formed some erroneous prejudices against Virginia, to visit Swallow Barn plantation and see southern life for himself. Although the reader suspects that this New Yorker may have antislavery leanings, Littleton makes it clear that he has an open mind about slavery, and that, in fact, he believes that one must study both sides of an issue in order to ascertain which is correct. In this way he both represents northerners who may have taken an antislavery stance without sufficiently investigating the matter and acts as an apparently impartial observer who is only interested in finding out the truth. The narrative that follows, Littleton's report to his friend Zachary Huddlestone, Esq., of Preston Ridge, New York, contains a number of descriptions of life on a Virginia plantation, as well as many observations about southern society.

Because these descriptions tend to be overwhelmingly sentimental, it is generally perceived that Littleton, with a few reservations, is won over by the genteel life of the plantation. The most important discussion of slavery offered by Kennedy is not presented by his narrator, however. Rather, we hear the words of kind, genial Frank Meriwether, the owner of Swallow Barn plantation and Littleton's cousin by marriage. In a chapter entitled "The Quarter," he and Littleton visit the cabins of the slaves, which the narrator describes as being a part of "an exceedingly picturesque landscape" (vol. 2, 223). Meriwether then takes this opportunity to present his opinions on the institution. His arguments predict what would become standard southern rhetoric on the slavery question.

Meriwether first points out that slavery, even to him, is "indefensible." He goes on to say that "It is theoretically and morally wrong; and, of course, it may be made to appear wrong in all its modifications" (vol. 2, 227). Here, however, Meriwether makes the point that it is actually the fault of those who have come before his generation, and perhaps of history itself, that plantation owners have come to be in this, to him, unenviable position.

But, surely, if these people are consigned to our care, and put upon our commonwealth, without our agency, the only duty that is left to us is to administer wholesome laws for their government, and to make their servitude as tolerable to them as we can. We are not bound to submit to internal convulsions to get rid of them; nor have we a right, in the desire to free ourselves, to whelm them in greater evils than they suffer here. . . . When we can part with them on terms easy to ourselves and to them, I would do it. In the mean time, we must treat them kindly and justly. As to the evils they suffer, I do not believe in them: – the evil generally is on the side of the master. (vol. 2, 227–8)

What Meriwether means, of course, is that it is the masters who suffer most of the evils of this system, in which they have to support these people who "do less work than any other labourers in society" (vol. 2, 228). He goes on to refute the claims that slaves are treated harshly by their masters, and finally makes an apparently reasonable statement concerning the only power that will be qualified to decide about matters such as abolition.

Whenever emancipation of slaves, or the abolition of slavery is to be required, the requisition must come from the slave-holding states themselves, as they are the only persons in this country who are able to deal with the subject. All other men will be deluded by the feeling which the abstract question of slavery excites in their minds, – a feeling of unmitigated abhorrence of its injustice. We, on the contrary, have every motive to calm and prudent counsel. Our lives, fortunes, families, – even our commonwealth – are put at the hazard of this resolve. (vol. 2, 229)

It is easy for modern observers to counter that this is precisely why plantation owners should not, and ultimately did not, have a part in the decision-making process. In 1832, however, when delivered by a generous, philosophical plantation owner like Frank Meriwether, this type of rationalization may have been persuasive to many northern readers who were theoretically opposed to the idea of slavery without ever having seen a plantation, or for that matter, a slave. Mark Littleton, an obviously intelligent visitor from New York, certainly seems to have been convinced of the expediency and humanity of this system. It is therefore ironic that, as William R. Taylor points out, by writing "sentimentally" about the feelings of the slaves, "Kennedy was unknowingly preparing the way for writers like Mrs. Stowe [and Emily Pearson] who were bent on showing the inhumanity and injustice of slavery through exploring the Negro consciousness."[19]

"Pocahontas," the nominal author of *Cousin Franck's Household* and of the letters that make up its epistolary text, is a young white woman who has traveled from Connecticut to visit her relatives in Port Royal, Virginia. The reader is never given any indication that this is anything but her actual name, and Pearson provides no explanation. One might conjecture, however, as one might about "Pocahontas Chadwick" of *Jamie Parker,* that this is a family name, which would lead the reader to the further supposition that our correspondent's family might be among those that trace their lineage back to Pocahontas and Rolfe. This would add irony to Pocahontas's indictment of slavery because she is thereby related to the gentry who have long profited from this system. Her letters are sent to her friend "S." back in New England, and, like Littleton's narrative, describe the life that this northerner finds on her cousin Franck's plantation in the Old Dominion.

From the beginning of her trip Pocahontas detests the idea of slavery, and she becomes more horrified by each encounter that she has with the institution. From her first meeting with a slave – a Topsy-like maid named Maria in a hotel in Washington, D.C. – to her descriptions of the life of the slaves on the plantation, Pocahontas's feelings change only in that her abstract dislike of slavery grows into an absolute hatred. She is able to see its terrible effects on all of the human beings involved, and often notes that the system is as bad for the masters as for the slaves. This assertion ultimately becomes one of the dominant themes of the novel.

The Cameron family is apparently headed by Cousin Franck, a transplanted New Englander, who has owned slaves only since his marriage. He has adjusted, however, and lives comfortably within the system and under the thumb of his strong-willed and "queenly" wife. Regina Cameron, the daughter of a great plantation owner, has strong beliefs about the correctness of their way of life, and she is passing them down to her pretty daughter Rosalie. It is to the other daughter, Ruth, a sensitive, sickly, humpbacked girl, that Pocahontas is drawn, because it quickly becomes clear that Ruth also detests everything having to do with slavery.

Throughout the novel various local people attempt to enlighten Pocahontas about what they perceive to be her overly sympathetic notions about the blacks. First among these is Doctor G., with whom she shares the stagecoach on her way to the Port Royal. Doctor G. has just bought a plantation in Florida and is attempting to purchase the slaves he will need to maintain it. Noticing Pocahontas's disgust after seeing a group of slaves working in the fields, he suggests that it is only her ignorance that is keeping her from appreciating the southern way of life. "I see," replied the Doctor, coolly, "that you have not been educated into the system; but, my word for it, you'll be charmed with it yet. It will recommend itself to your good common sense" (25). This is generally the line taken by the apologists for slavery; they point out its necessity and maintain that one will eventually come to see its positive, if not its "charming," side, if one gives it a fair chance.

Pearson seems to have realized that a totally one-sided presentation of the evils of slavery might not be convincing. Therefore, from the outset of the novel we meet characters like Dr. G., who argue in favor of maintaining this system. However, her proponents, far from being kind, philosophical individuals like Kennedy's Frank Meriwether, are instead portrayed as stereotypically cruel, in some way untrustworthy, or as people who have simply become immune through usage to the abuses of slavery. This numbness, however, serves as well as any violently proslavery response to show the weakness of their arguments.

Far more convincing statements are made by those individuals who are against slavery. From Murray Mackintosh, the young Blue Ridge philosopher who holds his own against a room full of slaveholders at Senator T.'s Christmas soiree, to Mrs. Briarly, a former housekeeper who had seen the horrors of this system in practice for forty years, we are presented with various characters who offer powerful evidence concerning the abuses of plantation life. Pearson's descriptions, however, are not set as unfortunate, singular depictions within a generally sentimental portrayal of the Old South. Rather, the experiences described by such characters are products of the charged, sinister atmosphere created by a system that survives by fear and violence. Foremost among these southern abolitionists is Ruth Cameron, whose opinions, and ultimately her actions, are incomprehensible to her mother, sister, and other "right-thinking" Virginians.

Much of *Cousin Franck's Household* will seem fairly stereotypical to the reader of *Uncle Tom's Cabin*. We meet a cruel overseer, Colonel Caleb Cutts; a minister, the Reverend Mr. Brincherhoff, who uses the Bible to defend slavery; and we are introduced to a number of vain, empty-headed southern belles and pseudo-chivalric young southern gentlemen. In terms of the plot, we find a sale that separates the members of a slave family, as well as separating the Camerons from their beloved servant, Aunt Selma; several escape attempts by slaves (one of which is aided by the kindhearted Ruth); and an almost Dickensian denouement involving the return of William, the long-lost brother of Aunt Selma, who, as it turns out, is also the half-brother of Regina Cameron. William, who now goes by the name of "Mr. Oglethorpe," was freed and adopted by his former master and has come into possession of both ample wealth and a will that declares him to be as much a rightful heir to the plantation as Regina. In the end he takes control of the plantation and frees the slaves, while, as Pocahontas is happy to report, the Cameron family relocates to New England, away from the "pestiferous atmosphere of the South" (258).

Pearson's attack in *Cousin Franck's Household* is more against the institution of slavery than against the slaveholders themselves. She constantly has Pocahontas and other sympathetic characters make the point that the whites suffer as much as the blacks under this system. As Mrs. Briarly puts it;

> There is, I am confident of it, something in the very nature of the system, which petrifies the kindly emotions of the heart, in dealing with the slaves. I do not fully understand it, but persons who are kind even to brutes, often prove perfect tyrants towards their oppressed brethren. They are elegant and accomplished, often, overflowing in hospitality to those of their own rank, and engaged in the enterprise of religion, but complete despots in their own little realm. (189)

The abolitionists in the novel emphasize a notion that was perhaps most eloquently stated by Jefferson in *Notes on the State of Virginia*.[20] The masters as well as the slaves suffer from this system, because, although both are dehumanized, the plantation owners also become desensitized to the suffering and degradation of others. (This is also the view expressed, ironically enough, by the proslavery Frank Meriwether of Kennedy's Swallow Barn plantation.)

Although the Pocahontas of *Cousin Franck's Household* always takes the side of the slaves, she does not really do anything particularly brave or heroic. Ruth Cameron, however, is a woman of courage and action. She aids in the escape of the slave Fayett and her family, thereby going against the wishes of her mother and the law, which would have allowed Regina to repossess both Fayett and her children. Ruth also, upon reaching the age of eighteen, immediately frees all of the slaves that have come into her possession. Finally, it is Ruth who makes the ultimate sacrifice by giving up her chance to marry Ferdinand T., the son of a wealthy neighbor and a man she truly loves, because she will not "become the mistress of slaves for life" (253).

Why, then, would Pocahontas be invoked by Pearson or by a proto-abolitionist like Hillhouse? On one level, her name was certainly first and foremost a "hook" to catch prospective readers, but this usage

would'have led people to expect a romantic text dealing with Indians, or at least with some issue involving Indian-white relations. We
must ask, therefore, if there could have been another reason why
Pocahontas was used in propagandist texts like these. What might a
contemporary reader have understood by such invocations?

On one level, the crucial issue of race relations in each of these
works is juxtaposed to a presentation of class relations and hierarchies within the white race. In *Pocahontas; A Proclamation*, the author
uses the figure of Pocahontas to attack both the Virginia aristocracy,
many of whom were proud to have been descended from her, and
the class system by which this aristocracy was able to maintain power.
By proclaiming the superiority of the southern planters to northern
whites as well as to their own slaves and then describing the cruelty
and foolishness of their way of life, Hillhouse, under his "royal"
pseudonym, is satirizing the institution that by 1820 had already
become one of the most familiar symbols of the South. It is important for Hillhouse to lampoon the aristocratic notions of the "royal
Virginians" he describes, because as his readers see the absurdity of
such archaic ideas, they must also notice the horror inherent in a
system that justifies the survival of these feudal notions. The invocation of the "princess" Pocahontas also necessitated the use of mo-
narchical terminology. This allowed Hillhouse to inject into his
pamphlet language that still would have been considered incendiary
by those who could remember the Revolutionary War, as well as
those who had fought in the War of 1812, which had concluded
only five years earlier.

Pearson breaks ground, in *Cousin Franck's Household*, in her portrayal of the forgotten victims of the slavery system, the "poor
whites." In what is perhaps the most important contribution of her
book, she spends a great deal of time on the plight of the these
people, who are the less obvious victims of the planter aristocracy.
Earlier writers had mentioned "poor whites" – Kennedy had acknowledged them in his portrayal of the Wingate family in *Horse-Shoe
Robinson*, and Simms had portrayed various types of lower-class white
families, including the Bloneys of *The Partisan* – but Pearson provides
a fairly detailed study of how they fit into, or, in fact, are left out of,
the southern plantation system.[21] As she notes in her preface, Pearson was well aware that she would be describing a class that would
not be familiar to most of her readers:

The "poor whites," a phase of Southern life not so well known
at the North, and to which we have given some prominence,
are not an accident of the slave system, but a necessary result,
bound to it by the immutable law of cause and effect. No picture

of Southern "institutions" is complete, in which this is not seen distinct in the back ground. (vi)

The poor whites of this novel, the family of Dijah Gray, appear after a coach accident in which Regina Cameron is injured. In her description of them, Pocahontas provides more information than an innocent girl from Connecticut probably would have known:

> It was late in the afternoon when we reached the rude settle-ment, composed of a few log huts scattered over a worn-out pine barren, which nobody claimed. The occupants of the huts are distinguished for their lazy, drunken habits, and their squalid degradation, – they being a portion of that great class called "poor whites," who constitute the worst excrescence and inev-itable product of the slave system. They resemble the Blaggs of Eastern Virginia, the Clay Eaters of Georgia, and the Piney Woods people of North Carolina. It is not pretended that they approach the slaves of Virginia in respectability and honesty of character. (125)

Regina is found, aided, and taken in by the Gray family, which at this point consists of Dijah's alcoholic wife and two small children. Gray's help is based solely on his perception that there would be money in helping a rich woman, perhaps enough to get his family through the winter and to replace the whiskey that had been acci-dentally spilled by his children.

The Gray's eldest child, Charley, had already been sold to a "nigger buyer," and the same fate probably awaited the younger children (131). Charley was by descent and appearance white, but, because of the large number of mulatto and octoroon slaves who appeared to be white, it was no problem to sell him into servitude. In this single inci-dent Pearson provides an ironic commentary on the Anglo-American fear of those "mixed-bloods" who could "pass for white," and points out the baseness that was aroused by the money that could be made in the buying and selling of human lives. The lot of the Gray family and people like them is actually worse than that of many slaves, and has led them to take such horrifying measures as the selling of their own chil-dren in order to survive. Our sense is that the slaves, who themselves can be bought and sold at will by white plantation owners, would never stoop to this level. Pearson does not have her characters discuss how the poor whites have gotten to this degraded state, but it is clear that they are useless, and therefore hopeless, in a system where the manual labor is done by slaves.

Pearson's descriptions of the poor whites are crucial to her anti-slavery arguments. Their lot is usually portrayed unfavorably in comparison with that of the slaves that Pocahontas has observed on the Virginia plantations. And since most of *Cousin Franck's Household* is made up of descriptions of the terrifying conditions of slavery, there can be no doubt as to the status of these less fortunate examples of what the plantation owners would have us believe is the "superior" race. By her vivid portrayal of how the white plantation owners, through their dehumanization, and the poor whites, through their degradation, suffer under the institution of slavery, Pearson provides powerful evidence that greatly bolsters her more traditional abolitionist arguments.

Because issues of class are crucial to both of these texts, the name "Pocahontas" is a perfect catalyst, in that both of these issues dovetail in her narrative. The original Pocahontas was an Indian, but she was just as importantly a princess, and we must remember that the anecdote about James I's objection to her marriage on the basis of class rather than race had become an accepted part of the tale. The princess Pocahontas was seen in the nineteenth century as the figurative mother of the Virginia aristocracy, who are lampooned by Hillhouse and implicitly indicted by Pearson.[22] "Her" approval of the ridiculous arguments made by Hillhouse undercuts her image and enhances his attempt to undercut both the racial and class distinctions upon which the southern, and particularly Virginian, Cavalier society was based.

In the Pocahontas narrative could also be found an interesting analogy to the fate of many African slaves, as well as a perhaps romantic hope for the ultimate assimilation of the black race into Anglo-American society. It must be remembered that Pocahontas was also tricked and taken prisoner on board a European ship by whites, and, while not enslaved, she had to learn to live in a foreign world that she was not free to leave. The fact that she was ultimately able to join that world through her baptism and marriage, and that her descendants had come to be accepted by the members of the capturing culture, at least allowed for the idea that one day such a future might be possible in America for those suffering under the bonds of slavery. (That future would, of course, have entailed the loss of their own culture, as it did with the original Pocahontas. Indeed, for African slaves this would be the second such loss.)

Pocahontas's most famous act was that of a mediator, who had attempted to stop the useless violence that one race was inflicting on a representative member of another. Also, as we have seen, her baptism placed her in the position as connector of two worlds. By the mid-nineteenth century, she had come to be accepted by whites as a model for the peaceful coexistence that perhaps could have existed between themselves and the Indians. In *Cousin Franck's House-*

hold, Pocahontas is again a mediator: at times between the slaves and their masters, and always, through her letters, between the two different societies of antebellum America. Her name, however, recalls the first Pocahontas and the possibility of salvation for those in bondage that the Indian princess had also come to represent. On the other hand, one could ironically view the actions of the historical Pocahontas at the moment of Smith's execution as typical of the lot of many black slaves, who, as in the engravings in *Pocahontas; A Proclamation,* sacrificed themselves for the benefit of their white masters. No matter what the specific interpretation, however, the use of Pocahontas in these texts would have contributed to a notion that a possible harmony between disparate races was possible, if only as the result of extraordinary heroism.

In *Alternative Americas,* her study of the cultural differences between the North and the South in the years before the Civil War, Anne Norton argues for the importance of the Pocahontas narrative to the growing sense of southern nationalism.

> In the South the Pocahontas myth became increasingly expressive of a peculiar sectional culture. The chivalrous conduct in the myth recalled the Cavalier, the rank and marriage of Pocahontas assured the legitimacy of the present residents. As an Indian princess, Pocahontas united a natural, Indian, character of noble savagery and natural virtue with a conventional preeminence, reconciling the conflicting demands of Jefferson and an ideology derived from the Enlightenment, with the Cavalier model.
>
> As Southern sentiment for rebellion . . . increased, Pocahontas was evoked with increasing frequency. These evocations associated Pocahontas as a sectional symbol with the violent independence considered characteristic of Indians in general.[23]

In her brief treatment of the princess as an ancestress, Norton is most interested in how the Indianness of Pocahontas and her descendants, such as John Randolph, came to be interpreted during the antebellum era. I am more concerned here with the rescue of Smith, because this incident was crucial to Virginians and ultimately became so to many Southern patriots, and because it attracted the wrath of northern historians during the period of heightening sectional tensions (Figure 29).

In a note in his *History of New England* (1858), John Gorham Palfrey casts a gentle doubt on the accuracy of Smith's descriptions of his precolonial adventures in Europe.

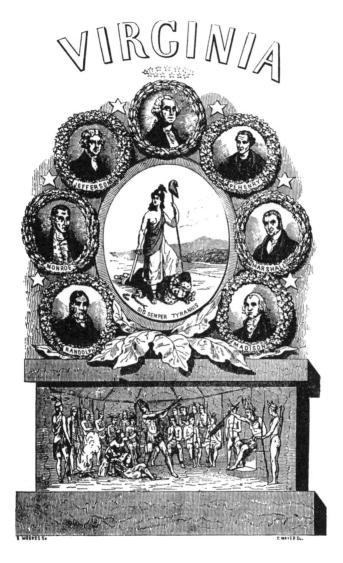

Figure 29. "Virginia." Frontispiece from Henry Howe, *Historical Collections of Virginia*, Charleston, SC, 1852. In this piece the rescue of John Smith is depicted as the foundation upon which the greatness of Virginia was built.

On the whole, the reader perhaps inclines to the opinion that John Smith was not the sole author of his books, but that they passed, for embellishment at least, through the hands of some craftsman, who was not perfectly possessed either of Smith's own story, or of the geography or public history to which it is related.[24]

Palfrey then immediately goes on to tell the story of "how first he planted Virginia," which would of course include his being saved by Pocahontas. While casting no direct aspersions on the New World material, Palfrey perhaps succeeds in planting a seed of doubt in the minds of his more suspicious readers. Whether this was done at the urging of his friend Charles Deane is not known, but Deane quickly seized this idea and became the most important northern voice in the ensuing Rescue debate.

In 1860, as a war between North and South began to seem inevitable, Deane of Massachusetts, himself a New England historian of some renown, first publicly challenged the veracity of the rescue story. This tale had had its early detractors, but over the preceding two hundred years had coalesced into a fairly consistent narrative.[25] Although particular details were adjustable, the bare bones of the story had come to be regarded as historical truth. The Indian princess had, in some more or less dramatic way, intervened between a prisoner and his executioner, appealed to her father, and saved the life of the brave captain who was the actual if not nominal leader of the Jamestown colony.

It is clearly more than a coincidence that Deane's comments, made in the notes to his new edition of *A Discourse of Virginia* by Edward Maria Wingfield, the first president of the Virginia colony, appeared during this time of heightened sectional turmoil.[26] Deane based his theory on the fact that the Rescue, which is detailed in Smith's *Generall Historie* of Virginia (1624), did not appear in his *True Relation* (1608) or in his earlier versions of his history.

> It was while on this expedition [to the Chickahominy], as we are told in one of the later publications of Smith, that his life, which was threatened by Powhatan, was saved by his daughter Pocahontas, just as he was about to suffer. The story is an interesting and romantic one. But the critical reader of the accounts of Smith's adventures in Virginia will be struck with the fact, that no mention whatever is made of this incident in his minute personal narrative covering this period, written at the time on the spot, and published in 1608 . . . .
>
> No one can doubt that the earlier narrative contains the truer statement, and that the passage last cited [the Rescue, in the *Generall Historie*] is one of the many embellishments with which Smith, with his strong love of the marvellous, was disposed to garnish the stories of his early adventures, and with which he or his editors were tempted to adorn particularly his later works.[27]

In one stroke, Deane's argument attempted to make a liar out of the first Cavalier, to undercut the best-known and loved incident of Virginia history, and to remove much of the luster from Pocahontas, the supposed heroine of the Jamestown colony.

Deane was certainly aware that this doubt, if successfully disseminated, would have a negative effect on readings of Anglo-American history that were sympathetic to the importance of Jamestown, the first permanent English settlement in the New World. Such attention was necessarily at the expense of the Plymouth and Massachusetts Bay colonies and therefore undoubtedly raised the hackles of any right-thinking Yankee, but especially of a historian like Deane, who had written extensively on early New England history, and in 1856 had edited Bradford's *History of Plymouth Plantation* for the Massachusetts Historical Society.[28] Deane was also attempting to deprive Pocahontas, one of the most important historical figures of the South, of her most famous contribution to the success of the British colonial enterprise, and her father of his great opportunity to display apparently nonsavage sentiments concerning the life of the prisoner and his love for his daughter.

Deane mentions the marriage of Pocahontas to John Rolfe in passing, but he gives it no emphasis and returns quickly to the anti-Smith thrust of his comments. Although it can be argued whether or not his theories are convincing, what he did manage to do successfully by his attack was to cast doubt on the Rescue and, by focusing contemporary discussions about Pocahontas on this question, he was able to direct attention away from the undeniable genealogical facts. The tradition of tracing one's ancestry had been kept alive in the South, and the importance of genealogy to the leading southern planters of the day is undeniable.[29] It had always been particularly crucial to those who could claim direct descent, or even a connection through marriage, to Pocahontas, and therefore to the primordial, hereditary aristocracy of America. (The most recent catalogue of her family had been produced by the prominent Virginia politician, former governor, and direct descendant of Pocahontas, Wyndham Robertson, in 1858.) The discussion of Deane's doubts was detrimental to such individuals, because, while it did not alter the legitimacy of their hierarchy through descent, which was based on her "royal" standing, it did tarnish the value of their inheritance of the heroic attributes that she had allegedly exhibited at the crucial moment of the Rescue (Figure 30).

As William Warren Jenkins points out, Deane was answered almost immediately.[30] In August 1860, in an article ostensibly written to clarify the events surrounding Pocahontas's marriage, Robertson again reminded readers of the genealogy of the princess, as well as her importance as the first native convert and first Indian to inter-marry with an Englishman, and argued strongly against the doubts expressed by Deane.[31] This defense, and the anonymous articles "Smith's Rescue By Pocahontas" and "Pocahontas; or, The Lady Rebecca," appeared, not surprisingly, in the *Southern Literary Messenger*, which at this point was using its rapidly lessening influence to defend southern culture and the Confederate cause.[32] The defense of the heroine of Virginia was necessarily an important part of their strategy.

The essay was not, however, the only course open to those who would respond to Deane's allegations. The January 1861 issue of *Harper's New Monthly Magazine*, which only two months earlier had carried a biography of John Smith that included an engraving of a curiously well-covered, extremely Caucasian-looking Pocahontas saving the life of the captain, contained a poem by John Esten Cooke, who later became a Confederate officer, a biographer of Robert E. Lee and Stonewall Jackson, and the author of perhaps the most admired novel about the princess, his 1885 *My Lady Pokahontas*.[33] In "A Dream of the Cavaliers" Cooke looks back to the great figures of the southern past, beginning, of course, with the first Cavalier, Smith, and his mythic companion.[34] The second section of the poet's "waking dream" is devoted solely to their relationship:

> They come in a great procession,
>   With firm but noiseless tread,
> From the mists of the far horizon –
>   Those ghosts of the mighty dead.
>
> In front of the glittering pageant,
>   With clear dark eyes serene,
> Behold, in his ruff and doublet,
>   The Knight of the Virgin Queen! –
>
> John Smith, the fearless captain
>   Of the mighty days of old,
> With the beard and swarthy forehead,
>   And the bearing free and bold!
>
> He has fought in the bloody battles
>   Of the Old World and the New,
> With a soul unmoved by peril –
>   A stout heart, kind and true!

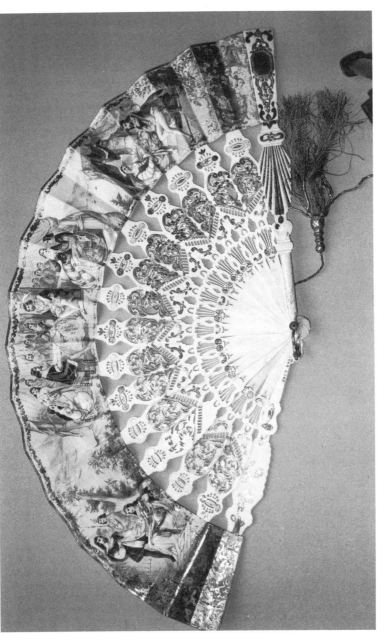

Figure 30. Unidentified artist. The "Pocahontas Fan," c. 1860. This fan, which has been identified as depicting events from the life of Pocahontas, does not include a vignette of the Rescue. The probable date of its construction suggests that the artist may not have wanted to include this scene, the veracity of which was at that time under attack. Reproduced courtesy of Mrs. Georgette Tilley, Woodford Green, Essex, England.

He has flashed his glittering falchion
    In the sun of Eastern lands,
And toilcd, a woe-worn captive,
    In the wild Caucasian sands!

He has bent with knightly homage
    To the beauty in her bower,
But here, in the purple sunset,
    He has met with a fairer flower!

She comes! – like a fawn of the forest,
    With a bearing mild and meek,
The blood of a line of chieftains
    Rich in her golden cheek.

With the tender, fluttering bosom,
    And the rounded shoulders, bare –
The folds of her mantle waving
    In the breath of the idle air.

With a crown of nodding feathers
    Set round with glimmering pearls;
And the light of the dreamy sunshine
    Asleep in her raven curls!

Our own dear Pocahontas!
    The Virgin Queen of the West –
With the heart of a Christian hero
    In a timid maiden's breast!

You have heard the moving story
    Of the days of long ago,
How the tender girlish bosom
    Shrunk not from the deadly blow:

How the valiant son of England,
    In the woodland drear and wild,
Was saved from the savage war-club
    By the courage of a child.

And now in the light of glory
    The noble figures stand –
The founder of Virginia,
    And the pride of the Southern land!

This identification of Pocahontas as "The Virgin Queen of the West" is somewhat peculiar in that we know of her subsequent marriage. John Rolfe, however, does not appear at all in the poem, nor do any references to Pocahontas's descendants or to her as the "mother" of the southern race, although one could argue that on one level Cooke's image invokes the Virgin Mary, the figurative mother of all Christians. Rather, we see the apparent transference of Smith's allegiance from his role as "The Knight of the Virgin Queen," who is clearly Elizabeth I, to "The Virgin Queen of the West." Pocahontas displaces Elizabeth as a foundress, thereby signifying that the freeing of the new Empire of America from the dominance of the older, British dominion began with the Jamestown founding.

Pocahontas's place as the progenitrix of many of the leading citizens of the Virginia was not open to Deane's attack, and so Cooke also ignores this issue, eschews any mention of Rolfe or her descendants, and directly challenges the New England historian on his own terms. Cooke implies that her mythic persona based on her relationship with Smith is primary, and indeed far more significant than anything that occurred after she had ceased to be a virgin. The "Our" that begins stanza 10 proclaims her to be specifically a southerner, not simply an American, and it is primarily because of her bravery in a life-threatening situation that she is invoked here as "the pride of the Southern land." Cooke clearly hoped that this aspect of her character, when coupled with a reminder of the great deeds of John Smith, would strike a responsive chord in the young men of the still-coalescing entity that would become known as the Confederacy. They too would soon be facing life-threatening situations and so would be in need of such models of bravery. Cooke in this poem, while attempting to refute Deane, encourages his southern audience to remember the gallant figures of their past, male and female, and to make use of their inspirational value during the troubling times ahead (Figure 31).

Laura Polanyi Striker has pointed out that "Smith, once scorned as a fellow without gentle birth, now ironically became the symbol of Southern honor. Northern historians attacked him as a way of undermining the South's symbol of itself."[35] Such attacks on Smith's veracity almost always centered on the Rescue, and therefore had the added advantage of also impugning the reputation of the woman James Kirke Paulding had called one of the "tutelary deities" of Virginia.[36] By the time of the Civil War, however, the facts of the case were no longer as relevant as her mythohistoric presence, which was firmly entrenched in the national consciousness.

Figure 31. Flag of the Powhatan Guards (Company E, 4th Virginia Cavalry). Courtesy of the Museum of the Confederacy, Richmond, VA. The creator of this flag attempts to provide a more realistic portrayal of Pocahontas, although the artist does seem to have been aware of the earlier of Robert Matthew Sully's portraits. The cross signifies her adoption of Christianity and perhaps suggests that as God had given her courage at a crucial moment, so He will favor those who follow her image into battle.

In *The Creation of Confederate Nationalism,* Drew Gilpin Faust argues that "The Confederacy's declaration of nationhood had, within the framework of nineteenth-century nationalist doctrine, made culture explicitly political, inextricably tied to the power of this new Confederate nation at home and abroad."[37] One foundation of Confederate culture was the memory of the Virginia-born Founding Fathers: Jefferson, Henry, Madison, and the archetypal personification of an oppressed people's fight for freedom, George Washington. Also important to the establishment of this new culture, however, was the actual beginning of the English settlement of the New World, which logically also became the first event in the history of the Confederacy. In this context, the significance of the founding of the colony at Jamestown, and the Indian princess without whom it would not have been possible, could be freely acknowledged without the "distraction" of the Pilgrims of Plymouth Rock and their ideological descendants.

Another aspect of the creation of this new culture was an insistence on the racial difference between northerners and southerners. This ethnic separation was a crucial part of southerners' attempts to establish their own identity, and evidence that a number of nationalist thinkers promulgated this theory is not hard to find. The *Southern Literary Messenger* of June 1860 leads off with an article specifically entitled "The Difference Of Race Between The Northern And Southern People," which argues that those descended from the "Saxons" in the North, are distinct from the "Norman" descendants of the South.[38] Faust points to the similar sentiments expressed in "Conflict of Northern and Southern Races," an article in the October–November 1861 *Debow's Review*, and notes that "In *Ivanhoe*, Scott contrasted 'churlish Saxons' and 'noble Norman knights.' "[39] And one of the most important poems of the period was Henry Timrod's "Ethnogenesis," which was "Written During The Meeting Of The First Southern Congress" by the man who would become known as the "laureate of the Confederacy."[40] In view of this occasion Timrod concentrated on the foundation of the new nation and looked ahead to its glorious future, but his title clearly suggests that with the founding of the Confederacy has come the acknowledgement that its citizens are the founding members of a new race.

An additional representation of this southern need to assert its difference is lifted from the editorial pages of the December 10, 1860, edition of the *New Orleans Bee*, in which the editor discusses the consequences of the recent presidential election.

Lincoln's triumph is simply the practical manifestation of the popular dogma in the free States that slavery is a crime in the sight of GOD, to be reprobated by all honest citizens, and to be warred against by the combined moral influence and political power of the Government. . . . If the North is sincere she must inevitably abhor the South. If this is a sentiment compatible with the endurance of a Union avowedly founded on the most perfect political equality and social harmony and fraternity, then we must ignore the history of our revolutionary struggles, our efforts in behalf of a sound government, and our success in the formation of the Constitution of the United States.

That instrument was designed to guide and govern a homogeneous nation – homogeneous in the patrimony of a common country, a common ancestry, and an independence achieved at

the point of the sword after years of sacrifice and struggle. The
events of the last quarter of a century prove distinctly and un-
deniably that the people have ceased to be homogeneous. . . .
There is no longer a union of heart or feelings, of patriotism
and nationality.[41]

To this editor, what once was true concerning the commonality of
the American people is no longer valid. The particular "unions"
that he mentions here as being broken are emblematic of the final
sectional split, which will leave southerners free to pursue their des-
tinies as a separate people.

Pocahontas and her narrative were crucial to the South's growing
sense of otherness. Indeed, one could argue that she was instrumental in the coalescing of the notion that there were two separate cultures inhabiting what was in mid-century the nominally "United"
States, in that many her powerful descendants thought of themselves
as being of a race that was distinct from the lineage of their northern
counterparts. As Anne Norton points out, "The first families of Virginia derived their aristocratic pretensions less from their English
than from their Indian blood. William Randolph was a gentleman,
but Pocahontas . . . was a princess and a noble savage."[42] The planters and politicians who could claim descent, and for whom John
Randolph had served as a model, were without doubt a different
genetic type from the northerner, no matter how reduced their
share of the Indian genetic inheritance may have become. Her presence at the beginning of the English colonial enterprise allowed
southerners to trace their genealogy back to a time before the existence of the Massachusetts settlements, and her royal blood presumably connected her descendants to a line whose power and
prestige far predated the European discovery of the New World.
(From our perspective, however, we can see that the prideful genealogical appeal to Pocahontas by her antebellum Virginia descendants proved that the southern obsession with "unmixed" white
blood was selective and hypocritical.)

The South's success in forming its own union would partly depend
on its ability to make manifest a national self-definition that would
be free from the northern, proto-Democratic model. It would also
need to find an alternative history to place against the northern,
typological, teleological model, in which the Indians had to give way
before the onslaught of civilization. The Pocahontas narrative made
possible the creation of an aristocracy-based, nontypological, non-
teleological history, with its own myth of origin, and in which the
Indian (or at least one Indian) survived "in the blood," as Thomas
Jefferson had put it.[43] The northern ideal of progress at all costs

could be contrasted with the genial plantation lifestyle, in which the maintenance of proper, "civilized" forms was crucial. The Pocahontas narrative also allowed this southern history to be self-contained, in that it provided a foundation myth, as well as the additional paternal figure of Powhatan to serve as a Saturn to Washington's Jupiter – a figure of greater antiquity, whose image recalled a primordial, if short-lived, age of peaceful relations between the races. And finally, her saving of Smith gave the South a great generative moment, a single act that was a turning point in the history of the continent, in which each of the founders of a specifically southern culture was at the height of his or her powers. Smith is courageous and stoic, Pocahontas is courageous and generous, and Powhatan tempers justice for the deaths of his warriors with the mercy inspired by his love for his daughter. It is therefore not surprising that northern propagandists attempted to undermine this crucial episode.

Indeed, the end of the Civil War did not bring the end of Deane's campaign. In his 1866 edition of Smith's *True Relation,* he again expressed his doubts concerning the Rescue.[44] However, the best-known member of the New England anti-Smith cabal did not become publicly involved in this attack until the following year. Henry Adams, a young New England historian of impeccable lineage, who was looking for a way to make a name for himself, or perhaps to free himself from his name, then took up the battle against the hero and heroine of the Jamestown colony. At the suggestion of Palfrey, who had told him "that an article in the *North American Review* on Captain John Smith's relations with Pocahontas would attract as much attention, and probably break as much glass, as any other stone that could be thrown by a beginner," and using the arguments put forward by Deane, Adams, in his first important essay, argues strongly for the untruth of much of Smith's *General Historie,* and especially of the heroism of Pocahontas.[45] In fact, Adams had been considering such an article for some time. In March of 1862 he wrote to Palfrey from London and expressed his true feelings about this topic, as well as his hoped-for result.

I hardly know whether I ought not to be ashamed of myself for devoting myself to a literary toy like this, in these times, when I ought to be helping or trying to help the great cause. But my pen is forced to keep away from political matters, unless I want to bring the English press down on me again, and in society I am a failure. So perhaps the thing is excusable, especially as it is in some sort a flank, or rather a rear attack, on the Virginia aristocracy, who will be utterly gravelled by it if it is successful.

I can imagine to myself the shade of John Randolph turn green at that quaint picture which [William] Strachey gives of Pocahontas "clothed in virgin purity" and "wanton" at that, turning somersets with all the little ragamuffins and "decayed serving-men's" sons of Jamestowne. Nevertheless, if it weren't for you and Mr Deane behind me, I hardly think I should dare to attack an article of American religious creed, so vital as this.[46]

Like those of the northern historians before him, Adams's attack on Smith was at least partially based on a sectionalist agenda. One could certainly argue, however, that had he decided that another subject would have "broken more glass," Adams probably would have left Smith and Pocahontas alone.

Adams did succeed in his main objective, which was to get himself attention. His article in the *North American Review* poured gasoline on the controversy that had been sparked by Palfrey and Deane, and engendered a number of responses from southern defenders of Smith's history. The most important of these were put forward by William Wirt Henry, who attempted to explain why the Rescue was missing from Smith's *True Relation,* but the rest of the nineteenth century would see attacks and rebuttals by historians on both sides of the issue.[47]

Adams and his followers, however, like Palfrey and Deane before them, were doomed to fail in their efforts to undercut the Rescue. The fact or fiction of this exploit had ceased to be an issue during the early part of the nineteenth century, when it had begun to take on national significance. And, as we shall briefly discuss, "Pocahontas" had by mid-century become so pervasive in American culture that no appeal to the historical record could have had any serious effect.

There have been few American narratives as popular and adjustable as the life of Pocahontas. We have seen something of that multiplicity in the uses of her story that we have examined, but her name and image were also widely disseminated in popular culture during the antebellum period.

As we saw in Chapter 3, Adolphe Bandelier used "Pocahontas" as his generic term for the depictions of romantic Indian princesses that had persisted despite the best efforts of anthropologists like Morgan and himself to discourage the public's belief in such mod-els.[48] Joseph Baldwin suggests that people with an Indian woman in their ancestry were generally thought to be descended from a "Po-cahontas."[49] The common name for a female cigar-store Indian fig-ure was "Pocahontas," and one could order standard or special

"Pocahontases."[50] Pictorial images of young Indian women, some of whom were explicitly identified as Pocahontas, were used to sell tobacco, as well as various types of medicines and tonics. Such figures were used extensively, and, especially when the illustration included a Caucasian male, the advertisement did not have to be selling "Princess Pocahontas Tobacco" for the archetypal Indian princess to be recalled.[51]

I have already mentioned some of the many ships christened *Pocahontas.* Her name was also popular for animals, including racehorses; indeed, the world record as the fastest horse in harness was held by the great pacing mare Pocahontas for twelve years during the mid-nineteenth century.[52] And it was the need for a snappy "walk-around" to close the Bryant Mistrels's adaptation of John Brougham's still very popular comedy *Pocahontas* that reputedly put Daniel Decatur Emmett to work one rainy weekend in New York in the spring of 1859. His composition, which was originally titled "I Wish I Was in Dixie's Land," was well received by the Bryants' audiences in the Northeast, and soon other road productions of *Pocahontas* began to include this lively number in their finales. "Dixie" was apparently introduced to the South in *Pocahontas, or The New Orleans Varieties,* a burlesque staged by Brougham in New Orleans in the fall of 1860, and, soon after the Bryant's Minstrels' production of *Pocahontas* opened in Montgomery, Alabama, "Dixie" was selected to be played at the upcoming inauguration of Jefferson Davis. One could argue that "The National Anthem of the Confederacy," which was also one of President Lincoln's favorite tunes, owed its existence and instant success in great part to the popularity of Brougham's play.[53]

One could go on at great length citing such commonplace usages, but I think that the point is clear. The crucial reason that Deane, Adams, Edward Neill, and the primarily northern historians who followed them failed in their debunking venture was not chiefly due to the superb counterarguments of her defenders. Rather, by the time of Deane's first attack, the name and accomplishments of the Indian princess Pocahontas were deeply ingrained in the collective American consciousness. By the second half of the nineteenth century, her heroic identity was far beyond the scope of any such attempts at demythologization.

POSTSCRIPT

<hr>

[Y]et God made Pocahontas the Kings daughter the meanes to deliver me.

– John Smith[1]

During my three years as Executive Director of the National Congress of American Indians it was a rare day when some white didn't visit my office and proudly proclaim that he or she was of Indian descent. . . .

All but one person I met who claimed Indian blood claimed it on their grandmother's side. I once did a projection backward and discovered that evidently most tribes were entirely female for the first three hundred years of white occupation. . . .

Within the next generation, if the trend continues, a large portion of the American population will eventually be related to Powhattan.

– Vine Deloria, Jr.[2]

Even though there had been a great deal of criticism of his colossal sculpture, *George Washington,* Horatio Greenough was commissioned by Congress in 1837 to do another large piece. *The Rescue,* which stood for many years at the east front of the Capitol, is described in the *Compilation of Works of Art and Other Objects in the United States Capitol* as portraying a scene in which "A frontiersman protects his wife and child from massacre by an Indian brave" (Figure 32).[3] The male savior is not clad in the traditional buckskins, however. Rather, this giant figure, as Vivien Green Fryd notes, appears in "a Renaissance-type flat hat and robe that resembles the clothing warn by Hans Holbein's humanists and officials of Henry VIII's court."[4] His calm demeanor is somewhat surprising, considering the drama of the moment. This white figure restrains the Indian, who is holding a tomahawk and whose arms are extended to a position reminiscent of a crucifixion victim, and therefore, of Christ on the cross.

The Rescue literally portrays the saving of the white woman and child, while also representing the triumph of reason or enlightenment, as represented by the white male figure, over the passion and savagery represented by the Indian. However, rather than appearing

Figure 32. Horatio Greenough, *The Rescue*. 1851. Courtesy of the Architect of the Capitol, United States Capitol Art Collection, Washington, D.C.

to be a frontiersman protecting his family, the great size and attire of the rescuer seems to portray the intercession at a critical moment of a supernatural being, who both saves the frontier family from death and saves the Indian from his own savagery. The tomahawk identifies the Indian with a particularly bloody form of murder and thereby deflects attention from the white violence that was being inflicted on the native peoples in Greenough's day. His enforced posture suggests that the Indian must be a sacrificial victim, whose demise will benefit contemporary Anglo-Americans and ultimately the future generations of Americans who will view Greenough's work. In fact, the artist wrote that his proposed piece would "serve as a memorial of the Indian race, and an embodying of the Indian character."[5] As we have seen, during the antebellum period it was often thought to be a sad but inevitable truth that the red race would ultimately have to be sacrificed, or domesticated like the dog in *The Rescue*, in order for the destined greatness of white America to be achieved. Anglo-Americans, like the woman and child in *The Rescue*, had been manifestly chosen to survive, and although the passing of the Indian was to be mourned, the savagery that was associated with the "Indian character" had to be eliminated.

It seems probable that the theoretical foundation for Greenough's work, as well as for many of the other rescue scenes in antebellum art and literature, was Pocahontas's rescue of Smith. Indeed, I would also hold that many nineteenth-century Americans believed that the Christian God had made manifest a choice similar to that made by the robed figure in Greenough's *Rescue* seconds before John Smith's planned execution through the intervention of this young Indian girl. As Jared Sparks had put it, "The protecting shield of divine Providence was over him, and the arm of violence was arrested."[6] During the antebellum period it would also have been clear that the ultimate result of Pocahontas's intercession was the ongoing sacrifice of "her people."

Pocahontas's role as the savior of Smith, whether based on love at first sight, her inherent humanity, or divine intervention, is to this day her best-known persona. Philip Young, after pointing out the importance of the Pocahontas narrative as a model of "self-sacrifice" and as "a tale of religious conversion," goes on to discuss an additional factor that may account for the popularity of this tale in America, and of similar myths elsewhere.[7]

> This story will work for any culture, informing us, whoever we are, that we are chosen, or preferred. Our own ways, race, religion must be better – so much better that even an Indian (Magian, Moor, Turk), albeit an unusually fine one (witness her recognition of our superiority), perceived our rectitude.[8]

Pocahontas chose to save Smith, and, by extension, all white Americans. Although the popularity of her narrative might be seen as something of a repayment for her heroism, more likely it is based on the feelings of superiority that this moment engendered.[9]

And as she chose Smith, white Americans seem to have chosen her. Vine Deloria Jr., explains why so many Caucasians seem to have an obsessive need to have an "Indian grandmother" in the family.

> It doesn't take much insight into racial attitudes to understand the real meaning of the Indian-grandmother complex that

plagues certain whites. A male ancestor has too much the aura
of a savage warrior, the unknown primitive, the instinctive ani-
mal, to make him a respectable member of the family tree. But
a young Indian princess? Ah, there was royalty for the taking.
Somehow the white was linked with a noble house of gentility
and culture if his grandmother was an Indian princess who ran
away with an intrepid pioneer.[10]

In practice one might claim a grandmother from the tribe that is
most geographically appropriate, but Deloria's later comment that
"a large portion of the American population will eventually be related to Powhattan" suggests another goal of such fantasies.[11] While
many white Americans seek a romantic connection to precolonial,
unspoiled America and to identify themselves with spirituality, en-
vironmentalism, stoicism, and other positively perceived "Indian"
traits, one could argue that they are also seeking a figurative connection to their archetypal protectress.

The debate about the veracity of the rescue story dominated much
of the critical writing about the Pocahontas narrative during the
latter half of the nineteenth century, but it had little effect on her
position in the pantheon of American cultural heroes. Both literary and visual representations of the narrative continued to be
produced, but with the occasional exception, such as John Esten
Cooke's novel *My Lady Pocahontas,* and Victor Nehlig's dramatic
painting of a more youthful than usual princess rushing to save
the captain, *Pocahontas and John Smith* (Figure 33), the renderings
were fairly standard.[12] In 1907, the celebration of the three hundredth anniversary of the founding of Jamestown inspired a new
generation of writers to reproduce the narrative and, if nothing
else, largely succeeded in tabling the Smith debate through the
course of the festivities.[13]

With her mythic position firmly established, some writers in the
early twentieth century began to concentrate on the physical body
and sexuality of the flesh-and-blood woman. Such depictions of Pocahontas, however, actually had an antebellum and ultimately a colonial source. In 1849 the Hakluyt Society published the first
printed version of William Strachey's *Historie of Travaile into Virginia Britannia* (1612). In this text readers discovered that Pocahontas may have been married to an Indian before she married
John Rolfe, and were treated to Strachey's now famous description
of the young princess:

> Pochahuntas, a well featured, but wanton yong girle, Powhatan's
> daughter, sometymes resorting to our fort, of the age then of

eleven or twelve yeares, get the boyes forth with her into the
markett place, and make them wheele, falling on their hands,
turning up their heeles upwards, whome she would followe and
wheele so her self, naked as she was, all the fort over.[14]

Strachey goes on to point out that young Powhatan women begin to
wear clothing upon reaching the age of twelve, but this fact did not
lessen the impact of his surprising description of the naked, cart-
wheeling Pocahontas.

Carl Sandburg invokes her body rather than her mythic persona
in "Cool Tombs," which in turn provides the epigraph for Vachel
Lindsay's "Our Mother Pocahontas."[15] This passage from Strachey
introduces the "Powhatan's Daughter" section of Hart Crane's *The
Bridge,* in which Pocahontas becomes the "body" and the "muse"
of America, in that she engenders both life and poetic inspiration,
and it is Strachey's description of her that appears in William Carlos
William's *In The American Grain.*[16] Later depictions, such as the sensual Pocahontas of David Garnett's romantic biography, the dramatic painting of the Rescue by Paul Cadmus (Figure 34), the
provocative bronze by David McFall (Figure 35), the lusty Pocahontas of Barth's *The Sot-Weed Factor,* and the object of desire in Neil
Young's "Pocahontas," in which the singer wishes he could sleep
with Pocahontas as part of his romantic yearning to return to a pre-
conquest, natural world, are rooted as much in Strachey's text as in
any of the attractive, but somewhat generic, nineteenth-century representations.[17] During the twentieth century the beautiful Indian
princess as rescuer of antebellum romances found a new home in
grade B westerns, and the salvation of heroic white male figures by
exotic women continues to be a successful and therefore often repeated motif.[18]

Charles R. Lawson has pointed out that we encounter no Pocahontas figures when we examine novels written by American Indian authors.[19] Indeed, few Indian artists of any media have chosen to make
use of Pocahontas material. Paula Gunn Allen, in *C'koy'u Old Woman,*
speaks somberly for La Malinche, Pocahontas, Molly Brant, and Sa-
cagawea, each of whom is represented as in some way regretful of
her relationship with the white world into which she was drawn, and
Gerald Vizenor makes a humorous, and ultimately tragic for Felipa
Flowers, hunt for the bones of Pocahontas an important incident in
The Heirs of Columbus, but the general sparsity suggests that problematic nature of the traditional Pocahontas story.[20] Whether or not she
was actually "a kind of traitor," as Lawson proposes, her mythic role
in the success of Anglo-America would necessarily make a portrayal
of Pocahontas's best-known actions from the perspective of her own
people difficult at best.[21]

Figure 33. Victor Nehlig, *Pocahontas and John Smith*. 1870. Courtesy of the Museum of Art at Brigham Young University.

The recent work of feminist and post-colonial critics has inspired attempts to mine less familiar aspects of the Pocahontas narrative. Annette Kolodny, in *The Lay of the Land,* focuses briefly on the marriage of Rolfe and Pocahontas and suggests why this union was viewed positively by their contemporaries: "The excitement that greeted John Rolfe's marriage to Pocahontas, in April of 1614, may have been due to the fact that it served, in some symbolic sense, as a kind of objective correlative for the possibility of Europeans' actually possessing the charms inherent in the virgin continent."[22] Ann Norton similarly suggests that "Pocahontas, in her marriage to John Rolfe, enhanced the claim of the interloping colonists to the land they settled. Herself embedded in nature, she provided the sanction of natural, maternal authority to the descendants of those settlers."[23]

Figure 34. Paul Cadmus, *Pocahontas Saving the Life of Captain John Smith.* 1938. Photograph courtesy of the Still Picture Branch, National Archives, Washington, D.C. We see it here as it looked in the Richmond, Virginia, Parcel Post Building, flanked by William Byrd and Sir Walter Raleigh.

Ron Scapp points out that Pocahontas was in fact appropriated twice. He sees her baptism, with its provision of the "Christian" name Rebecca, as well as her marriage, which provided her with a European surname, as part of the European attempt to return to Eden, which was "marked by a certain desire to (re)claim and master the land [the New World] and its inhabitants." With her new names and status "came the erasure of any real identity of something other [than European]."[24] J. Martin Evans goes so far as to compare one of Gilbert Osmond's apparent goals in his relationship with Isabel Archer in Henry James's *Portrait of a Lady* to what he sees as Rolfe's attempt to transform Pocahontas:

> His [Osmond's] self-appointed mission is to perform upon her the same mental operation that John Rolfe had aspired to perform upon Pocahontas, to transform her into a replica of his own mind, a mirror in which to admire his own rectitude, piety, and good taste. . . .
>
>   In the firm belief that he is restoring her womanly identity to her, Osmond proposes to obliterate her national identity altogether.[25]

Such readings, which suggest that the marriage of Pocahontas and Rolfe can be usefully interpreted as having constituted a symbolic appropriation of the New World by its English colonizers, have helped to extend the range of possible correspondences of the narrative.

Pocahontas's persona as an exile from her culture and homeland has encouraged the use of her name and story in recent texts that have called attention to the dangers faced by those who would

Figure 35. David McFall, *Pocahontas*. 1956. Courtesy of Cassell and Company, London, England.

choose, or be forced, to abandon the heritage of their birth. Even these readings are not wholly original, however. For instance, in *The Good Soldier* (1915) Ford Madox Ford has John Dowell and his new wife Florence Hurlbird Dowell leave for Europe on the *Pocahontas*.[26] she tragic nature of this journey and their subsequent life in Europe, from which Florence, like Pocahontas in England, will never return, is foreshadowed by Dowell's, and Ford's, choice of ship.

In the past few years there have been two wonderful expressions in fiction of the potential for innovative inclusions of Pocahontas material. The first is contained in Michelle Cliff's novel, *No Telephone to Heaven*.[27] Here the reader is told the story of Clare Savage, a young half-blood woman from Jamaica who is living in England. In a crucial scene, as she wanders away from the class reunion of her British friend Liz, where she was by definition an outsider, Clare finds herself in the cemetery of St. George's Church in Gravesend. She is drawn to, and is soon standing in front of, a statue that had been placed there by the "Colonial Dames of America in 1958, in loving memory of their countrywoman, Pocahontas" (136). After gathering what information she could about this strange figure, Clare takes a moment to consider "the woman under the weight of all these monuments. She thought of her, her youth, her color, her strangeness, her unbearable loneliness. Where was she now?" (137). While these thoughts are apparently about Pocahontas, they are just as surely

about Clare's own life in England. Her meeting with this much earlier exile has much to do with Clare's eventual decision to return to
her homeland.

The second occurs early in Arturo Islas's recent novel, *Migrant
Souls*.[28] Islas describes a family scene on the American side of the
Texas-Mexico border. It is late November in the Salazar home, and
the youngest daughters, Josie and Serena, who are learning history
in an American public school, are expressing their happiness at the
fact that their mother has decided to cook a turkey for Thanksgiving.
Their father Sancho, however, is against the idea, since he sees it as
yet another manifestation of the process that is making *gringas* out
of his daughters. " 'Oh, Daddy, please! Everybody else is going to
have turkey.' The girls, wearing colored paper head-dresses they had
made in art class, were acting out the Pocahontas story and reciting
from 'Hiawatha' in a hodgepodge of Indian sentiment that forced
Sancho to agree in order to keep them quiet" (22). It is probable
that the girls were acting out the rescue scene, but another aspect
of the narrative is immediately brought into play. There follows a
discussion of deportation, which includes the mention of young
Mexicans who had been left to die in a boxcar. This somber image
serves to remind readers of a second, more melancholy persona of
Pocahontas, who died during an attempt to return to her home in
Virginia. Indeed, throughout *Migrant Souls* the dangers of alienation
from one's homeland and culture are crucial to Islas's portrayals of
people who have been raised "on the border" between two countries (the United States and Mexico) and three societies (Mexican,
Indian, and Caucasian).

Such uses of Pocahontas will become more prevalent as contemporary critics continue to discuss the often ambivalent and poignant
positions of people who have been taught to give up their native
cultures in favor of that of the dominant political power. This was
the position of the kidnapped Pocahontas, who was forced to remain
at Jamestown so as to make sure that Powhatan maintained the peace
with the colonists and, while a captive was indoctrinated into English
colonial culture. These applications of the narrative, like Chapman's
portrayal of her baptism, require that the audience attempt to balance her traditional, heroic role with more problematic adaptations
of her story.

Cliff's powerful description of the young woman buried in the
churchyard demands that the reader look beyond her heroic persona and consider whether or not her heroism, and her subsequent
relations with the English, were worth the price of the early death
far from home that this young Indian woman had to pay. Similarly,
in *Migrant Souls*, the somewhat lighthearted debate about the dinner

Figure 36. R. L. Morgan Monceaux, *Matowaka*. 1992. Courtesy of the Morgan Rank Gallery, East Hampton, NY.

menu and the mention of the "Pocahontas story" in the context of "Hiawatha" and Thanksgiving dinner invoke an image of her most famous mythohistoric exploit. Islas's discussions of the deportation of "aliens," some of whom are in fact American citizens, and of the potential perils faced by those who willingly cross the border, however, reinforce the danger of cultural transition embodied in Pocahontas's transportation to England and death at Gravesend. These contemporary adaptations, along with such recent works as R. L.

Morgan Monceaux's portrait, *Matowaka* (Figure 36), Steve Shill's drama, *Just a Piece of Pocahontas,* and *Pocahontas,* the forthcoming animated feature from Walt Disney Studios, point to the ongoing generative power of her story and exemplify the continuation of the tradition begun in the eighteenth century of applying her name and narrative to presentist concerns.[29]

Karen Robertson, in her discussion of the last meeting of Pocahontas and John Smith in England, asserts that it is in her reproachful silence at this moment that the true Pocahontas is most clearly visible.[30] After an interval during which his own consternation is evident, Smith begins to ventriloquize her spoken vexation, but, Robertson argues, "His report of her speech is marked by his own resentment over his failure to achieve patronage at court."[31] Pocahontas's words here, like her actions elsewhere, are formulated to serve those telling her story. Robertson's reading exemplifies one of the few constants in the reproductions of the narrative, and concurrently points to the untrustworthiness of the historical record where Pocahontas is concerned. While the actual daughter of Powhatan may well have been an extraordinary woman, she left no verifiable words of her own. The ultimate reality of Pocahontas, therefore, is in the cumulative power of the often contrasting representations of her in the multifarious narratives ironically made possible by her silence. A study of a tradition like that of Pocahontas reminds us that every new era interprets the cultural documents of the past in the service of prevailing agendas. Our contemporary awareness of the issues being explored by post-colonial and feminist critics gives us new perspectives that should augment, rather than replace, those readings that have long been at our disposal.

Despite the recent emphasis on other aspects of the narrative, Pocahontas will probably always be best known as the rescuer of Captain John Smith. When we are reminded that she was a young exile, who died at age twenty-two in a foreign country, or the first of her people to be converted to Christianity, or the wife of John Rolfe and the mother of Thomas, the enduring power of her most popular image is actually magnified. Indeed, it is the reintroduction of these alternative personae that make contemporary, innovative uses of the narrative so compelling.[26]

NOTES

Extracts

1 John Smith, *The Generall Historie of Virginia, New-England, and the Summer Isles;* reprinted in *The Complete Works of Captain John Smith,* ed. Philip L. Barbour, 3 vols. (Chapel Hill: University of North Carolina Press, 1986), vol. 2, 258–9. (Originally published in 1624.) This passage is from a letter ostensibly written by Smith to Queen Anne in 1616 in which he begs that Pocahontas be treated well at the English court.

2 William Wirt, *The Letters of the British Spy* (Richmond: Printed by Samuel Pleasants, Junior, 1803), 16.

3 Jared Sparks, *Lives of Alexander Wilson and Captain John Smith,* in *The Library of American Biography,* vol. 2 (Boston: Hilliard, Gray, 1839), 239–41.

4 William Watson Waldron, *Pocahontas, Princess of Virginia: and Other Poems* (New York: Dean & Trevett, 1841), 9.

Introduction

1 William Watson Waldron, speaking of the Pocahontas narrative in the "Preface" to his poem, *Pocahontas, Princess of Virginia,* in *Pocahontas, Princess of Virginia: and Other Poems* (New York: Dean & Trevett, 1841), 7.

2 James Chamberlayne Pickett, *The Memory of Pocahontas Vindicated Against the Erroneous Judgment of the Hon. Waddy Thompson* (Washington: Printed by J. and G. S. Gideon, 1847), 5. (See my detailed discussion of Thompson and Pickett in Chapter 3.)

3 Richard Slotkin, *Regeneration Through Violence* (Middletown, Conn.: Wesleyan University Press, 1973), 313.

4 Slotkin, 313.

5 Helen C. Rountree, *Pocahontas's People* (Norman: University of Oklahoma Press, 1990).

6 Asebrit Sundquist, *Pocahontas & Co.* (Atlantic Highlands, N.J.: Humanities, 1987).

7 Mary V. Dearborn, *Pocahontas's Daughters* (New York: Oxford University Press, 1986).

8 Stuart E. Brown, Jr., Lorraine F. Myers, and Eileen M. Chappell, *Pocahontas' Descendants* (Berryville, Va.: Pocahontas Foundation, 1985).

9 Many critics have commented on the emergence of the Pocahontas myth. See, for example, Elémire Zolla, *The Writer and the Shaman: A Morphology of the American Indian,* trans. Raymond Rosenthal (New York: Harcourt

Brace Jovanovich, 1973), 14; Peter Hulme, "John Smith and Pocahontas," in *Colonial Encounters: Europe and the Native Caribbean, 1492–1797* (London: Methuen, 1986), 140–1.

10 Grace Steele Woodward, *Pocahontas* (Norman: University of Oklahoma Press, 1969); Philip L. Barbour, *Pocahontas and Her World* (Boston: Houghton Mifflin, 1970); Frances Mossiker, *Pocahontas* (New York: Knopf, 1976).

11 Philip L. Barbour, *The Three Worlds of Captain John Smith* (Boston: Houghton Mifflin, 1964), 441. Barbour reasons that the Rescue was part of a ceremony in which the idea was to pose the threat of imminent death and then have Smith be saved by Pocahontas.

See Hulme, "John Smith and Pocahontas," 136–73 (esp. 149–61); and Karen Ordahl Kupperman, *Captain John Smith: A Collection of His Writings* (Chapel Hill: University of North Carolina Press, 1988), 65. See also Mossiker, 81–9; Jean Fritz, *The Double Life of Pocahontas* (New York: Putnam, 1983); and most recently J. A. Leo Lemay, *The American Dream of Captain John Smith* (Charlottesville: University of Virginia Press, 1991), 8, 51–2, for agreement with Barbour. Rountree, however, argues that although the Rescue may have been part of such a ritual, we have no evidence of this from Smith, nor do we have enough of an understanding of Powhatan adoption rituals to infer this to be the case. A bit later, in reference to the question of who actually sent the provisions to Jamestown, she points out that "the person who sent the food that saved the colony was Powhatan, not Pocahontas, as Smith claimed in 1624. Indians and English alike lived in a world in which prepubescent girls had little real power" (39–40). Alden Vaughan states simply that "The truth lies buried with the captain and his Indian captors." See Alden Vaughan, *American Genesis: Captain John Smith and the Founding of Virginia* (Boston: Little, Brown, 1975), 37.

Another text that has been extremely useful to me is William Warren Jenkins's Ph.D. dissertation, "Three Centuries in the Development of the Pocahontas Story in American Literature: 1608–1908," University of Tennessee, 1977. His bibliography is excellent, and I have at times turned to Jenkins's analysis when presenting my own arguments about the Pocahontas narrative.

12 Philip Young, "The Mother of Us All: Pocahontas Reconsidered," *Kenyon Review* 24, 3 (Summer 1962), 391–415. This is perhaps the best short piece on the Pocahontas narrative. See also Jay B. Hubbell, "The Smith-Pocahontas Story in Literature," *Virginia Magazine of History and Biography* 65, 3 (July 1957), 274–300; and Rayna Green, "The Pocahontas Perplex: The Image of Indian Women in American Culture," *Massachusetts Review* 16, 4 (1975), 698–714; Hulme, "John Smith and Pocahontas" (see note 11 to the introduction); and Charles R. Lawson, "The Children of Pocahontas," in *American Indian Fiction* (Albuquerque: University of New Mexico Press, 1978), 17–33.

13 The story of his earlier rescue by the Lady Tragabigzanda is included in what Barbour calls "John Smith's only outright autobiographical work," *The True Travels*, which was originally published in 1630, one year before Smith's death. See *The True Travels, Adventures, and Observations of Captaine John Smith*, in *The Complete Works of Captain John Smith*, ed. Philip L. Barbour, 3 vols, (Chapel Hill: University of North Carolina Press, 1986), vol. 3, 123–251 (esp. 125, 186–8, and 200; see also 334, 337, 355–7); see also De Soto, Ferdinando, *The Discovery and Conquest of Terra Florida*, trans. Richard Hakluyt, reprinted from the 1611 edition (New York: B. Franklin, 1970), 29–33, 173–4.

14   For a discussion of the "Squaw," see Leslie Fiedler, *The Return of the Vanishing American* (New York: Stein & Day, 1969); and Green, "Pocahontas Perplex" (note 12 to this chapter).

15   The term "miscegenation" was coined in a pamphlet of the same name. See David Goodman Croly, *Miscegenation: The Theory of the Blending of the Races, Applied to the American White Man and Negro* (New York, 1863; reprint, London: Trübner, 1864). In this fascinating, ostensibly pro-intermarriage work, Croly takes credit for coining "miscegenation" and all of its related forms and explicitly provides his reasons for doing so.

> *Reasons for coining these words.* – (1.) There is, as yet, no word in the
>
> language which expresses exactly the idea they embody. (2.) Amalgamation is a poor word, since it properly refers to the union of metals with quicksilver, and was, in fact, only borrowed for an emergency, and should now be returned to its proper signification. (3.) The words used above are just the ones wanted, for they express the ideas with which we are dealing, and, what is quite important, they express nothing else. (vii)

Croly also states that "miscegenation," a word that is now regarded as a biased expression reflecting racial prejudice and the assumption that intermarriage is unnatural and wrong, was at its inception seemingly meant to be a positive term. Croly begins, "The word is spoken at last. It is Miscegenation – the blending of the various races of men – the practical recognition of the brotherhood of all of the children of the common father" (v). He makes clear not only that he favors the mixing of the black and white races, but that intermixture with the Indians would be a positive eventuality as well. (For his comments about Indian-white relationships on the frontier, see pages 86–7.) George M. Fredrickson, however, argues that *Miscegenation* was "an ingenious hoax designed to discredit the Republican Party [and therefore President Lincoln] in the election of 1864." See *The Black Image in the White Mind* (New York: Harper & Row, 1972), 171–4. See also Dearborn (note 7 above), esp. 97–193, and the discussion of miscegenation in Margo Hendricks, "Civility, Barbarism, and Aphra Behn's *The Widow Ranter*" in Margo Hendricks and Patricia Parker, eds., *Women, "Race," and Writing in the Early Modern Period* (London: Routledge, 1994), 225–39.

    The term "Manifest Destiny" was first used by journalist John L. O'Sullivan. See his "Annexation," *United States Magazine and Democratic Review* 17 (July/August, 1845), 5–10; and his editorial, "The True Title," *New York Morning News* (December 27, 1845). For documentation that these are the first such uses of the term, see Julius W. Pratt, "The Origin of 'Manifest Destiny,' " *American Historical Review* 32 (July 1927), 795–8.

16   Sharon Larkins, "Using Trade Books to Teach about Pocahontas," *Georgia Social Sciences Journal* 19, 1 (1988), 21–5. Larkins's discussion is useful for anyone teaching Pocahontas material.

17   Larkins, 23.

Chapter 1. Miscegenation and the Pocahontas Narrative

1   Powhatan, quoted in John Smith, *The Proceedings of the English Colony in Virginia*, in *The Complete Works of Captain John Smith*, ed. Philip L. Barbour, 3 vols. (Chapel Hill: University of North Carolina Press, 1986), vol. 1,

247. (I have used Barbour's edition of the *Complete Works* throughout this book.)

2 William Wirt, *The Letters of the British Spy* (Richmond: Printed by Samuel Pleasants, Junior, 1803), 18.

3 Marquis de Chastellux, *Travels in North America in the Years 1780, 1781, and 1782*, translated from the French by an English Gentleman (London: G. G. J. and J. Robinson, 1787; reprint, New York: New York Times and Arno Press, 1968), vol. 2, 131. The information concerning the Chevalier's not yet having been elevated to Marquis is from Howard C. Rice's introduction to his translation: Marquis de Chastellux, *Travels in North America in the Years 1780, 1781, and 1782*, a revised translation, with introduction and notes by Howard C. Rice, Jr. (Chapel Hill: University of North Carolina Press, 1963), vol. 1, 28. The brief portrayal of the princess provided by Chastellux becomes, for reasons I will discuss at length in Chapter 2, the version of the narrative best known to Americans of the post-Revolutionary period. This continued to be true until the explosion of romantic versions finally usurped it early in the nineteenth century.

4 Chastellux, 1787, 135–6. The elder Robert Bolling mentioned here is usually identified as "Robert Bolling of Bollingbrook," whereas the younger is most often referred to as "Robert Bolling of Centre Hill, Petersburg." See *Pocahontas' Descendants*, ed. Stuart E. Brown, Jr., Lorraine F. Myers, and Eileen M. Chappell (Berryville, Va.: Pocahontas Foundation, 1985), 39.

5 Chastellux, 1787, 144. The strange interpretation of the Pocahontas narrative by Chastellux is not the only peculiar rendering by a European visitor during this period. For another example, see the *Viaggio* of Luigi Castiglioni (1790), in which Smith is to be burned at the stake rather than clubbed, Pocahontas and Smith travel to England together, and, after he "no longer showed her the affection that he had manifested in America," *she returns to Virginia* and marries Rolfe. Luigi Castiglioni, *Viaggio*, ed. and trans. Antonio Pace (Syracuse: Syracuse University Press, 1983), 191–2.

6 Samuel Stanhope Smith, *An Essay on the Causes of the Variety of Complexion and Figure in the Human Species*, ed. Winthrop D. Jordan (Cambridge, Mass.: Harvard University Press (Belknap Press), 1965), 201–2. Smith's *Essay* was originally published in 1787 and was reprinted in an expanded version in 1810. Jordan reprints the 1810 edition (New Brunswick, N.J.: J. Simpson; New York: Williams & Whiting). Smith refers to Lord Kames as "Lord Kaims" in his response to the "Discourse." The sentence from Lord Kames is quoted from Jordan's edition of Smith's text, 201. Jordan points out that Smith must have read the Philadelphia, 1776, edition of Kames's *Six Sketches of the History of Man*. (See Jordan's introduction, xiii–xv, and page 260 of the text.) This is the only edition of Kames's text so titled; all other editions are simply called *Sketches of the History of Man*.

Other writers of the late eighteenth and nineteenth centuries also provided descriptions of members of this august family. For instance, see James Kirke Paulding, *Letters From the South*, 2 vols. (1817; reprint, New York: Harper & Brothers, 1835), vol. 1, 13–23. He spends most of these pages describing John Randolph, but at the end also provides a brief description of Randolph's cousin, Bolling Robertson. Their supposed Indianness, based on their descent from Pocahontas, is clearly of great interest to Paulding.

7 William J. Scheick, *The Half-Blood: A Cultural Symbol in Nineteenth-Century American Fiction* (Lexington: University Press of Kentucky, 1979), 3. The phrase from Albert Keiser's *The Indian in American Literature* (New York: Oxford University Press, 1933) is quoted in Scheick.

8 See Bernard W. Sheehan, *Seeds of Extinction: Jeffersonian Philanthropy and the American Indian* (New York: Norton, 1973), 175. Sheehan cites as his source Samuel Whitcomb, Jr., "Copy of an Interview with Thomas Jefferson by My Father, the Late Samuel Whitcomb, Formerly of Dorchester Mass., June 1, 1824," Jefferson Papers, Alderman Library, University of Virginia, Charlottesville, Va. See also William Peden, "A Book Peddler Invades Monticello," *William and Mary Quarterly*, Ser. 3, vol. 6, no. 4 (October 1949), 631–6. This article claims that it was really Samuel Whitcomb, Jr. who interviewed Jefferson, not his father, and places the Whitcomb manuscript in the Samuel Whitcomb, Jr. Papers, which are owned by the Massachusetts Historical Society, Boston.

Concerning the marriage of Martha Jefferson to Thomas Mann Randolph, see also Augustus John Foster, *Jeffersonian America*, ed. Richard Beale Davis (San Marino, Ca.: Huntington Library, 1954), 153. (Foster's notes were collected from 1805–7 and 1811–12.)

Although the claim is sometimes made that Thomas Jefferson was a member of the family, he was not a direct descendant of Pocahontas. His father, Peter Jefferson, married Jane Randolph, eldest daughter of Isham and Jane Rogers Randolph of Dungeness. The "Pocahontas blood" was brought into the Randolph family by Isham's younger brother, Richard Randolph of Curles, who married Jane Bolling. See Jonathan Daniels, *The Randolphs of Virginia* (Garden City, N.Y.: Doubleday, 1972), x–xxi, 43.

9 Sheehan, 175. Sheehan's chapter 6, "Manipulation," provides an excellent study of Indian-white relations during the Jeffersonian era. (See esp. pp. 161–81.)

10 For the derivation of the term "miscegenation" see note 14 to the Introduction.

11 William Symonds, *Virginia. A Sermon Preached At White-Chappell, In the Presence of the Adventurers and Planters for Virginia* (London: Printed by I. Windet for Eleazar Edgar and William Welby, 1609).

12 Symonds, 25.

13 Scheick, 4.

14. For a discussion of the importance of the marriage of Pocahontas and Rolfe to the establishing of more peaceful relations between the Powhatan Confederation and the Virginia colonists, see J. Frederick Faust, "An 'Abundance of Blood Shed on Both Sides': England's First Indian War, 1609–1614," *Virginia Magazine of History and Biography* 98, 1 (January 1990), 3–56 (esp. 46–9).

15 John Rolfe, "Letter to Sir Thomas Dale," reprinted in Ralph Hamor, *A True Discourse of the Present State of Virginia* (London: printed by John Beale for William Welby, 1615; reprint, Richmond: Virginia State Library Press, 1957), 63. Hereafter cited as *Hamor*.

16 Samuel Sewall, *The Diary of Samuel Sewall, 1674–1729*, ed. M. Halsey Thomas (New York: Farrar, Straus & Giroux, 1973), vol. 1, 532.

17 Although there is no specific mention of intermarriage in the earliest statutes of the Virginia colony, there was from the outset a clear attempt to regulate various types of intercourse between the Europeans and Indians. The first set of written laws drawn up in the English New World, the *Lawes Divine, Morall And Martiall*, compiled by William Strachey in

1612, contains a warning against illicit contact and unauthorized trade with the Indians. See William Strachey, *Lawes Divine, Morall And Martiall,* ed. David H. Flaherty (Charlottesville: University of Virginia Press, 1969), 15. Such trade, as well as any violence found to be perpetrated against any Indians coming to trade, was punishable by death. Attempts to "ravish or force any woman, maid or Indian, or other," carried a similar penalty (12). The *Proceeding of the First Assembly of Virginia* of 1619, two years after the death of Pocahontas, and, not coincidentally, the year of the arrival of the first blacks brought to Jamestown, state some of the same concerns about covert meetings between Indians and whites, and add a new expression to the fear of the possibility of any kind of New World–Old World amalgamation (352). This code contained a statute that forbade the gift or sale of any dogs of quality of the "English race" to the Indians. This law showed explicitly the phobia of the Virginia settlers about any type of interbreeding, ostensibly because it could lead to a corruption of the European stock. There can be no doubt about what was implied by this statute concerning the human inhabitants of the colony.

In 1630, we get the first explicit notice of the dangers of the mixing of the human races – in this case a white man with a black woman. While these events were not common, they apparently did occur fairly regularly, and by 1662 the colonial government saw the need for a law specifically prohibiting all intermarriage in Virginia. Antifraternization and antimiscegenation laws were passed in other states as well. At times they allowed for ambiguous interpretations of terms such as "colored" person or "mulatto." Such definitions often became cloudy and therefore could be used to suit the needs of the moment. See James Hugo Johnston, *Race Relations in Virginia and Miscegenation in the South* (Amherst: University of Massachusetts Press, 1970), esp. 165–314. See also David H. Fowler's *Northern Attitudes toward Interracial Marriage* (New York: Garland, 1987). Both of these texts provide references to the statutes that pertain to interracial marriage. Fowler's appendix is invaluable as a resource for anyone studying the problems of race relations in antebellum America. See also *Records of the Governor and Company of the Massachusetts Bay in New England,* ed. Nathaniel B. Shurtleff (Boston: William White, 1853), vol. 1, 140.

18 Fowler, 26. An interesting account of such differences is also to be found in Thomas Shourds, *History and Genealogy of Fenwick's Colony* (1876; reprint, Baltimore: Genealogical Publishing, 1976). On page 6 he describes the feelings of the English who settled this territory as they approached the Delaware River. "The natives, they looked upon as savages in a literal sense, and dreaded the necessity of any intercourse with them; regarding the wild beasts of the forest with less fear, and more easily controlled." After a short time, however, as Shourds points out, at least some of the colonists apparently had a change of heart.

> The early emigrants, finding in the Aborigines excellent neighbors, and reliable associates, the relations brought about marriages between the emigrants and natives, involving the genealogy of a number of families in the Salem tenth, and likewise all West Jersey. It is always to be regretted that so little pains has been taken to trace the Indian blood, distributed in these latter generations, and although much diluted, occasionally crops out, in feature or form.

Although, black hair, dark skin, and exact, graceful form, may not
always be taken as coming from this line, yet the presumption is a
fair one, that the parents of such with several removes, were of this
people, and the manor born. (8)

Shourds is the rare commentator who follows S. S. Smith in his positive
description of the physical appearance of at least some of the descendants of these early intermarriages.

One could argue that the proliferation of antimiscegenation and antifraternization laws was a response to the substantial numbers of Europeans who apparently found Indians of the opposite sex, and Indian
life, to be an attractive alternative. See William Christie Macleod, *The
American Indian Frontier* (New York: Knopf, 1928), 357–62, 550–1.

19 For a note on the Massachusetts law, see Sewall, vol. 1, 532. For the
Virginia law, see W. W. Hening, ed., *Statutes at Large; Being a Compilation
of All the Laws of Virginia from the First Session of the Legislature in the Year
1619* (Richmond: 1810–23), vol. 3, 86–8. The quoted passage is reprinted in Fernando Henriques, *Children of Conflict* (New York: Dutton,
1975), 59. (On the fear of intermarriage in Virginia, see note 17 to this
chapter.)

In Massachusetts, William Bradford uses an instance of an "unnatural
joining" – the case of Thomas Granger, who was convicted of buggery
in 1642 – to ponder "[H]ow came it to pass that so many wicked persons and profane people should so quickly come over into this land?"
William Bradford, *Of Plimoth Plantation* (Boston: Wright & Potter, 1898),
476. Part of his answer is that those who began to transport people to
the colony were not concerned with the character of the people they
brought, but only with whether or not they could pay for the trip. What
makes this dangerous, however, is that "one wicked person may infect
many" (Bradford, 476). One sin can multiply and spread even in a God-
fearing settlement, and therefore such sins, and those who commit
them, must be done away with as efficiently as possible. And so, while
it is clear that according to the law of Leviticus 20:15 both the human
and the animals involved must die, practically, since this sinful infection
could be passed on to others, Granger must die so that he cannot pass
it on, and the animals must die so that this sin is not perpetuated in
the issue.

This may sound strange to the modern reader, but corroboration
comes from the case of George Spencer in New Haven. He too was
convicted of buggery, and the evidence was irrefutable. From a litter of
pigs born to the sow of John Wakeman, one was brought to the court
for examination.

> The monster was come to the full growth as the other pigs . . . butt
> brought forth dead. Itt had no haire on the whole body, the skin
> was very tender, and of a reddish white collour like a childs; the
> head was most straing, itt had but one eye in the midle of the face,
> and that large and open, like some blemished eye of a man; . . . .
> Some hand of God appeared in an impression upon Goodwife
> Wakemans speritt, sadly expecting, though she knew not why, some
> strange accedent in that sows pigging, and a strange impression was
> allso upon many thatt saw the monster, (therein guided by the
> neare resemblance of the eye,) that one George Spencer . . . had
> beene actor in unnatureall and abominable filthynes with the sow.

George Spencer was convicted on the evidence of that eye. He too had a deformed eye, and so the "impression" that the pig's eye made on those who saw it, an impression made by the "hand of God," pointed incontrovertibly in his direction. The deformity of the parent had been passed on to the offspring and had been the manner of his sin being made manifest. Again, death was the penalty, for both the sow and the human being who had supposedly taken part in this act. See Bradley Chapin, *Criminal Justice in Colonial America, 1606–1660* (Athens: University of Georgia Press, 1983), 128–9.

A third example, and perhaps the most famous case where offspring are "read" to discern the moral character of a parent, concerns some of the more bizarre happenings of the Antinomian controversy. The "misconceptions" of Anne Hutchinson and her follower Mary Dyer were reflected in their giving birth to monsters. In these cases the monstrous births were seen to be the results of linkings with the devil or one of his minions, and, like their heresies, were public symbols of their spiritual decay. The sins grew out of these women and moved into the community, and so birth imagery was used as the vocabulary best suited to express the progression of their sins. The births of the monsters, first to Mrs. Dyer and then to Anne Hutchinson herself, were clear evidence of their inner corruption, which must have come from a consent to, if not a literal physical joining with, the powers of evil. One can see the use of birth imagery in the contemporary accounts of these events. See, for instance, David D. Hall, *The Antinomian Controversy, 1636–1638* (Middletown, Conn.: Wesleyan University Press, 1968). (One might ask whether God actually creates the monsters in the wombs of these women, or whether He is most crucial in making sure that others bear witness to these monsters.)

20   Alexander Whitaker, "To my verie deere and loving *Cosen* M. G. *Minister of the* B. F. in London"; reprinted in Hamor, 59–61. The quoted passage is on 59–60.

21   Thomas Dale, "To the R. and my most esteemed *friend Mr. D. M. at his house at* F. Ch. in London"; reprinted in Hamor, 51–9. The quoted passages are on 55.

22   William Alexander, *The Mapp and Description of New-England* (London, 1630), 28.

23   Karen Ordahl Kupperman, *Settling with the Indians* (Totowa, N.J.: Rowman & Littlefield, 1980), 119.

24   Hamor, 41–2.

25   Robert Beverley, *The History and Present State of Virginia*, ed. Louis B. Wright (Chapel Hill: University of North Carolina Press for Institute of Early American History and Culture, 1947), 38.

26   Beverley, 38.

27   Beverley, 44.

28   Beverley, 44.

29   Smith, in Beverley, 42. One should remember Richard Pots's comment that Smith might have married Pocahontas and thereby "made himselfe a king." See Smith, *The Proceedings of the English Colonie in Virginia*, in Barbour *Complete Works*, vol. 1, 274.

30   Beverley, 44.

31   William Byrd, *The History of the Dividing Line*, in *The Prose Works of William Byrd of Westover*, ed. Louis B. Wright (Cambridge, Mass. Harvard University Press [Belknap Press] 1966), 160–61. (Originally published in

1738.) Byrd also makes clear that the ideal union is one between an Indian woman and a white man. Bernard Sheehan points out that the other possibility would have been unacceptable.

> Intermarriage took place between white men and Indian women. Hence the subtle defenses of civilized superiority would be maintained, the father presumably would bring into the wilderness the ways of civilization. The most publicized unions between white female and Indian male had taken place in captivity, which meant the subjection of the white and the preservation of savagery. As a means of fostering civilization, intermarriage had to be part of the white man's expanding way of life. The surrender of his women to the savage scarcely conformed to the necessary pattern. (178)

Unions between male colonists and female Indians should have been theoretically possible. The idea of a union between an Indian man and a white woman, however, no matter what the potential gain, was and would remain too repulsive for most Europeans colonists to support.

32 Roy Harvey Pearce, *Savagism and Civilization: A Study of the Indian and the American Mind* (1953; reprint, Baltimore: Johns Hopkins University Press, 1967), 85. Pearce goes on to discuss "savage virtues," the first of which he describes as "a devotion to freedom and independence." Perhaps it was this that the colonists sought to emulate when they chose to dress as Indians at the Boston Tea Party? See also Brian W. Dippie, *The Vanishing American* (Middletown, Conn.: Wesleyan University Press, 1982). He goes so far as to say that "Red-white amalgamation was seen as a marriage of common types because the native's fabled independence and love of freedom were in line with core American values" (260).

33 Francis Paul Prucha, *American Indian Policy in the Formative Years* (Lincoln: University of Nebraska Press, 1962), 13. Numerous government documents also show that Indians, usually as tribes, did "own," in the European sense of the word, certain lands. See, e.g., the "Resolution on Unclaimed Western Lands" of March 3, 1791, reprinted in *Legislative Histories*, ed. Charlene Bangs Bickford and Helen E. Veit (Baltimore: Johns Hopkins University Press, 1986), vol. 6, 2127–8. Much has been written on the feelings of the Indians for their land. See for instance, Angie Debo, *A History of the Indians of the United States* (Norman: University of Oklahoma Press, 1970), 3–18. See also William Cronon, *Changes in the Land: Indians, Colonists, and the Ecology of New England* (New York: Hill & Wang, 1983), esp. 3–15, 159–70. This book contains an excellent discussion of the changes in the ecology of New England brought on by the coming of the Europeans.

Prucha also argues that peace with the frontier Indians was imperative during America's first years as a nation. The dream represented by assimilation was that warfare, while necessarily an option in the quest for land, might thereby have been avoided. See also Robert F. Berkhofer, *The White Man's Indian* (New York: Random House, 1979), 142.

34 Prucha, 1–2.

35 John Oldmixon, *The British Empire in America* (London: Printed for J. Brotherton et al., 1741); reprint, New York: Kelley, 1969.) vol. 1, 366. As mentioned, the comment about inheritance is not included in the original 1708 edition. (See note 38 to this chapter.)

36 Oldmixon, 366.

37 Oldmixon, 367. See also, Sir William Keith, *The History of the British Plan-*

tations in America (London: Printed at the expense of the Society for the encouragement of Learning, by S. Richardson, 1738), 129.

38 John Oldmixon, *The British Empire in America* (London: Printed for John Nicholson et al. 1708), 232–3.

39 Peter Fontaine to Moses Fontaine, March 30, 1757, reprinted in Ann Maury, *Memoirs of a Huguenot Family* (New York: Putnam, 1872), 349. Fontaine notes here that intermarriage had long been a feature of French-Indian relations on the frontier. However, trappers and explorers usually led nomadic lives and needed women who knew how to travel, produce meals from what could be found, serve as an interpreters, and, perhaps most important, whose very presence told other Indians that her group could not possibly be a war party. (Sacagewea, of Lewis and Clark fame, is an example of how invaluable such a woman could be to an expedition.) Settlers, on the other hand, brought white women with them and could not be persuaded to choose Indian women over those of their own kind, even if there was something as valuable as land to be gained. It is also interesting to note Fontaine's interpretation of Rolfe's letter. Rolfe explains his reasoning and attempts to portray his marriage as a positive thing for all concerned. Fontaine, however, sees his need to write such a letter, and the discussion that followed his request, as deterrents to future intermarriages.

40 Fontaine, 350–1. One cannot fault Fontaine for his theory concerning the possibility of the Indians "changing color," since this notion was common during the period.

41 For Beverley, see note 25 to this chapter.

42 William Robertson, *The History of America, Books IX and X: Containing the History of Virginia to the Year 1688; and of New England to the year 1652* (Philadelphia: Printed from the London edition by James Humphries, 1799; reprint, New York: J. & J. Harper, 1828), 411.

43 Thomas Jefferson, *Notes on the State of Virginia* (New York: Harper & Row, 1964), 59. (Originally published in 1785.)

44 Robertson, 411. See also William Stith, *The History of the First Discovery and Settlement of Virginia* (Williamsburg: Printed by William Parks, 1747), 146. Stith was himself a distant relation of Thomas Rolfe.

45 Thomas Jefferson, "To Captain Hendrick, the Delawares, Mohicans, and Munries," in *The Writings of Thomas Jefferson*, ed. Andrew A. Lipscomb and Albert Ellery Bergh (Washington, D.C.: The Thomas Jefferson Memorial Association, 1903), vol 16, 452. Reginald Horsman, in *Race and Manifest Destiny* (Cambridge, Mass., Harvard University Press, 1981), quotes this strangely problematic passage in a slightly different form: "After telling the Indians to adopt farming and private property, he [Jefferson] asserted 'you will become one people with us; your blood will mix with ours: and will spread with ours across this great island'" This construction provides more clearly for a "mixing of the blood." (108). Bernard Sheehan's version is also slightly different: "Your blood will mix with ours; and will spread, with ours, over this great island" (174). See also, Dippie, 260.

46 Jefferson to Benjamin Hawkins, February 18, 1803. *Writings of Jefferson*, 10, 363.

47 Thomas Jefferson, The Declaration of Independence, in *The Life and Selected Writings of Thomas Jefferson*, ed. Adrienne Koch and William Peden (New York: Random House, 1944), 22.

48 The issue here is how any trace of Indian blood will manifest itself. Perhaps it might be in one's physical appearance, or in the possessing of certain Indian abilities (what Natty Bumppo would call Indian "gifts"), or it may be that, as in the case of Mary Burton Bolling, the Indian part is buried deep beneath the surface but emerges as part of one's character. Either way, the descendant in question would be, by definition and affiliation, white.

49 See Scheick, 1. He describes this distancing as from "the remote past or the far-off frontier" and discusses Pearce's idea that the Indians themselves must be placed in the past, or at some other such distance, in order to be portrayed as noble. Pearce, *Savagism*, 194–5. I agree, but also suggest that to the Jeffersonians the survival of the Indian could only be posited in terms of an amalgamation with the whites, and such an amalgamation could only be presented as a possibility of the distant future. Scheick argues that the "half-blood" is a figure of the "present." I again agree, to a point, but would also mention that such people were thought to be too close to their Indian roots to be accepted by white society.

50 See my discussions of selected works of John Davis in Chapter 2.

51 John Burk, *The History of Virginia, from Its First Settlement to the Present Day* (Petersburg, Va.: Dickson & Pescud, 1804–16), vol. 1, 188.

52 Richard Slotkin, "Myth and the Production of History," in *Ideology and Classic American Literature*, ed. Sacvan Bercovitch and Myra Jehlen (Cambridge: Cambridge University Press, 1986), 86.

53 Rayna Green, "The Only Good Indian: The Image of the Indian in American Vernacular Culture," Ph.D. diss., Indiana University, 1973, 382.

54 Angie Debo, *A History of the Indians of the United States* (Norman: University of Oklahoma Press, 1970), 42.

55 Because the great majority of Anglo-American colonists continued to frown on the idea of intermarriage, eighteenth-century attempts to promote it had little or no success. As early as 1709, however, intermarriage was being actively encouraged. John Lawson, in *A New Voyage to Carolina*, does not recommend that all Anglo-Americans choose this road, but says that for some it would be an appropriate and well-rewarded choice. "But it is highly necessary to be brought in Practice, which is, to give Encouragement to the ordinary People, and those of lower Rank, that they might marry with these *Indians*, and come into Plantations, and Houses, where so many Acres of Land and some Gratuity of Money, (out of a publick Stock) are given to the new-married Couple" (244). Earlier in his text Lawson had mentioned the attractiveness of Indian women, as well as the fact that "*Indian* Girls that have convers'd with the *English* and other *Europeans*, never care for the Conversation of their own Countrymen afterwards" (189, 193). After the passage just quoted, Lawson goes on to point out several other advantages, including the acquiring of "a true Knowledge of all the *Indians* Skill in Medicine and Surgery" (245). It seems clear, however, that the potential for monetary recompense would have been the most powerful part of his argument. And although Wilbur R. Jacobs has interpreted parts of Lawson's text as suggesting that there were more intermarriages than white commentators wanted to admit, not even such advantages as those described by Lawson were enough to promote a widespread amalgamation of the races. See Wilbur R. Jacobs, *Dispossessing the American Indian* (New York: Scribner, 1972), 210, note 42.

Bernard Sheehan points out that in 1719 in Nova Scotia the English offered ten pounds and fifty acres to any Englishman who would marry an Indian woman, or even any Englishwoman who would marry an Indian man, but there were apparently few takers. Edmund Atkin's 1755 *Plan For Imperial Indian Control* encouraged soldiers on the frontier, and convicts who had served out their time at frontier forts, to marry Indian women, but marriages, while certainly more numerous there than in more "civilized" areas, were still relatively rare.

See John Lawson, *A New Voyage to Carolina,* ed. Hugh Talmage Lefler (Chapel Hill: University of North Carolina Press, 1967), 244, 189, 193, and 245 (originally published in 1709); Sheehan, 175; and Wilbur R. Jacobs, ed., *The Appalachian Indian Frontier: The Edmond Atkin Report and Plan of 1755* (Lincoln: University of Nebraska Press, 1967), 80, 91. (The difference between soldiers, and even prisoners, who might someday return to the East and mountain men who were fleeing civilized society is in part the reason for the failure of this aspect of Atkin's scheme.)

Patrick Henry brought back the idea of offering a bounty to encourage intermarriage in 1784, in an attempt, as William Wirt describes it, "to implant kind affections in bosoms which at present were filled only with reciprocal and deadly hatred" (257–8). Henry's bill to the Virginia legislature suggested that

> [E]very white man who married an Indian woman should be paid ten pounds, and five for each child born of such a marriage; and that if any white woman married an Indian she should be entitled to ten pounds with which the county court should buy them livestock; that once each year the Indian husband of this woman should be entitled to three pounds with which the county court should buy clothes for him; that every child born to the Indian man and white woman should be educated by the state between the ages of ten and twenty-one years.

The true goal of this bill was to make life safer for Virginia frontiersmen. In Wirt's note about horrors perpetrated by the Indians, he makes clear just how bad things had gotten through this resonant comparison: "The adventure of Captain Smith and Pocahontas, if you put aside the dignity of their characters, is cold and tame, when compared with some which are related among the Western inhabitants of this state" (256).

In Henry's scenario, the child of a white father would of course be "raised English," whereas some steps would have to be taken to ensure the education of the child of an Indian father. This all became moot, however, because the bill did not pass, primarily because Henry left the Assembly before the final debate to begin a term as governor. This well-intentioned statute ultimately failed, as did the other attempts to institutionalize intermarriage. For all of their humanitarian motives, and despite the presence of the aristocratic descendants of Pocahontas, those who championed this cause simply could not overcome the general feeling of revulsion at the idea of racial mixing. See William Wirt, *Sketches of the Life and Character of Patrick Henry,* 15th ed. (Hartford: Silas Andrus & Son, 1832), 256–8. The passage quoted is reprinted in Fernando Henriques, *Children of Conflict* (New York: Dutton, 1975), 58.

56 Latrobe's was the first serious attempt to catalogue her descendants. He read a paper to the American Philosophical Society on February 18, 1803, entitled "Account of the descendants of Pocahontas, daughter of Powhatan, king or chief of the tribe of Powhatan, who inhabited the

country about the falls of the James River, Virginia." *Proceedings of the American Philosophical Society* 23 (1885), 333. It is interesting that the greatest minds in America saw this as a topic worthy of their investigation.

Other genealogies were drawn up during the nineteenth century, culminating with those of Wyndham Robertson, who wrote a short family history in 1858 and a longer version, *Pocahontas alias Matoaka and Her Descendants* (Richmond: J. W. Randolph & English) in 1887. Modern attempts to provide a more complete lineage include Marilyn J. Burns's *Pocahontas Blood* (Silver Spring, Md.: Virginia Tree, 1983), and the recent *Pocahontas' Descendants* (Brown et al.), which its modern editors describe as a continuation of Robertson's work.

57   Benjamin Latrobe, *The Virginia Journals of Benjamin Latrobe, 1795–1798*, ed. Edward C. Carter II et al. (New Haven: Yale University Press for Maryland Historical Society, 1977), vol. I, 111–22. Nor is Latrobe the only writer to comment on the hardiness of the descendants of Pocahontas and Rolfe. In our century, Dixon Wecter has pointed out that other than the descendants of Pocahontas and "John Rolfe, a man of petty rank, there is not a single American family today which stems from the first settlers of Jamestown." Dixon Wecter, *The Saga of American Society* (New York: Scribner, 1937), 16. The great proliferation of this family, as testified to by the sheer magnitude of the listings in *Pocahontas' Descendants*, provides additional corroboration. (See note 8 to the Introduction to the present volume.) The original edition runs to 443 pages, 318 of which consist of a single-spaced listing of most of her descendants. (As of this writing, two supplements, each containing some corrections and many additions, have been published.)

58   Paulding, vol. 1, 23.

59   Burk, 190. Burk claims to know many of the descendants he describes as "amiable." Perhaps he had never met Thomas Mann Randolph, a son-in-law of Thomas Jefferson, whose amiability was, to say the least, not usually thought of as his strong point.

60   Burk, 190–1.

61   Burk, 191. See also Stith, 146.

62   George Brandburn, in "House Report, No. 7, Commonwealth of Massachusetts, in the House of Representatives, Jan. 19, 1841." Quoted in Johnston, *Race Relations*, 338. See also the comments of Thomas Bouldin before Congress in 1835, quoted in Michael Paul Rogin, *Fathers and Children* (New York: Knopf, 1975), 5. Bouldin points out that "Many of our first families and most distinguished patriots are descended from the Indian race." There can be little doubt about to what families the Virginia congressman was referring. Bouldin goes on to say, however, that he himself does not have any Indian blood.

63   The "Pocahontas Exception" is quoted in Walter Wadlington, "The *Loving* Case: Virginia's Anti-Miscegenation Statute in Historical Perspective," *Virginia Law Review* 52B, 5, (1966), 1202.

64   Wadlington, 1202. See also H. Pleckman, "The New Family and Health Improvement," *Virginia Health Bulletin Extra* 12, New Family Series, 5 (1925), 25–6.

65   Wadlington, 1189, note 1.

66   See *Acts and Joint Resolutions of the General Assembly of the Commonwealth of Virginia* (Richmond: Department of Purchases and Supply, Commonwealth of Virginia, 1968), chap. 318, 428.

67   Mary Jane Windle, *Life At The White Sulpher Springs* (Philadelphia: Lip-

pincott, 1857); Charlotte Barnes, *The Forest Princess*, in *Plays, Prose and Poetry* (Philadelphia: E. H. Butler, 1848), 145–270. This play was first produced in England in 1844 and opened in Philadelphia four years later. Charlotte Barnes's mother, Mary, was the original Pocahontas of G. W. P. Custis's 1830 New York production of *Pocahontas; or, The Settlers of Virginia*, which I discuss in Chapter 3. See also Jenkins, 303–9.

68 Vachel Lindsay, "Our Mother Pocahontas," in *The Chinese Nightingale and Other Poems* (New York: Macmillan, 1917), 40. The poet goes on to renounce the "Saxon blood" and "Teuton pride" of the white race.

69 Herman Melville, *White-Jacket or The World in a Man-of-War*, ed. Harrison Hayford (Evanston and Chicago: Northwestern University Press and Newbery Library, 1970), 141, 378; *Moby-Dick or, The Whale*, ed. Charles Feidelson, Jr. (Indianapolis: Bobbs-Merrill, 1964), 27; *Pierre or The Ambiguities*, ed. Harrison Hayford (Evanston and Chicago: Northwestern University Press and Newbery Library, 1971) 3–14.

70 Melville, *Pierre*, 10.

71 Ebenezer Baldwin, *Observations on the Physical, Intellectual, and Moral Qualities of Our Colored Population* (New Haven: L. H. Young, 1834), 45. Quoted in Joseph R. Washington, Jr., *Race and Religion in Early Nineteenth-Century America*, 2 vols. (Lewiston, Queenston, Lampeter: Edwin Mellen Press, 1988), vol. 2, 679–80.

72 Helen C. Rountree has filled in many of the gaps in our knowledge about Powhatan Indian culture in her two excellent studies, *The Powhatan Indians of Virginia: Their Traditional Culture* (Norman: University of Oklahoma Press, 1989), and *Pocahontas's People* (Norman: University of Oklahoma Press, 1990). The quoted passage is from page 187 of *Pocahontas's People*, which in large part deals with the struggles of the Powhatan people to maintain their cultural and racial identities. See also, William Rasmussen and Robert S. Tilton, *Pocahontas: The Life and Legend*. Forthcoming publication of the Virginia Historical Society, Richmond, 1994.

73 Quoted in Henriques, *Children of Conflict*, 60.

74 Ibid.

75 B. Drummond Ayres, Jr., "Last Stand Nears for Tiny Indian Tribe's Identity," *New York Times*, natl. ed. (January 16, 1989), 8.

76 Brown et al., *Pocahontas' Descendants*. (See note 8 to the Introduction to the present volume.)

77 John Davis, *The Farmer of New Jersey, or, A Picture of Domestic Life* (New York: Furman and Loudon's Type, 1800), 10–11.

Chapter 2. The Pocahontas Narrative in Post-Revolutionary America

1 John Davis, *Travels Of Four Years And A Half In The United States Of America During 1798, 1799, 1800, 1801, And 1802*, ed. A. J. Morrison (New York: Holt, 1909), 321. (Originally published, 1803.) (All parenthetical page numbers in the text refer to this edition.)

2 See the "Publisher's Preface" in John Marshall, *The Life of George Washington* (New York: Wise, 1925), vol. 1, vii. (Originally published, 1804–7.)

3 Washington is first referred to as the "Father of his country" in the *Lancaster Almanack* for 1778. See Jay Fliegelman, *Prodigals and Pilgrims: The American Revolution Against Patriarchal Authority, 1750–1800* (Cambridge: Cambridge University Press, 1982), 200.

4 Marshall, "Preface," xvi.

5   Marshall, 24, 28, 41-2.

6   Marshall, 28.

7   Davis's *Travels* was not the first text to posit that the love of the princess for Smith prompted her actions, it was the first to construct a fairly complex fictional narrative around this scene.

8   Davis, *Travels*, 321. The text of Chastellux to which Davis refers is the Frenchman's earlier *Travels:* Marquis de Chastellux, *Travels in North America in the Years 1780, 1781, and 1782*, translated from the French by an English Gentleman, 2 vols. (London: G. G. J. and J. Robinson, 1787; reprint, New York: New York Times and Arno Press, 1968. (Unless specified, all references to Chastellux's *Travels* are to this edition.)

9   See Lawrence W. Towner, "*Ars Poetica et Sculptura:* Pocahontas on the Boston Common," *Journal of Southern History* 28, 4 (November 1962), 485.

10   William Wirt, *The Letters of the British Spy* (Richmond: Printed by Samuel Pleasants, Junior, 1803), 18. (The first edition, which was also printed by Pleasants in 1803, is entitled *The Letters of A British Spy.*)

11   "Anecdote of Pocahunta, An Indian Princess, From Whom Several Respectable Families in Virginia Are Descended," *Columbian Magazine* (July 1787), 548-51.

12   The Chastellux narrative is not in the earliest editions of *An American Selection*, but it appears by the early part of the nineteenth century. See Noah Webster, *An American Selection of Lessons in Reading and Speaking* (Elizabethtown, [N.J.]: Printed by John Woods, for Evert Duyckinck, 1802), 84-7. This edition also includes Jefferson's story of Chief Logan and an excerpt from Gay's account of "The Captivity of Mrs. Howe."

13   See Henri Petter, *The Early American Novel* (Columbus: Ohio State University Press, 1971), 389-90, note 6. Among the versions of the narrative that would have been available are Jeremy Belknap, "John Smith," in *American Biography*, vol. 1. Published According to Act of Congress (Boston: Printed by Isaiah Thomas and Ebenezer T. Andrews, 1794), 240-319; John Burk, *The History of Virginia, From Its First Settlement To The Present Day* (Petersburg, Va.: Dickson & Pescud, 1804-16). The Pocahontas material is in volume 1 of Burk's *History* and therefore was published in 1804. See also William Robertson, *The History of America, Books IX and X: Containing the History of Virginia to the Year 1688; and of New England to the Year 1652* (Philadelphia: Printed from the London edition by James Humphreys, 1799). The Pocahontas-Rolfe material became more accessible when complete versions of Robertson's *History* were published. See, for example, the "Harper's Edition" (New York: J. and J. Harper, 1828), 403-11.

14   Mason Locke Weems to Mathew Carey, January 20, 1797, in Emily Ellsworth (Ford) Skeel, ed., *Mason Locke Weems, His Works and Ways*, 3 Vols. (New York, 1929; Printed for the Plimpton Press, Norwood, MA), vol. 2, 70. Quoted in Richard Beale Davis, *Intellectual Life in Jefferson's Virginia* (Chapel Hill: University of North Carolina Press, 1964), 313. (See his section, "The Pocahontas-John Smith Theme," 313-19.)

15   Chastellux, *Travels*, vol. 2, 139-40.

16   Robert Beverley, *The History and Present State of Virginia*, ed. Louis B. Wright (Chapel Hill: University of North Carolina Press for Institute of Early American History and Culture, 1947), 44.

17   Chastellux, *Travels*, vol. 2, 142.

18   This note is on pages 137-9 of volume 2 of the reprint of the 1787 edition of Chastellux's *Travels*. In the introduction to his translation the

Travels, Howard C. Rice, Jr. identifies George Grieve as almost certainly the translator. See Marquis de Chastellux, *Travels in North America in the Years 1780, 1781, and 1782,* 2 vols. A revised translation, with introduction and notes by Howard C. Rice, Jr. (Chapel Hill: University of North Carolina Press, 1963), vol. 1, 29–35. This passage contains a sketch of the rather exciting life of Grieve, as well as Rice's assertions. One should be sure to notice the paragraph that precedes the section entitled "Something About the Translator," and see also vol. 2, 591–2.

19 John Davis, *Travels.* See also, John Davis, *The Farmer of New-Jersey* (New York: Furman and Loudon's Type, 1800).

20 Richard Beale Davis, in *Intellectual Life,* calls this version "anonymous" (314). However, Kevin J. Hayes identifies the author. See Edward Kimber, "A Short Account of the British Plantations in America," *London Magazine* 24 (July, 1755), 307–12. See also Hayes's *Captain John Smith: A Reference Guide* (Boston: Hall, 1991), 9.

21 Davis, 311. As Davis describes it, Smith feared that Pocahontas would seek revenge against the English when she discovered that he had left Virginia, and so she was told that he had died.

22 William Warren Jenkins, "Three Centuries in the Development of the Pocahontas Story in American Literature," Ph.D. diss., University of Tennessee, 1977, 232.

23 Davis, 282–3. One could argue that Richardson and his successors (including Susanna Rowson) were the first to attempt to create a "captive" audience of women readers. There can be little doubt that Davis was trying to tap into the already existing audience for sentimental fiction.

24 He begins the *Travels* with his correspondence with Jefferson concerning the president's patronage and ends *Captain Smith and Pocahontas, An Indian Tale* (Philadelphia: T. C. Plowman, 1805) with a list of his subscribers, among whom, not surprisingly, is Jefferson (159–73). Davis also takes a moment to point out that "Thomas Mann Randolph [son-in-law to Thomas Jefferson, then President of the United States] is lineally descended from the princess; and his first cousin is called Powhatan Randolph, after the great king her father" (134).

25 We can gauge how popular the Pocahontas material was, or perhaps the type of wishful thinker that Davis was, by his publishing later in 1805, *The First Settlers of Virginia, An Historical Novel* (New York: Printed for I. Riley and Co. by Southwick and Hardcastle, 1805). This did, however, earn him the right to call himself the first author in America to build a novel around the Pocahontas material. Davis had only expanded the narrative a bit between the *Travels* and *Captain Smith,* but in *The First Settlers* he adds a number of subplots. One of the most interesting is an attempt to convince Powhatan to give another of his daughters in marriage to a colonist. The scene in which West speaks to Powhatan for Mr. Throgmorton is reminiscent of Hamor speaking to Powhatan for Sir Thomas Dale. West, however, unlike Hamor, is finally successful, and Mr. Throgmorton marries his beloved Watoga, the sister of "Pokahontas." See *The First Settlers,* 2d ed. (New York: Printed for I. Riley and Co., 1806), 241–2. (Davis claims that this second edition is "enlarged," but both it and the first edition are 284 pages long.)

26 John Davis, *Captain Smith,* ix.

27 John Davis, *Captain Smith,* 114–15.

28 Davis, *Travels,* 322.

29 Barbara Ruf, "John Davis: Poet, Novelist, and Traveler," Ph.D. diss., University of Tennessee, 1974, 235.

30   James Nelson Barker, *The Indian Princess* (Philadelphia: Printed by T. & G. Palmer, 1808). It is interesting to note how much more intense the love scenes between Pocahontas and Rolfe are in this 1808 play than they are in the plays of later in the nineteenth century, such as those of George Washington Parke Custis and Robert Dale Owen. *The Indian Princess* can be seen as something of a transitional play, in that while Pocahontas has strong feelings for Smith, these are the feelings of a sister for a brother, rather than those of a lover.

31   William J. Free, The Columbian Magazine and *American Literary Nationalism* (The Hague: Mouton, 1968), 139.

32   Joseph Croswell, *A New World Planted* (Boston: Gilbert & Dean, 1802). *A New World Planted* is the first of many instances of the Pocahontas material being co-opted for use in tales of New England.

33   Croswell, 43–5.

34   Croswell, 20.

35   Free, 139–40.

36   Joel Barlow, *The Columbiad*, vol. 2 in *The Works of Joel Barlow*, 2 vols., facsimile, intro. William K. Bottorff and Arthur L. Ford (Gainesville: Scholars' Facsimiles and Reprints, 1970). *The Columbiad* was originally published in 1807, but Bottorff and Ford use the Washington City, 1825, edition. (The page numbers in the following citations refer to *The Works* rather than *The Columbiad* itself.)

37   Joel Barlow, *The Vision of Columbus* (Hartford: Printed by Hudson and Goodwin for the author, 1787).

38   Barlow, *Columbiad*, 539–40.

39   Barlow, *Columbiad*, 540.

40   Samuel Lorenzo Knapp, *Lectures on American Literature* (New York: Elam Bliss, 1829); reprinted in *American Cultural History, 1607–1829*, ed. Richard Beale Davis and Ben Harris McClary (Gainesville, Florida: Scholars' Facsimiles & Reprints, 1961), 145.

41   Davis, *Travels*, 318. Interestingly, this usage reverses the roles. In this case, Pocahontas is the traveler, and she comes upon Smith, whom she had believed dead.

42   This celebration marked the two-hundredth anniversary of the founding of Jamestown. Blanchard's was one of many works written for the Jubilee.

43   "Eminent Roman Writers," *American Gleaner and Virginia Magazine* (May 30, 1807), 152–5. The passage dealing with Virgil is on pages 153–4.

44   C. K. Blanchard, "Ode," in "National Jubilee," *American Gleaner and Virginia Magazine* (May 30, 1807). The coverage of the celebration runs from pages 155 to 160. Blanchard's "challenge" is on page 160.

45   Edmund Randolph, *History of Virginia*, ed. Arthur H. Shaffer (Charlottesville: University of Virginia Press for Virginia Historical Society, 1970), 24–5.

46   See Arthur Shaffer's introduction to his edition of Randolph's *History*, xxxi.

47   John Gould Fletcher, *John Smith – Also Pocahontas* (New York: Brentano's, 1928; reprint, New York: Kraus, 1972), 125.

48   Fliegelman, 200.

49   Mason Locke Weems, *The Life of Washington*, ed. Marcus Cunliffe (Cambridge, Mass.: Harvard University Press [Belknap Press], 1962), 12. The "cherry tree" incident first appears in the 5th edition of Weems's *Life* (1806). Cunliffe uses the 9th edition (Philadelphia: Mathew Carey, 1809).

50 Richard Beale Davis, *Intellectual Life*, 314.

51 Richard Beale Davis, 314.

52 For instance, the July 1787 *Columbian Magazine,* the October 1788 *American Magazine,* and the August and September 1812 *Port Folio* were among the numerous periodicals in which the Pocahontas-Smith relationship was presented.

53 William Allen, *An American Biographical and Historical Dictionary* (Cambridge, Mass.: William Hilliard, 1809).

54 Mary Webster Mosby [Mrs. M. M. Webster], preface to *Pocahontas: A Legend* (Philadelphia: H. Hooker, 1840), vii. This phenomenon has survived into the present. For example, in their *Native Americans: Five Centuries of Changing Images* (New York: Abrams, 1989), Patricia Trenton and Patrick T. Houlihan mention the painting that is the subject of my Chapter 4: "Her best known memorial is probably the large mural *The Baptism of Pocahontas* . . . painted by John Gadsby Chapman (1808–1889). It now hangs in the rotunda of the Capitol, in Washington, D.C., one of the few pictures that honors a national heroine, and, even more remarkable, a native American woman" (23). Rather than their simply stating that the painting is a study of Pocahontas, it still seems important to describe the *Baptism* as a "memorial." She is not simply the subject of such works; they pay tribute to her.

55 Rev. of *Biography and History of the Indians of North America,* by Samuel G. Drake, *North American Review* 44 (n.s. 35), 95 (April 1837), 301–4.

56 Rev. of Drake, 327.

Chapter 3. The Pocahontas Narrative in the Era of the Romantic Indian.

1 Herman Melville, *The Confidence Man: His Masquerade* (Evanston and Chicago: Northwestern University Press and the Newberry Library, 1984), 140.

2 W. H. Gardiner, rev. of *The Spy,* by James Fenimore Cooper, *North American Review* 15, 36 (n.s. 6, 11), (July 1822), 255.

3 Gardiner, 256.

4 Gardiner, 256.

5 There were a number of attempts to encourage Indian-white intermarriage in the nineteenth century, but these, like their eighteenth-century predecessors, had little chance of success. Secretary of War William H. Crawford recommended, in a report of 1816, that if all else failed, intermarriage with the Indians should be encouraged by the government as a way of ensuring their survival. It was not. In 1824, he attempted to have a bill encouraging the intermarriage of "Americans" and Indians passed, but it did not make it through Congress. Some commentators suggested conditions for such mixings, as did the Reverend Jedidiah Morse in his *Report to the Secretary of War of the United States, on Indian Affairs* (New Haven: S. Converse, 1822), 73–5: "While Indians remain in their present state, the minds of civilized people must revolt at the idea of intermarrying with them. It is natural and decent that it should be so." He then points out that a number of such marriages, "or, that which amounts to the same thing," have taken place, and that the "complexion" of the offspring is not a problem. What is still needed, however, is more education, especially of Indian women. "Let the Indians, therefore, be taught all branches of knowledge pertaining to civilized man; *then* let intermarriage with them become general, and the end which the Government has in view will be completely attained. They

would be literally one blood with us, be merged in the nation, and saved from extinction." These, and other last-gasp suggestions made before the removal policies of the late twenties and thirties, were doomed to fail, and although such an amalgamation continued to be posited occasionally until the advent of the assimilation policies of the Grant administration, there was never any real chance for success. See also D. G. Croly, *Miscegenation* (London, 1864), 86–7, for a positive view of the mixing of the races on the frontier. To Croly, joining with the whites will be the salvation of the Indians, who will live on as members of an "ethnographically composite yet socially homogeneous population." Another such proassimilation text is Lydia Maria Child's *Appeal for the Indians* (New York: W. P. Tomlinson, 1868).

Reginald Horsman points out, however, that "there is considerable evidence to show that after 1830 neither the mass of the American people nor the political leaders of the country believed that the Indians could be melded into American society." This was, in fact, always the majority position among Anglo-Americans. Reginald Horsman, *Race and Manifest Destiny* (Cambridge, Mass.: Harvard University Press, 1981), 190.

6   Charles M. Lombard, "Chateaubriand's American Reception," in *Chateaubriand Today,* ed. Richard Switzer (Madison: University of Wisconsin Press, 1970), 221–8.

7   Charles M. Lombard, ed., *The Romantic Indian: Sentimental Views from Nineteenth Century American Literature* (Delmar, N.Y.: Scholars' Facsimiles and Reprints, 1981), vol. 2, x.

8   See, for example, the appendix to James Chamberlayne Pickett, *The Memory of Pocahontas Vindicated* (Washington: Printed by J. and G. S. Gideon, 1847), 25–39 which includes passages from the 1707 and 1757 French translations of Smith. Pickett also includes nineteenth-century translations into Italian and German.

9   For the most complete survey of European versions of the Pocahontas narrative, as well as of other texts about American Indians, see Leslie A. Fiedler, "The Indian in Literature in English," and Christian F. Feest, "The Indian in Non-English Literature," both in *History of Indian-White Relations,* ed. Wilcolm E. Washburn: volume 4 of *Handbook of North American Indians,* genl. ed. William C. Sturtevant (Washington, D.C.: Smithsonian Institution, 1988), 573–81, 582–6. The individual texts mentioned here include Unca Eliza Winkfield's novel *The Female American* (London, 1767); Carl Friedrich Scheibler's novel *Reisen . . . des Schifs – Captain J. Schmidt* (1781); and the drama *Pocahontas,* by Johann Wilhelm Rose (Ansbach, 1784). Feest notes that this play was actually written in 1771 but published in 1784, "due to the current interest in such things" (583). Feest also mentions *La Sauvagesse* and *Les Mariages de Canada* here, as well as other eighteenth-century French dramas set in the New World. For an interesting study of the importance of the Inkle and Yarico tradition, see Peter Hulme, "Inkle and Yarico," in his *Colonial Encounters* (London: Methuen, 1986), 224–63. Finally, Chateaubriand could also have been aware of the story of Juan Ortiz (see note 13 to the Introduction). This Pocahontas-like tale had been published in Hakluyt's *Voyages* early in the seventeenth century. Indeed, skeptics have speculated that this may have been Smith's source for the Rescue.

10 François-René de Chateaubriand, *Atala/René,* trans. Irving Putter (Berkeley and Los Angeles: University of California Press, 1952), 75. (*Atala* was originally published in 1801, *René* a year later.)

11 Chateaubriand, *Atala*, 17–19.

12 Chateaubriand, *René*, 85.

13 François-René de Chateaubriand, *Chateaubriand's Travels in America*, trans. Richard Switzer (Lexington: University of Kentucky Press, 1969), xv. (Originally published in 1828.) See also the section entitled "Present State of the Savages of North America" for corroboration of Chateaubriand's pessimistic outlook concerning the survival of the Native American cultures. Chateaubriand was apparently a devout believer in Catholic dogma, and so to him the deaths of priests and converts may not have seemed terrible because such individuals were going to their reward.

14 Leslie A. Fiedler, *The Return of the Vanishing American* (New York: Stein 8 Day, 1969), 70.

15 Fiedler, *Return,* 70.

16 William Scheick provides an excellent discussion of the historical and literary "half-breed" in *The Half-Blood: A Cultural Symbol in Nineteenth-Century American Fiction* (Lexington: University of Kentucky Press, 1979).

17 James Fenimore Cooper, *The Prairie* (New York: New American Library, 1964), 29 (originally published in 1827). Cooper's note informs his readers about "Half-breeds; men born of Indian women by White fathers. This race has much of the depravity of civilization without the virtues of the savage." His Rousseauvian description of the dominant traits of each society is interesting, as are his belief in the white man–Indian woman formula and his apparent sense that only male children are produced by such unions. He would soon, however, tell the story of such a male child born of the marriage of an Indian man and a white woman in *The Wept of Wish-Ton-Wish.*

18 Unless otherwise indicated, the following are the texts used in this discussion: James Wallis Eastburn and His Friend [Robert Sands], *Yamoyden, A Tale of the Wars of King Philip* (New York: Published by James Eastburn; Clayton & Kingsland, Printers, 1820); Lydia Maria Child, *Hobomok, A Tale of Early Times,* ed. Carolyn L. Karcher (New Brunswick, N.J.: Rutgers University Press, 1986) (originally published in 1824); James Fenimore Cooper, *The Wept of Wish-Ton-Wish* (Columbus, Ohio: Merrill, 1970) (originally published in 1829).

19 Eastburn and Sands, 69.

20 See Carolyn L. Karcher's introduction to her edition of *Hobomok,* xvii–xx.

21 Child, 139.

22 Child, 140.

23 Child, 148.

24 Child, 150.

25 Rev. of *The Last of the Mohicans,* by James Fenimore Cooper, *United States Literary Gazette* 4 (May 1826), 87–94. Reprinted in *Fenimore Cooper: The Critical Heritage,* ed. George Dekker and John P. McWilliams (London: Routledge & Kegan Paul, 1973), 100.

26 Dekker and McWilliams, 100.

27 Robert F. Berkhofer, *The White Man's Indian* (New York: Random House, 1979), 94.

28 Washington Irving, "Philip of Pokanoket," in *The Sketch Book of Geoffrey Crayon, Gent.* (New York: New American Library, 1981), 283–99. (originally published in 1819.)

29 Cooper, *Wept*, 381.

30 Cooper, *Wept*, 383.

31 Cooper, *Wept*, 388–9.

32 Cooper, *Wept*, 320.

33 Cooper, *Wept*, 400. The same themes occur in the story of the Bush family, as told in *The Prairie*, the Leatherstocking Tale which immediately precedes *The Wept*. Here too, hardships must be endured by two races to ensure the success of one.

34 Cooper, *Wept*, 399.

35 James Fenimore Cooper, "Dedication," *The Wept of Wish Ton-Wish* (Philadelphia: Carey, Lea & Carey, 1829), iii–iv. (In this first American edition, there is no hyphen between the first "Wish" and "Ton.") For the first British edition, see *The Borderers* (London: Henry Colborn and Richard Bentley, 1829), iii–iv.

36 In the first editions, Pocahontas and Powhatan are both mentioned in the catalogue of great Indian figures that ends with the protagonists of the novel. By the 1833 edition, Cooper had combined the titles of the first British and American editions and done away with the dedication, as well as his references to the Virginia Indians. See *The Borderers; or, The Wept of Wish-Ton-Wish* (London: Richard Bentley, 1833). Both reappear, however, in the first edition of *The Wept* published after Cooper's death in 1851 (New York: Stringer and Townsend, 1854).

37 The-best known dramatic renderings of the Pocahontas narrative written during the antebellum period are James Nelson Barker, *The Indian Princess; or, La Belle Sauvage* (Philadelphia: T. & G. Palmer, 1808), reprinted in Lombard, ed., *Romantic Indian*, vol. 2, 1–74. George Washington Parke Custis, *Pocahontas, or The Settlers of Virginia* (1830), reprinted in *Representative American Plays from 1767 to the Present*, 7th ed., ed. Arthur Hobson Quinn (New York: Appleton-Century-Crofts, 1953), 165–92. Robert Dale Owen, *Pocahontas: A Historical Drama* (New York: George Dearborn, 1837), reprinted in Lombard, ed., *Romantic Indian*, vol. 2, 1–240. (Each text is paginated separately in Lombard.) Charlotte Barnes, *The Forest Princess, or Two Centuries Ago* in *Plays, Prose, and Poetry* (Philadelphia: E. H. Butler, 1848), 145–270. (Barnes's mother Mary originated the role of Pocahontas in Custis's drama.) John Brougham, *Po-ca-hon-tas, or The Gentle Savage* (1855), reprinted in *Dramas from the American Theatre, 1762–1909*, ed. Richard Moody (Cleveland: World, 1966), 397–421. For an interesting discussion of these plays and information on Gilliam's lost *Virginia*, see Jenkins, "Three Centuries," 286–318. (For Lombard, see note 7 to this chapter.)

38 Arthur Hobson Quinn, introduction to Custis's *Pocahontas*, in Quinn, 167.

39 Custis, 192.

40 Custis, 173.

41 Owen, 21.

42 Smith's obviously rightful leadership is based on his natural abilities rather than on a royal appointment. Owen's more liberated Pocahontas is all that is generally remembered about his play.

43 Owen, 149.

44 Richard Moody points out, in his introduction to *Po-ca-hon-tas*, that "Brougham's burlesque was not aimed at Barker's *The Indian Princess* or

at Custis's *Pocahontas* so much as at the blustering performance of [Edwin] Forrest and his company in *Metamora*," which was by far the most popular of the Indian dramas (Brougham, 402).

45 Brougham, 413.

46 Brougham, 419. After their duet, "King" [Powhatan] objects to her wish to free Smith by invoking the facts: *"On no account, can I run counter to / Virginia records which relate to you"* [Pocahontas]. This ceases to be a problem as the play moves toward its comedic climax.

47 Brougham, 421.

48 "The New England Pocahontas," reprinted in G. Waldo Browne, ed., *Real Legends of New England* (Chicago: Whitman, 1930), 28–34. "Malee – Pocahontas of Florida" was printed in consecutive issues of the *National Republic*: 31, 4 (August 1933), 5–6; 31, 5 (September 1933), 21–2, 32. The "Malee," or "Milly," story was a popular alternative to the traditional Pocahontas narrative during the antebellum period. (See note 67 to this chapter.)

49 James Kirke Paulding, *Koningsmarke, the Long Finne*, ed. Daniel A. Wells (Schenectady: Union College Press, 1988), (originally published 1823); Catharine Maria Sedgwick, *Hope Leslie, or Early Times in the Massachusetts*, ed. by Mary Kelley (New Brunswick, N.J.: Rutgers University Press, 1987), (originally published 1827); William A. Caruthers, *The Cavaliers of Virginia* (New York: Harper & Brothers, 1834); reprint Ridgewood, N.J.: Gregg, 1968. Although the heroines of these works – Aonetti, Magiwisca, and Wyanokee – are suitable examples of Pocahontas-like maidens, a number of others could have been used. One of the most interesting is the protagonist of Lewis Deffebach's *Oolaita; or, The Indian Heroine* (Philadelphia: printed for the author, 1821). See Werner Sollars's discussion of *Oolaita* in *Beyond Ethnicity* (New York: Oxford University Press, 1986), 107–9, 114.

50 Paulding, 125.

51 Paulding, 160–1.

52 Paulding, 161. This notion that the gods, or, specifically, the Christian God, played a hand in the rescue of white captives from Indians became a fairly standard view. Whether one believed that God was ultimately in control of the entire situation, as in Mary Rowlandson's *Narrative*, or that maidens like Pocahontas were in some way divinely inspired to undertake their inexplicable actions of saving the lives of white men, the sense was that the Christian God was overseeing, and approved of, the conquest of the Americas by the Europeans.

53 Paulding, 115–18.

54 Sedgwick, 6.

55 Caruthers, vol. 1, 3.

56 Michael Davitt Bell, "History and Romance in Catharine Sedgwick's *Hope Leslie*," *American Quarterly* 22, 2 (Summer 1970), 217.

57 Sedgwick, 92–3.

58 It was apparently almost universally held that such unions would not have been welcomed in the white world. Even the most obviously successful relationships between captive white women and Indian men, such the marriage of Faith Leslie and Oneco in *Hope Leslie*, the marriages of Mary Jemison to Sheninjee and Hiokatoo, or the love between the Indian brave and the white captive in John Rollin Ridge's "Stolen White Girl," to name only a few, were portrayed in such a way as to

make clear that these unions could only have so prospered in the freedom that existed away from civilized society.

59 Sedgwick, 189.

60 Caruthers, vol. 2, 16.

61 Caruthers, vol. 2, 18.

62 Caruthers, vol. 2, 19.

63 Curtis Carroll Davis, *Chronicler of the Cavaliers: A Life of the Virginia Novelist Dr. William A. Caruthers* (Richmond: Dietz, 1953), 168.

64 There are a number of possible candidates, including Mrs. Ann S. Stephens's fascinating novel of 1860, *Malaeska: The Indian Wife of the White Hunter* (reprint, New York: Day, 1929). This text, which had been previously serialized in the February, March, and April 1839 issues of the *Ladies' Companion*, includes the requisite selfless rescue scene. However, as the melancholy narrative suggested by the title unfolds, it describes as well the killing of Malaeska's Indian father by her white husband, who also dies as a result of their fight; the often excruciatingly painful life of a woman forced to deny the maternity of her son; the suicide of that son when the truth – that his beloved nurse is actually his mother – comes out; the death of the mother, "the heart-broken victim of an unnatural marriage" (253); and various other sorts of mayhem. However, the editors at Irwin P. Beadle and Company claimed that they chose it to begin their "Dime Novel" series in 1860 because of "the chaste character of its delineations" and the fact that it was "pure in its tone" and "elevating in its sentiments." One would also guess that it was selected because its extreme subject matter almost guaranteed a large audience. (See the "Publishers' Notice," in the 1929 ed., xv.)

65 *The Wept of Wish-Ton-Wish*. A Drama, in Two Acts, From J. Fennimore [*sic*] Cooper's Novel of the Same Name (New York: Samuel French, n.d. [1856?]).

66 Diana Reep, *The Rescue and Romance* (Bowling Green, Ohio: Bowling Green State University Popular Press, 1982), 92–3.

67 See, for instance, John Frost, *Pictorial Life of Andrew Jackson* (Hartford: Wm. Jas. Hamersley, 1846), 426–8. In Frost's text the reader is both told about the dramatic rescue of M'Krimmon by Milly and provided with a small sketch of the crucial scene. The biography could easily have done without this short anecdote, and its inclusion illustrates how such rescues came to be used as generic plot devices.

68 William Hickling Prescott, *History of the Conquest of Mexico*, ed. John Foster Kirk 3 vols. (Denver: Tandy, Wheeler, 1873). (Originally published in 1843.) Doña Marina is the "La Malinche" figure.

69 John Smith, *The Generall Historie*, in *The Complete Works of Captain John Smith* ed. Philip L. Barbour (Chapel Hill: University of North Carolina Press, 1986), vol. 2, 198–9.

70 Prescott, vol. 2, 15.

71 Prescott, vol. 2, 15.

72 Prescott, vol. 2, 16.

73 Walter O'Meara, *Daughters of the Country* (New York: Harcourt, Brace & World, 1968), 93. See also Charles R. Larson, *American Indian Fiction* (Albuquerque: University of New Mexico Press, 1978), 27.

74 Cynthia Enloe makes this point in her description of what her readers are to believe is a typical elementary school class's encounter with the Pocahontas narrative: "A school teacher plans a lesson around the life

of Pocahontas, the brave Powhantan [*sic*] 'princess' who saved Captain John Smith from execution at Jamestown and so cleared the way for English colonization of America. The students come away from the lesson believing the convenient myth that local women are likely to be charmed by their own people's conquerors." Enloe argues that this aspect of the narrative reinforces a view of the captivating natural superiority of the white colonizers. See her *Bananas Beaches and Bases* (Berkeley and Los Angeles: University of California Press, 1990), 1.

75 Waddy Thompson, *Recollections of Mexico* (New York: Wiley & Putnam, 1846), v.

76 Thompson, 29.

77 Pickett, *Memory* (see note 8 to this chapter).

78 Pickett, 5.

79 Pickett, 25–39.

80 Jenkins, 146–7.

81 Prescott's text was in fact a source for Leutze. See William H. Truettner, "Prelude to Expansion," in *The West as America*, ed. William H. Truettner (Washington, D.C.: Smithsonian Institution Press, for National Museum of American Art, 1991), 59.

82 Robert Levine, *Conspiracy and Romance* (Cambridge: Cambridge University Press, 1989), 4.

83 Melville, *Confidence Man* (see note 1 to this chapter), 140.

84 Melville, 140.

85 Adolphe F. Bandelier to Thomas Janvier, September 2, 1888, in *The Unpublished Letters of Adolphe F. Bandelier* (El Paso: Hertzog, 1942), 3. This passage is reprinted in Elémire Zolla, *The Writer and the Shaman*, trans. Raymond Rosenthal (New York: Harcourt Brace Jovanovich, 1973), 166. I have yet to find a clear explanation of what Bandelier meant by the " 'vuelta abajo' trade." My sense of the idiom was that it meant "return below," and so I thought that Bandelier's comment had to do with "low-brow" or pulp fiction, in which such Pocahontases would have been popular and enduring figures. However, in a personal communication Professor John Rick of the Department of Anthropology at Stanford University hypothesized that the idiom meant something closer to "return back." Therefore Bandelier was complaining about the old, traditionally romantic portrayals of Indian maidens, such as "statuesque" Pocahontases.

86 Fiedler, *Return*, 64.

87 See Georg Lukács, *The Historical Novel*, trans. Hannah Mitchell and Stanley Mitchell, intro. Fredric Jameson (Lincoln: University of Nebraska Press, 1983), 34–48.

88 One could view Pocahontas as one of those figures who "can only act and express himself in situations of historical importance." Lukács, 45.

89 Review of *Gleanings in Europe*, by James Fenimore Cooper, *North American Review*, 46 (n.s. 37), 98 (January 1838), 3. See also Lukács's description of the "leaders of the warring classes and parties," who generally play only minor roles in Scott's fiction (45).

90 Owen, 61–2.

91 "Als" is an abbreviation for "alias."

Chapter 4. Chapman's Baptism of Pocahontas

1 The quotation in the title to this chapter is from John Gadsby Chapman, "The Subject Of The Picture," in Chapman, *The Picture Of The Baptism*

Of Pocahontas (Washington: Peter Force, 1840), 5. He is paraphrasing Smith, who, in the abstract of his letter to Queen Anne, calls Pocahontas "the first Christian ever of that Nation."

We owe almost everything that we know about John Gadsby Chapman and *The Baptism of Pocahontas* to the efforts of two scholars. Georgia Stamm Chamberlain spent a number of years studying Chapman and his work. She wrote a series of articles about him that have been collected in her *Studies on John Gadsby Chapman* (Annandale, Va.: Turnpike Press, 1963), hereafter cited as *Studies*. William P. Campbell, former assistant chief curator at the National Gallery of Art, also did a great deal of research on Chapman and was the author of the companion catalogue to the "John Gadsby Chapman: Painter and Illustrator" exhibit at the National Gallery of Art (Washington D.C.: H. K. Press for the National Gallery of Art, 1962). Campbell amassed a tremendous number of documents about Chapman and his work, now in the William P. Campbell Papers, Archives of American Art, Smithsonian Institution, hereafter cited as Campbell Papers. The collection has not been edited or catalogued, and there are a number of items, including letters, for which Campbell does not supply sources. Each of these scholars planned to write a full-length biography of Chapman but passed away before such a work could be completed. Campbell, however, did leave parts of a first draft of his manuscript, which is in the Campbell Papers.

Although the effort to convert the Indians has traditionally been considered to have been less significant to the Virginia colonists than it was to their New England successors, a number of scholars have pointed out the importance of this aspect of the Jamestown founding. See Perry Miller, "Religion and Society in the Early Literature of Virginia," in Miller, *Errand into The Wilderness* (New York: Harper & Row, 1964), 99–140, and more recently, David R. Ransome, "Pocahontas and the Mission to the Indians," *Virginia Magazine of History and Biography* 99, 1 (January 1991), 81–94. (Ransome supplies additional bibliography on this topic.)

2   This letter is included in Lawrence W. Towner, *"Ars Poetica et Sculptura:* Pocahontas on the Boston Common," *Journal of Southern History* 28, 4 (November 1962), 484–5.

3   Robert Beverley, *The History and Present State of Virginia* (London: Printed for R. Parker, 1705).

4   Towner, 483.

5   John Burk, *The History of Virginia From Its First Settlement to The Present Day*, vol. 1 (Petersburg, Va.: Dickson & Pescud, 1804), 187.

6   Ann Uhry Abrams, "The Pocahontas Paradox: Southern Pride, Yankee Voyeurism, Ethnic Identity or Feminine Heroics," paper delivered at the annual meeting of the American Studies Association, October 1988, 6.

7   Joseph Croswell, *A New World Planted* (Boston: Gilbert & Dean, 1802), 20. Other critics have observed this convention. See, for example, Rayna Green, "The Pocahontas Perplex," *Massachusetts Review* 16, 4 (1975), 704.

8   A second representation of the Rescue, a frieze designed by Constantino Brumidi, was later added to the Rotunda.

9   John Quincy Adams, quoted in *Register of Debates in Congress*, 23rd Congress, 2nd Session (December 1, 1834–March 3, 1835), vol. II, pt. 1 (Washington: Gales & Seaton, 1835), 791.

10 Henry Alexander Wise, quoted in *Register of Debates*, 791. Wise's state-

ment is interesting in that he seems to be saying that there is something in the nature of the country itself that inspires fine art.

Wise was not the only one angered by Adams's comment. See, for example, James Kirke Paulding to Richard Henry Wilde, February 13, 1835, in *The Letters of James Kirke Paulding*, ed. Ralph M. Aderman (Madison: University of Wisconsin Press, 1962), 164–5.

11 See John Quincy Adams, *Memoirs of John Quincy Adams*, ed. Charles Francis Adams, (Philadelphia: Lippincott, 1876), vol. 9, 189.

12 Wise, *Register*, 791–2.

13 It is interesting that Wise, at this relatively early date, uses the words of John Randolph, a member of one of the great aristocratic families of the South and a direct descendant of Pocahontas, to attack both a Connecticut artist and Adams, the distinguished representative from Massachusetts and a member of one of the great aristocratic families of the North. Although the matter at hand was not of the greatest importance, the delegates of both regions would no doubt have understood the greater message contained in Wise's precocious display of sectionalist rhetoric.

14 My biographical sketch of Chapman was gleaned from the manuscript of Campbell's uncompleted biography of Chapman, Campbell Papers; his exhibit catalog, *John Gadsby Chapman: Painter and Illustrator;* and two articles by Georgia Stamm Chamberlain: "John Gadsby Chapman, Painter of Virginia," *Art Quarterly* (Detroit Museum of Arts Founders Society) 24, 4 (Winter 1961), 378–90; and " 'The Baptism of Pocahontas': John Gadsby Chapman's Gigantic Mural in the Rotunda of the National Capitol," *Iron Worker* (Lynchburg, Va.: Lynchburg Foundry Company) 23, 3 (Summer 1959), 15–22. Both of the Chamberlain articles are reprinted in *Studies.*

15 Frances Trollope, *Domestic Manners of the Americans*, ed. Donald Smalley (New York: Random House, 1949), 326–7 (originally published in 1832).

16 Jesse Brown's Indian Queen Hotel was one of the most famous establishments of its kind in Washington City. See James D. Horan, *The McKenney-Hall Portrait Gallery of American Indians* (New York: Bramhall House, 1986), 21. See also Herman J. Viola, *The Indian Legacy of Charles Bird King* (Washington, D.C.: Smithsonian Institution Press and Doubleday, 1976), 25–6.

17 Chapman to Johnston, March 10, 1832, Campbell Papers, 8–10.

18 Chapman to Johnston, 14.

19 Chapman to Wise, June 29, 1836, Campbell Papers, 4–5.

20 As Samuel Morse's son, Edward Lind Morse, describes it, "Morse, president of the National Academy of Design, and enthusiastically supported by the best artists in the country, had every reason to suppose that he would be chosen to execute at least one of the paintings." Fate, in the form of John Quincy Adams, intervened. When Adams suggested that the competition for the commissions should be open to foreign as well as American artists, he was answered with "an indignant and remarkably able reply" by an anonymous correspondent to the *New York Evening Post.* Samuel Morse was accused of the authorship of this article, which insulted and angered Adams, and so he used his considerable clout to make sure that Morse was denied a commission. According to Edward Lind Morse, James Fenimore Cooper was the actual author of this inflammatory letter. (It must be mentioned that had Samuel Morse gotten the commission and continued his career as a painter, he might not

have gotten around to inventing the telegraph.) See Samuel F. B. Morse, *Samuel F. B. Morse: His Letters and Journals*, ed. Edward Lind Morse (Boston: Houghton Mifflin, 1914), vol. 2, 28–35.

21 "Paintings For The Rotundo," Report of the Select Committee to the House of Representatives, H.R. Rep. No. 294, 24th Congress, 2nd Session, February 28, 1837 (Washington: Blair & Rives).

22 "American Historical Paintings," *New-York Mirror*, March 4, 1837, 288. After announcing the names of the artists chosen – "Vanderlin [*sic*], Inman, Chapman, and Weir" – the writer makes his or her opinion of these artists clear: "This appointment will, probably, give general satisfaction, though there are artists of distinguished ability passed by. If some member of Congress would offer a resolution for adorning the president's house with historical paintings illustrative of the revolution, an opportunity might be afforded of doing justice to some artists of superior genius, who are now neglected. . . . Let our best artists be employed, and there will be no difficulty in finding appropriate places for their works."

23 I have discussed the dinner conspiracy in Chapter 3. Chapman completed two paintings of *The First Ship*. In his initial version, now lost, he portrayed a young, Pocahontas-like Indian princess seeing the incoming Europeans. In his second attempt he used the more traditional Indian brave.

24 When we recall the 1734 letter, which was discussed at the beginning of this chapter, her baptism is the one major event of Pocahontas's life that even this correspondent failed to mention.

It is interesting to compare Chapman's choice of subject with that made by a contemporary literary artist. In his *Pocahontas, Princess of Virginia: and Other Poems* (New York: Dean & Trevett, 1841), William Watson Waldron goes out of his way to deemphasize her baptism. Indeed, in the introduction to his poem, Waldron suggests that making a Christian out of her might somehow detract from what is most remarkable about her narrative: "Unenlightened by revelation, we find her loving her enemies, doing good to those who despitefully used and persecuted her, without knowing that such obligations were imposed on us by "a teacher come from God" (9). Waldron clearly believes that her natural benevolence should be seen as primary, and he goes on to say almost nothing about her becoming a Christian in the text of his *Pocahontas*.

25 See Chamberlain, "Baptism," 19–20 (cited in note 13 to this chapter).

26 Sir Thomas Dale was the governor of Virginia at the time of the baptism. He and his wife are often given credit for helping to instruct Pocahontas in the Christian faith. The Reverend Alexander Whitaker, author of *Good News From Virginia* (1613), was the leading clergyman in the Jamestown colony and is known to have performed her baptism.

27 Abrams (see note 6 to this chapter).

28 Owen makes his claim in a note to the 1837 edition of his play, *Pocahontas; A Historical Drama*, which is reprinted in *The Romantic Indian*, ed. Charles M. Lombard (Delmar, N.Y.: Scholar's Facsimiles & Reprints, 1981), 216–17.

29 Most recent scholarship on the *Booton Hall Portrait* suggests that it was probably painted in the mid-eighteenth century. This effectively has ended what had been a lively debate about which came first, the portrait or the Van de Passe engraving. See, for instance, Philip L. Barbour, "Notes on So-called Relics of Powhatan and Pocahontas" in his *Pocahontas and Her World* (Boston: Houghton Mifflin, 1970), 233–4. As to its

"discovery," this is mentioned, without elaboration, in the *Boston Evening Transcript* 48, 14 (October 19, 1875), 874.

30 Chapman to Bolling, November 28, 1837, January 27, 1838, and March 13, 1838. Cited in Campbell Papers as Virginia Historical Society (Richmond, Va.) manuscripts 2B6386b6, 2B6386b7, and 2B6386b8. "Cobbs," in Chesterfield County, Va., was the home of this branch of the Bolling family from the mid-eighteenth century until it was sold by William Bolling to Edward Lynch in the late 1820s. The portraits had been acquired by Thomas Bolling after the death of Ryland Randolph. (See note 31.)

31 William Bolling, quoted in Ella Loraine Dorsey, *Pocahontas* (Washington, D.C.: Howard Press, 1906), 48. The *Turkey Island Portrait* got its name from the environs of the home of Ryland Randolph. Randolph had offered to buy the portraits of Pocahontas and John Rolfe from their English owner, but they were ultimately given to him gratis, in the mid-eighteenth century because of Randolph's status as a direct descendant.

32 Dorsey, 49.

33 Thomas McKenney and James Hall, *The History of the Indian Tribes of North America*, 3 vols, (Philadelphia: Daniel Rice and J. G. Clarke, 1836–44). (Rice and Clarke are listed as publishers in the three volumes of the first edition that I was able to see. However, this text is often cited as having been published by E. C. Biddle of Philadelphia. The problem apparently has to do with the rights to the engravings.)

34 See "Melville's Indian-Hating Source," in Herman Melville, *The Confidence-Man*, Harrison Hayford, Hershel Parker, and G. Thomas Tanselle, eds. (Evanston and Chicago: Northwestern University Press and Newberry Library, 1984), 501–10.

35 L. Cleo Mullins, a senior conservator at the Richmond (Virginia) Conservation Studio, has done extensive research on the *Turkey Island Portrait* and the works supposedly derived from it. As of this writing, she is preparing an article in which she will sort out the complex histories of these paintings. Sully's first copy of the *Turkey Island Portrait*, which was long thought to have been lost, may have been rediscovered by the author during his research for the "Pocahontas: The Life and Legend" exhibition. We await the results of Ms. Mullins's examination of a portrait that is clearly from the "Turkey Island" school, but is less stylized than Sully's later efforts.

    Robert Matthew Sully was apparently obsessed with Pocahontas. In a March 1855 letter to Lyman Draper, he calls her "the idol, of my romantic dreams, since boyhood." See Louise Phelps Kellogg, "Pocahontas and Jamestown," *Wisconsin Magazine of History and Biography* 25 (September 1941), 38–42; see also Charles E. Hatch, Jr., "Robert Sully at Jamestown, 1854," *William and Mary Quarterly* 22, 4 (October 1942), 343–52. I believe that Mullins's forthcoming article will address this issue as well.

    For an antebellum commentary on midcentury visual representations of Pocahontas, see J. E. C. [John Esten Cooke], "Wanderings on the Banks of the York," *Southern Literary Messenger* 26, 26 (June 1858), 457–65.

36 Chapman to Bolling, January 27, 1838. Cited in the Campbell Papers as Virginia Historical Society manuscript 2B6386b7, 1–2.

37 Chamberlain argues that the portrait of Hayne Hudjihini (in this article "Hudijihini") may have been used as a model. She points out that Chapman owned a version of this portrait in 1837 and notes some sim-

ilarities. See Chamberlain, "Baptism," 18–19. Campbell speculates that a "Miss Gardiner" may have been Chapman's model but provides no argument. See Campbell Papers. Jessie Poesch, in *The Art of the Old South* (New York: Knopf, 1983) states flatly that "Cooke's daughter posed for Pocahontas" but likewise provides no proof.

38 It should also be noted that the young Indian woman with the baby in the *Baptism,* who is identified in the "Key" as the sister of Pocahontas, bears something of a resemblance, both in appearance and pose, to the Pocahontas of Chapman's version of the Rescue. This earlier princess may, in fact, be the truest model for the later figure.

39 Wanda Corn has suggested to me that this pose is also reminiscent of Mary Magdalene, another young woman with long, dark hair who is transformed from sinner to saved.

40 "Preparations in the Capitol – Paintings in the Rotunda" (Letter from a "correspondent" dated November 30, 1840), *New York Herald* 6, 64, whole no. 1629, December 3, 1840, 2.

41 "Preparations," 2.

42 "Mr. Chapman's Painting Of The Baptism Of Pocahontas," *Daily National Intelligencer* 28, 8673 (December 1, 1840), 3.

43 John Gadsby Chapman, *The Picture Of The Baptism Of Pocahontas* (Washington: Peter Force, 1840). For a time there was a controversy concerning whether the baptism of Pocahontas took place before or after her wedding. Bishop William Meade finally sorted this out, opting for the more canonically correct baptism – marriage order. See his 1857 *Old Churches, Ministers and Families Of Virginia* (Philadelphia: Lippincott, 1891), 77–80.

44 Chapman, *Picture,* 4.

45 Chapman, *Picture,* 4–5.

46 Abrams, 12–13.

47 "W.," "Chapman's Painting," *Daily National Intelligencer* 28, 8686, (December 16, 1840), 3.

48 Ibid.

49 Ibid.

50 "Landscape," "Mr. Chapman's Picture – The Baptism of Pocahontas," *Daily National Intelligencer* 28, 8690, (December 21, 1840), 3.

51 William Gilmore Simms, "Pocahontas: A Subject For The Historical Painter," in *Views and Reviews In American Literature, History and Fiction* (New York: Wiley, 1848), 91. This essay was originally published in *Southern and Western Magazine* 2 (September 1845), 145–54.

52 Simms, 91–2.

53 Simms, 92.

54 Simms, 92.

55 William Gilmore Simms, *The Life of Capt. John Smith* (New York: Geo. F. Cooledge & Brother, 1846).

56 Abrams, 1.

57 Abrams, 13. In fact, Weir's painting was placed in the Rotunda after *The Baptism of Pocahontas,* and so, if anything, the *Embarkation* was a northern counterpart to Chapman's work.

   George Dekker has reminded me that Pocahontas is almost always kneeling in representations of the Rescue as well. One could argue that she is in position to be "blessed" in both instances.

58 Chapman to Bolling, January 27, 1838. Cited in Campbell Papers as Virginia Historical Society manuscript 2B6386b7, 2.

59 Chapman, *Picture,* 3–4.

60 Chapman, *Picture,* 6.

61 Chapman, *Picture*, 11–12.

62 Both "Pocahontas" and "Matoaka," or "Matoax," have been translated as "playful." This has been variously presented as meaning that she was what one might today call a "tomboy"; that she was "pleasing," especially to Powhatan; or that she was a "little wanton," in the modern sense of the word. Her detractors tend to stress the final translation. For a discussion, see Charles Edgar Gilliam, "His Dearest Daughter's Names," *William and Mary Quarterly*, 2nd ser., 21, 3 (July 1941), 239–42.

63 Nathaniel Hawthorne, *The Scarlet Letter*, Sculley Bradley, Richmond Groom Beatty, E. Hudson Long, and Seymour Gross, eds. (New York: Norton, 1978), 140. It has been argued that Hester's entreaty, which is emblematic of her growing sense of personal freedom, is reminiscent of the beliefs of Anne Hutchinson, the central figure of the seventeenth-century Antinomian controversy. See Michael J. Colacurcio, "Footsteps of Anne Hutchinson: The Context of *The Scarlet Letter*," *ELH* 39 (1972), 459–94.

64 Abraham Lincoln, "Address Delivered at the Dedication of the Cemetery at Gettysburg," in *The Norton Anthology of American Literature*, 2nd ed., ed. Nina Baym et al. (New York: Norton, 1985), vol. 1, 1464–5. (Originally delivered in 1863.)

65 Both Mozier's *Pocahontas* (1859) and Erastus Dow Palmer's *The Girl or the Dawn of Christianity* (1856) portray a young Indian woman holding a Christian cross in her right hand. Joy S. Kasson has commented that such works "suggest a kind of reverse captivity theme." The subjects "signal their willing 'captivity' by gazing at a cross. . . . [B]ut in the tradition of the captive and dying maiden, it also suggests the subject's willingness to forego temporal power for the sacrificial spiritual power of the woman's sphere." See her "Power and Powerlessness: Death, Sexuality and the Demonic in Nineteenth-Century American Sculpture," *Women's Studies* 15 (1988), 355. For Hawthorne's comments, see *The French and Italian Notebooks*, ed. Thomas Woodson (Columbus: Ohio State University Press, 1980), 153–4.

66 Osceola, the great chief of the Seminoles, went to a meeting with Brigadier General Joseph M. Hernandez, the commander of the U.S. Forces, on October 21, 1837, under a flag of truce. While there he was arrested and ultimately sent to Fort Moultrie, where he died a prisoner on January 30, 1838. See the two issues of *Florida Historical Quarterly* 33, 3–4 (January–April 1955) that are wholly dedicated to Osceola. His courageous death was noted by a number of authors, including Walt Whitman in his poem, "Osceola" (in *Good-Bye My Fancy*, 1891).

67 As Peter Hulme points out concerning this painting, "Virginia is represented by Pocahontas, but the picture, . . . shows neither the famous 'rescue' nor her marriage with John Rolfe. Instead it depicts Pocahontas's baptism, shrewdly choosing the moment when European ritual symbolized her rejection of her own culture and her incorporation into the ranks of the saved." See "John Smith and Pocahontas," in his *Colonial Encounters: Europe and the Native Caribbean, 1492–1797* (London: Methuen, 1986), 170.

68 For other discussions of the Figures of Jacob and Esau in American culture, see Michael Paul Rogin, *Fathers and Children* (New York: Knopf, 1975), 126–8, 162–3; Anne Norton, *Alternative Americas: A Reading of Antebellum Political Culture* (Chicago: University of Chicago Press, 1986), 144–7; Hulme, 145–7.

69 For an excellent study of nineteenth-century opinions about the origins of Native Americans, see Robert E. Bieder, *Science Encounters the Indian, 1820–1880* (Norman: University of Oklahoma Press, 1986). See also, Rogin, esp. 3–37.

70 Matthew Baigell, "Territory, Race, Religion: Images of Manifest Destiny," *Smithsonian Studies in American Art* 4, 3–4 (Summer / Fall 1990), 3–21. This article is written in the revisionist spirit of "The West as America" exhibit, which sparked so much controversy during its stay at the National Museum of American Art.

71 Baigell, 3.

72 Baigell, 16–17.

73 Opechancanough, who would become the leader of the Indian confederacy after the death of Powhatan in 1618, is by far the most interesting figure in the painting. From his expression it is clear that he is unhappy with the ceremony that is taking place and is perhaps already plotting against the English. He was to lead the Indian uprisings of 1622 and 1644.

74 Baigell, 8.

75 Baigell, 9.

76 William Cullen Bryant, "The Prairies," in *The Complete Poems of William Cullen Bryant*, ed. H. C. Edwards (New York: Stokes, 1894), 131, lines 46–50.

77 Bryant, lines 58–60.

78 Bryant, lines 75–85.

79 Julie Schimmel, "Inventing 'the Indian,'" in *The West As America*, ed. William H. Truettner (Washington, D.C.: Smithsonian Institution Press, 1991), 148–89. On the "doomed Indian," see 168–78. Albert Gelpi has suggested to me that perhaps the most poignant representation of the last days of the Indians is Albert Bierstadt's painting *The Last of the Buffalo*, which is as certainly about the end of the Indians as it is about their dwindling prey.

80 Schimmel, 169.

81 Powers's *Last of the Tribes* stands in the National Museum of American Art in Washington, D.C. Unfortunately the museum did not have a photograph available for use here.

82 See George Catlin, quoted in Baigell, 10.

83 One could argue that other "first" Indians, such as Chapman's brave who watches the colonists ship approaching in *The First Ship*, or the single Indian in Thomas Birch's *Landing of William Penn*, can also be seen symbolically as "last" Indians because the landing of the Europeans forecasts the end of their race.

84 "Presidential Election," next to "Mr. Chapman's Painting Of The Baptism Of Pocahontas," *Daily National Intelligencer* 28, 8673 (December 1, 1840), 3.

85 It is interesting to look at James Hall's *Memoir of the Public Services of William Henry Harrison* (Philadelphia: Key & Biddle, 1836). After a brief sketch of Harrison's youth and the post-Revolutionary War situation in the Northwest, Hall spends 258 of his remaining 295 pages on Harrison's military career, most of which was spent as an Indian fighter.

One of the ironies of the presidential campaign of 1840 was that General Harrison and John Tyler defeated President Van Buren and his vice-president, Colonel Richard M. Johnson, whose fame was based on his claim that he had killed Tecumseh at the Battle of the Thames.

86 R. David Edmunds, *The Shawnee Prophet* (Lincoln: University of Nebraska Press, 1983), esp. 3–117.

87 Quoted in Edmunds, 38.
88 Indeed, it was even suggested that *The Baptism of Pocahontas* be removed from its place in the Rotunda. See the passage from U.S. *House of Representatives, Executive Document no. 315* (41st Congress, 2nd Session), quoted in Charles E. Fairman, *Art and Artists of the Capitol of the United States of America* (Washington, D.C.: U.S. Government Printing Office, 1927), 245.
89 "The Indians in American Art," *The Crayon* 3 (January 1856), 28.
90 "Editor's Table," *Southern Literary Messenger* 28, 21 (May 1959), 395.
91 "Editor's Table," 395–6.
92 "Editor's Table," 396.
93 "Editor's Table," 396.

Chapter 5. The Figure of Pocahontas in Sectionalist Propaganda

1 Emily Clemens Pearson [Pocahontas, pseud.], *Cousin Franck's Household, or, Scenes in the Old Dominion*, 4th ed. (Boston: Upham, Ford & Olmstead, 1853; reprint, Freeport, N.Y.: Books for Libraries, 1972), 29. (All parenthetical page numbers within the text refer to the reprint edition.)
2 *Official Records of the Union and Confederate Navies in the War of the Rebellion*, published under the direction of the Hon. H. A. Herbert, Secretary of the Navy, by Lieut. Commander Richard Rush, U.S.N. and Mr. Robert H. Woods, ser. 1, vol. 4 (Washington, D.C.: U.S. Government Printing Office, 1896), 236.
3 For information on any U.S. naval vessel, see the *Dictionary of American Naval Fighting Ships*, 8 vols. (Washington, D.C.: Navy Department, Office of the Chief of Naval Operations, Naval History Division, 1959–81). For specific information on the *Powhatan* or the *Pocahontas*, see vol. 5 (1970). See also *"The Launch of the Powhatan," Virginia Historical Register* 3, 1 (1850), 111. The United States Navy had a *Powhatan* and a *Pocahontas* in commission during both the First and the Second World Wars.
4 See David Lindsey, "Perry in Japan," *American History Illustrated* 13, 5 (August 1978), 4–8, 44–9. The Treaty of Kanagawa "called for: (1) peace and friendship between the two countries; (2) the ports of Shimoda Hakodate to be open to American ships for supply of 'wood, water, provisions and coal' and other necessities involving limited trade; (3) shipwrecked American sailors to be transported to one of the above ports for delivery to their countrymen, these and other Americans to be allowed to move freely in these ports" (48). The last item, while in fact the least important, was of great concern to American sailors, as stories of the abuses committed by the Japanese upon shipwrecked American seamen were well known.
5 In 1850, as Melville was working on *Moby-Dick*, two events occurred that should have increased the believability of his novel, although they clearly did not aid in bettering the public and critical reception. The first took place on the "off-shore ground" in the South Pacific, when the whale ship *Ann Alexander* of New Bedford, under the command of Captain John S. Deblois, "was sunk by the charge of a maddened whale after the whale had attacked and smashed two of the ship's boats." On December 12 of this same year, off the coast of Brazil, the whaler *Pocahontas* of Holmes Hole, under the command of Captain Joseph Dias, "was rammed by a whale . . . , her bow badly stove and leaking beyond the capacity of her pumps, barely stated afloat long enough to make

Rio de Janeiro." News of this latter event reached the United States early in 1851, and the dramatic story of the encounter was told in the May 17, 1851, edition of *Gleason's Pictorial Drawing Room Companion*. See William Armstrong Fairburn, *Merchant Sail*, 6 vols. (Center Lovell, Maine: Fairburn Marine Educational Foundation, 1945–55), vol. 2, 1026–7.

6 John Tyler's rowboat *Pocahontas* is mentioned in Curtis Carroll Davis, *Chronicler of the Cavaliers: A Life of Virginia Novelist Dr. William A. Caruthers* (Richmond, Va.: Dietz, 1953), 167.

7 For information about commissioned ships, see *Official Records*, ser. 1, vol. 4, 248. The list of Indian names was gleaned from the *Dictionary of American Naval Fighting Ships* (cited in note 3 to this chapter).

8 Herman Melville, *Moby-Dick or, The Whale*, ed. Charles Feidelson, Jr. (Indianapolis: Bobbs-Merrill, 1964), 104.

9 Rayna Green, "The Only Good Indian: The Image of the Indian in American Vernacular Culture," Ph.D. diss., Indiana University, 1973, 224. One could also argue that a more subtle way of making this same point is evident on another symbol that was publicly displayed on all United States vessels. The alternating red and white stripes on the U.S. flag could, in this context, be seen as symbolic of a "joining of forces," even when there were no Indians present.

10 The absorption of such tribes would obviously mean their destruction. The naming of ships (or trains, or automobiles) after them represents a sentimental attempt to portray that something of them still survives. Those who named ships of war probably had quite specific traits in mind.

11 Erik Heyl, *Early American Steamers* (Buffalo: Published by the author, 1964), Vol. 3, 291–4. See also, "Editor's Table," *Southern Literary Messenger* 28, 21 (May 1859), 395–7, for the Everett sighting.

12 Robert Selph Henry, *The Story of the Confederacy* (New York: Grosset & Dunlap, 1936), 69.

13 William Hillhouse, *Pocahontas; A Proclamation: With Plates* (New Haven: J. Clyme, 1820). (All parenthetical page numbers within the text refer to this edition.)

14 Colin McEvedy, *The Penguin Atlas of North American History to 1870* (London: Penguin, 1988), 78.

15 David M. Potter, *The Impending Crisis, 1848–1861*, completed and edited by Don E. Fehrenbacher (New York: Harper & Row, 1976), 56.

16 Pearson, *Cousin Franck's Household*. (See note 1 to this chapter.)

17 Emily Catharine Pierson, *Jamie Parker, The Fugitive* (Hartford: Brockett, Fuller, and Co., 1851). John Greenleaf Whittier, in his review of *Cousin Franck's Household* in the *National Era*, immediately recognizes the author of *Cousin Franck's Household* as the author of the previously "favorably noticed" *Jamie Parker*. See Whittier, Rev. of *Cousin Franck's Household*, *National Era* 7, 319 (February 10, 1853), 1. (Pearson's name, however, is not mentioned in the review.)

18 Sterling Brown, *The Negro in American Fiction* (Port Washington, N.Y.: Kennikat Press, 1968), 34. Brown is one of the rare twentieth-century critics who has taken notice of *Cousin Franck's Household*, although it was fairly popular in its day.

John Pendleton Kennedy, *Swallow Barn; or, A Sojourn in the Old Dominion*, 2 Vols. (Philadelphia: Carey and Lea, 1832). Brown calls *Swallow Barn* the first example of what would become the "plantation tradition" (18). (All parenthetical page numbers within the text refer to this edition of *Swallow Barn*.)

In the revised, 1851 edition, perhaps to make the novel more palatable to his northern audience, Kennedy omits a thirty-five-page chapter called "A Chronicle of the Life of Captain John Smith." Littleton still begins and ends his journey, however, musing about the man he calls "the unmatchable Smith." See the recent reprint (Baton Rouge: Louisiana State University Press, 1986), which contains an excellent introduction by Lucinda H. MacKethen.

19 William R. Taylor, *Cavalier and Yankee* (New York: Harper & Row, 1969), 305.

20 Thomas Jefferson, *Notes on the State of Virginia* (New York: Harper & Row, 1964), 155–6 (originally published in 1785).

21 John Pendleton Kennedy, *Horse-shoe Robinson* (Philadelphia: Carey, Lea & Blanchard, 1835); William Gilmore Simms, *The Partisan* (New York: Harper & Brothers, 1835). See also the mention of the role played by poor whites in the recapturing of slaves, in Kenneth M. Stampp's *Peculiar Institution* (New York: Random House, 1956), 153. The subject of poor whites remained important to Pearson. In 1864, after the reissue of *Cousin Franck's Household* as *Ruth's Sacrifice*, Pearson published *The Poor White; or, The Rebel Conscript* (Boston: Graves and Young, 1864.)

22 I would argue that they are not explicitly indicted because Pocahontas does not generalize about the Virginia aristocracy. She only comments on the Cameron family and life on their plantation.

23 Anne Norton, *Alternative Americas: A Reading of Antebellum Political Culture* (Chicago: University of Chicago Press, 1986), 183.

24 John Gorham Palfrey, *History of New England*, 3 vols. (Boston: Little, Brown, 1899), vol. 1, 92 (originally published in 5 volumes, 1858–90).

25 The first doubter of Smith was probably Thomas Fuller. See his 1662 *The Worthies of England*, ed. John Freeman (London: Allen & Unwin, 1952), 75–6. One could argue, however, that Fuller was refuted in his own century. See Henry Wharton, *The Life of John Smith, English Soldier*, translated from the Latin, with an introductory essay by Laura Polanyi Striker (Chapel Hill: University of North Carolina Press, 1957). There was also the occasional early nineteenth-century detractor. For instance, see the highly critical review of John Davis's *Travels* in *Edinburgh Review* 2 (July 1803), 443–53.

26 Edward Maria Wingfield, *A Discourse of Virginia*, ed. Charles Deane, in *Transactions and Collections of the American Antiquarian Society* (Worcester, Mass.: American Antiquarian Society, 1860), vol. 4, 67–103. Deane's edition was published privately, in a run of one hundred copies, in 1859 (Boston: Privately printed [J. Wilson and Son], 1859).

27 Deane, in Wingfield, 92–4.

28 William Bradford, *History of Plymouth Plantation*, ed. Charles Deane, Massachusetts Historical Society Collections, ser. 4, no. 3 (Boston: Massachusetts Historical Society, 1856).

29 See Bertram Wyatt-Brown, *Southern Honor* (New York: Oxford University Press, 1982).

30 William Warren Jenkins, "Three Centuries in the Development of the Pocahontas Story in American Literature," Ph.D. diss., University of Tennessee, 1977, 164.

31 Wyndham Robertson, "The Marriage of Pocahontas," *Southern Literary Messenger* 31, 6 (July 1859), 81–91.

32 The anonymous articles "Smith's Rescue By Pocahontas" and "Pocahontas; or, The Lady Rebecca," appeared in the *Southern Literary Mes-*

senger 36 (November/December 1862), 627–31, 641–7. The *Messenger* ceased publication in 1864.

33 John Esten Cooke, *My Lady Pokahontas* (Boston: Houghton Mifflin, 1885).

34 John Esten Cooke, "A Dream of the Cavaliers," *Harper's New Monthly Magazine* 32, 128 (January 1861), 252–4.

35 Laura Polanyi Striker and Bradford Smith, "The Rehabilitation of Captain John Smith," *Journal of Southern History* 28, 4 (November 1962), 480–1.

36 James Kirke Paulding, *Letters from the the South,* 2 vols. (New York: Harper & Brothers, 1835), vol. 1, 25.

37 Drew Gilpin Faust, *The Creation of Confederate Nationalism* (Baton Rouge: Louisiana State University Press, 1988), 14–15.

38 "The Difference of Race Between the Northern and Southern People," *Southern Literary Messenger* 30 (June 1860), 401–9. The July 1861 issue of this journal contained a similar article, entitled "The True Question: A Contest for the Supremacy of Race, as Between the Saxon Puritan of the North, and the Norman of the South," 30 (July 1861), 19–27.

39 Faust, 10–11, 90.

40 Henry Timrod, "Ethnogenesis," reprinted in *Poems of Henry Timrod* (Richmond: B. F. Johnson, 1901), 150–4. The title "laureate of the Confederacy" is borrowed from Henry Tazewell Thompson's biography of Timrod, *Henry Timrod: Laureate of the Confederacy* (Columbia, S.C.: State, 1928). Timrod is generally thought of as the best of the southern poets who were writing during the Confederate era.

41 "The President and the Union," *New Orleans Bee* (December 10, 1860); reprinted in Dwight Lowell Dumond, ed., *Southern Editorials On Secession* (New York: Century, 1931), 315–16.

42 Norton, 182.

43 Thomas Jefferson, cited in Reginald Horsman, *Race and Manifest Destiny* (Cambridge, Mass.: Harvard University Press, 1981), 108, 325.

44 John Smith, *A True Relation,* ed. Charles Deane (Boston: Wiggins and Lunt, 1866).

45 Henry Adams, *The Education of Henry Adams* (Boston: Houghton Mifflin, 1918), 222; Henry Adams, "Captain John Smith," *North American Review* 104, 214 (January 1867), 1–30.

46 Henry Adams to John Gorham Palfrey, March 20, 1862, in J. C. Levenson et al., eds. *The Letters of Henry Adams* (Cambridge, Mass.: Harvard University Press [Belknap Press], 1982), vol. 1, 287. Earlier in this letter Adams asks Palfrey "who Mr Deane is." This leads one to believe that Adams had yet to begin a serious study of the Smith material at this point. It should also be mentioned that in an earlier letter to Palfrey, Adams seemingly has not yet begun to doubt the authenticity of the Rescue. See Adams to Palfrey, October 23, 1861, in *Letters,* vol. 1, 258–60.

   The "Strachey" text to which Adams refers is William Strachey, *Historie of Travaile into Virginia Britannia* (London: Printed for the Hakluyt Society, 1849). In this work, about which more will be said in the Postscript, Strachey describes the young Pocahontas as "wanton" and tells of the naked princess doing somersaults with the young boys of the Jamestown settlement (65).

47 Henry published a number of pieces in defense of Smith and Pocahontas. See, for example, William Wirt Henry, "The Rescue of Captain John Smith by Pocahontas," *Potters American Monthly* 4–5 (1875), 523–8, 591–7; "The Settlement at Jamestown, With Particular Reference to the Late

Attacks upon Captain Smith, Pocahontas, and John Rolfe," *Proceedings of the Virginia Historical Society* (Richmond: Published for the Society, February 24, 1882), 10–62; "A Defence of Captain John Smith," *Magazine of American History* 25 (1891), 300–13; "Did Percy Denounce Smith's History of Virginia?" *Virginia Magazine of History and Biography* 1 (1893–4), 473–6.

48 Adolphe F. Bandelier to Thomas Janvier, September 2, 1888, in *The Unpublished Letters of Adolphe F. Bandelier* (El Paso: Carl Hertzog, 1942), 3. (See my discussion of this letter in Chapter 3.)

49 Joseph G. Baldwin, *The Flush Times of Alabama and Mississippi,* intro. William A. Owens (New York: Sagamore Press, 1957), 17. (First published in 1853.)

50 Edwin O. Christensen, *Early American Wood Carving* (Cleveland: World, 1952), 50. Christensen uses "Pocahontas" as a generic term often in his chapter, "Shop Figures and Amusement Props," 36–64.

51 See Rayna Green, "The Only Good Indian: The Image of the Indian in American Vernacular Culture," Ph.D. diss., Indiana University, 1973, esp. 263–301. Green amassed a prodigious number of visual representations of male and female Indians. Princess Pocahontas Tobacco (284) and Pocahontas Perfume (278) are only two of the literally hundreds of images of Indians discussed.

It is not surprising that Pocahontas and her figurative sisters were used to sell tobacco. This is, in fact, why the historical Pocahontas went to England. John Rolfe was trying to get investors interested in tobacco production, and who would better represent the New World and the intoxicating product he wanted to grow than his enchanting young wife?

There was something about these young Indian women that antebellum white manufacturers believed would help to sell their products to white consumers. Some of these advertisements, especially those for tobacco, played on the seductive nature of "dusky" maidens, but in others the prospective consumers were being asked to trust that these Indian women had their best interests at heart. I would argue that Pocahontas stands behind these figures, both as the best-known Indian princess and as the model for such trustworthiness. Her reputed saving of the Jamestown colony earned her this trust, which, through her and her symbolic descendants, became the tool of advertisers, politicians, and other agents who wanted to win the support or sympathy of the public.

James F. O'Gorman describes a particularly interesting "show-card" advertisement for "Dr. Stephen Jewetts Justly & Highly Celebrated Health Restoring Bitters[,] Pulmonary Elixir and Strengthening Plasters": "On the right side of the card, Aesculapius stands as a Roman god of medicine, and on the left is Hygia, a Pocahontas-like figure whose image and name were contrived to symbolize hygrastics, the science of health and hygiene." By 1850 (the date of the card), Pocahontas-like figures had long been associated with various types of medicines. Here, however, the young woman seems also to represent the possibility of changing one's lifestyle. In this advertisement, according to O'Gorman, the Pocahontas-like figure combines "natural" health (based on her being an Indian) with the learned aspects of hygiene. See James F. O'Gorman, *Aspects of American Printmaking, 1800–1950* (Syracuse: Syracuse University Press, 1988).

52 Sidney Lerner, letter to the author, July 4, 1990. (See also *Wallace's American Trotting Register,* vol. 3, 1879.) Harness (standardbred) horses trot or pace, rather than gallop as do thoroughbred horses. Pocahontas

held her record from June 21, 1855, until it was broken by the great trotter Dexter on August 14, 1867.

There were a number of standardbred and thoroughbred horses named Pocahontas over the years, but there will almost certainly never be another. The World Champion pacing mare of the 1850s and 1860s has recently been enshrined in the Hall of Fame of the Trotter in Goshen, New York. The last thoroughbred to wear this name was the mare Pocahontas, who was chosen "Broodmare of the Year" in 1965, primarily on the basis of her being the dam of a champion three-year-old, the appropriately named "Tom Rolfe." Such honors usually disqualify the name from being used again. (The names of champion horses are almost always retired. So, there will never be another thoroughbred Citation or Secretariat, nor another standard-bred Dan Patch or Greyhound.)

53   I must first thank Thomas C. Moser, Jr., for putting me on the trial of the "Dixie"–"Pocahontas connection. Much of the information provided here is due to the courtesy of Patrick M. Reynolds, who graciously sent me the contents of his file on "Dixie." See his two-part "Unofficial Confederate Anthem" in "Flashbacks," comics sec., *Washington Post* (May 16 and May 23, 1993). See also Maymie R. Krythe, *Sampler of American Songs* (New York: Harper & Row, 1969), 100–11; Richard Jackson, *Popular Songs of Nineteenth-Century America* (New York: Dover, 1976), 61–4, 268; John Lair, *Songs Lincoln Loved* (New York: Duell, Sloan & Pearce, 1954), 39–41; and Hans Nathan, *Dan Emmett and the Rise of Early Negro Minstrelsy* (Norman: University of Oklahoma Press, 1962), 243–75.

Although "Dixie" has long been credited to Daniel Emmett, Harold and Judith Sachs have recently argued that this song was actually taught to him by Ben and Lou Snowden, two black musicians from Ohio. See Howard L. Sachs and Judith Rose Sachs, *Way up North in Dixie* (Washington, D.C.: Smithsonian Institution Press, 1993).

Postscript

1   John Smith, *New England's Trials*, in *The Complete Works of Captain John Smith*, 3 vols., ed. Philip L. Barbour (Chapel Hill: University of North Carolina Press, 1986), vol. 1, 432. (Originally published in 1620.)

2   Vine Deloria, Jr., *Custer Died for Your Sins* (New York: Avon, 1969), 10–11.

3   In this postscript, *The Rescue* refers to the Greenough sculpture; the Rescue remains my abbreviation for the rescue of Captain John Smith. On the sculpture, see *Compilation of Works of Art and Other Objects in the United States Capitol*. Prepared by the Architect of the Capitol Under the Direction of the Joint Committee on the Library (Washington, D.C.: United States Government Printing Office, 1965), 365. This piece was erected in 1853.

The companion piece to *The Rescue,* Luigi Persico's *Discovery of America* (1844), is described on the same page as portraying a moment when "Columbus holds aloft the globe, while an Indian maiden cowers at his side with surprise and awe." One might argue that this "awe" is the first step toward a joining with the Europeans in the process of conquest. By the mid-nineteenth century, it was widely believed that at least three young Indian women (Pocahontas, Sacajawea, and Doña Marina), perhaps because of their susceptibility to the charms of charismatic European males, had played important roles in the establishing of European dominance in the New World. (*The Rescue* and *Discovery of America* are currently in storage.)

There may be a connection, albeit a tenuous one, between Chapman's *Baptism of Pocahontas* and Greenough's *The Rescue*. Among the Campbell Papers is a quotation from a letter from Greenough to James Kirke Paulding in which he mentions that Chapman had sent him "casts and drawings" for "The Group." (Nathalia Wright, who owned the letter while Campbell was amassing materials for his book on Chapman, presumes that the "casts and drawings" were of Indians.) Campbell gives us the date as December 14, 1939, which is clearly an error. If the correct date is December 14, 1839, it places this letter during the period after Greenough had gotten his commission, as well as during the completion of the *Baptism*. There are slight compositional similarities, especially between the positions of Nantequas and Pocahontas in the *Baptism* and the Indian brave and pioneer woman in *The Rescue*.

4   Vivien Green Fryd, "Two Sculptures For The Capitol: Horatio Greenough's *Rescue* and Luigi Persico's *Discovery of America*," *American Art Journal* 19, 2 (1987), 31. In this article Fryd provides an excellent study of the cultural climate that inspired both works.

5   Horatio Greenough to John Forsyth, July 1, 1837, in *Letters of Horatio Greenough; American Sculptor*, ed. Nathalia Wright (Madison: University of Wisconsin Press, 1972), 214.

6   Jared Sparks, *Lives of Alexander Wilson and Captain John Smith*, in *The Library of American Biography*, vol. 2 (Boston: Hilliard, Gray, and Co., 1839), 240.

7   Philip Young, "The Mother of Us All: Pocahontas Reconsidered," *Kenyon Review* 24 (Summer 1962), 412.

8   Young, 413.

9   Beyond the inherent romantic appeal of the tale and the explanations suggested by Young, there are any number of other theories about the continued popularity of this story. For instance, when Pocahontas mediates between the violence of her father and his intended victim she in effect performs the first successful appeal for clemency in American legal history. Justice is done in the end in that Smith, who, under some duress, had actually been guilty of killing a number of Indians, continues to be a prisoner and is given some menial tasks to perform, but it is tempered with mercy. Pocahontas wins her case, and her success as an advocate can be seen as an exemplar to those who would view the American legal system as typically just and temperate.

Indeed, Pocahontas might also be viewed as an American Athena figure in that she, like the goddess at the end of the *Oresteia*, was able to stop (if only briefly) what would have been a continuing cycle of revenge between the colonists and the Indians and to redirect what had appeared to be uncontrollable violence. One could argue that her action was even more impressive than that of the goddess, because to accomplish it she literally had to put her own life on the line.

The Rescue might also be seen to represent an aspect of the "Frog Prince" fairy tale. Barry Gordon and Richard Meth point out that the frog (in this case Smith) "only becomes a prince when the princess defies her father and acts autonomously. Out of her strength to be herself comes the Frog's chance to be liberated." See their "Men as Husbands," in Richard L. Meth and Robert S. Pasick, *Men in Therapy: The Challenge of Change* (New York: Guilford Press, 1990), 56.

10 Deloria, 11. See his discussion of "Indian Princesses" on pages 11–12.

11 Deloria, 11.

12 John Esten Cooke, *My Lady Pokahontas* (Boston: Houghton Mifflin, 1885). For a detailed discussion of Nehlig's *Pocahontas and John Smith*, see Linda Joans Gibbs, *One Hundred and Fifty Years of American Painting: An Exhibition from the Permanent Collection of the Museum of Art at Brigham Young University* (Provo, Utah: Brigham Young University Press, 1994).

13 See Jenkins for discussions of many of these texts. See also, William Rasmussen and Robert S. Tilton, *Pocahontas: The Life and Legend*, Forthcoming publication of the Virginia Historical Society, Richmond, 1994.

14 William Strachey, *The Historie of Travaile into Virginia Britannia* (1612; reprint, London: Printed for the Hakluyt Society, 1849), 65. The reference to her "first husband" Kocoum is on page 54.

15 Carl Sandburg, "Cool Tombs," in *Cornhuskers* (New York: Holt, 1918), 120; Vachel Lindsay, "Our Mother Pocahontas," in *The Chinese Nightingale and Other Poems* (New York: Macmillan, 1917), 39–42.

16 Hart Crane, "Powhatan's Daughter," in *The Bridge* (New York: Liveright, 1970) 9–29 (originally published in 1930); William Carlos Williams, *In The American Grain* (New York: New Directions, 1956), 78 (originally published in 1925). For a useful discussion of Lindsay, Crane, and Williams, see Michael Castro, *Interpreting the Indian* (Albuquerque: University of New Mexico Press, 1983), 47–69.

17 David Garnett, *Pocahontas, or The Nonparell of Virginia* (London: Chatto & Windus, 1972); John Barth, *The Sot-Weed Factor* (New York: Doubleday, 1960); Neil Young, "Pocahontas" (Silver Fiddle-BMI, 1977). One should also consider the lyrics of the fourth verse and chorus of John Davenport and Eddie Cooley's "Fever," which discusses the romantic entangling of John Smith and Pocahontas. John Davenport and Eddie Cooley, "Fever" (Fort Knox Music Inc. and Trio Music Company, Inc., 1956).

18 Peter Conn has recently reminded me of the opening of the film *Ruggles of Red Gap* (1935), in which the humorous exchange between Ruggles and the earl of Burnstead is dependent on the audience's familiarity with the story of historical Pocahontas. And I would be remiss if I did not also make mention of the wonderful revisionist portrayal of Pocahontas by Christina Ricci as Wednesday Addams in the recent film, *Addams Family Values*.

19 Larson, Charles R., "The Children of Pocahontas," in *American Indian Fiction* (Albuquerque: University of New Mexico Press, 1978), 32–3.

20 Paula Gunn Allen, *C'Koy'u, Old Woman*, in *Skins and Bones: Poems 1979–87* (Albuquerque: West End Press, 1988), 1–23; Gerald Vizenor, *The Heirs of Columbus* (Hanover: Published by University Press of New England [Wesleyan University Press], 1991), esp. 93–117.

21 Larson, 27.

22 Annette Kolodny, *The Lay of the Land* (Chapel Hill: University of North Carolina Press, 1975), 5.

23 Anne Norton, *Alternative Americas: A Reading of Antebellum Political Culture* (Chicago: University of Chicago Press, 1986), 148.

24 Ron Scapp, "Lack and Violence: Towards a Speculative Sociology of the Homeless," *Practice* 6, 2 (Fall 1988), 39.

25 J. Martin Evans, *America: The View from Europe* (New York: Norton, 1976), 121.

26 Ford Madox Ford, *The Good Soldier* (New York: Bantam, 1991), 69. (The *Pocahontas* is mentioned a number of times thereafter.) I must thank

Thomas Moser, Sr., of Stanford University for reminding me of the fictional existence of this vessel.

27 Michelle Cliff, *No Telephone to Heaven* (New York: Dutton, 1987), 136–7. (Page numbers in the text refer to this edition.) I must thank Judith Raiskin of the University of California at Santa Barbara for calling this novel to my attention.

28 Arturo Islas, *Migrant Souls* (New York: Avon, 1990). (Page numbers in the text refer to this edition.)

29 As this book goes to press, we look forward to two events that will mark the quadricentennial of Pocahontas's birth. In October 1994, the Virginia Historical Society in Richmond will open an exhibition entitled "The Life and Legend of Pocahontas." This exhibit will examine what we know about the historical Pocahontas and her world, display reproductions of her image and scenes from her narrative, and discuss the importance of the figure of Pocahontas in Virginian and American culture.

In the summer of 1995, we will see the release of what almost certainly will become the most popular interpretation of the Pocahontas narrative in the twentieth century: Walt Disney Studios's animated feature, *Pocahontas*. While its producers are apparently going to some pains to reproduce Powhatan Indian life as it would have been in her day, they are also, as so many artists have done before, taking a number of liberties in their attempts to fill in the gaps in her biography. It will be interesting to see whether this film inspires a renewed interest in the historical Pocahontas, or whether the power of the widescreen image is such that it overwhelms the narrative upon which it is, of necessity, loosely based.

30 Karen Robertson, "Pocahontas at the Masque," A paper delivered at the meeting of the Shakespeare Association of America, Philadelphia, April 12, 1990.

31 Robertson, 30.

BIBLIOGRAPHY

Primary Sources

I. Seventeenth Century

Alexander, William. *The Mapp and Description of New-England*. London, 1630.

Bradford, William. *History of Plymouth Plantation*. Ed. Charles Deane. Massachusetts Historical Society Collections, ser. 4, vol. 3. Boston: Massachusetts Historical Society, 1856.

Of Plimoth Plantation. Boston: Wright & Potter, 1898.

Dale, Thomas. "To the R. and my most esteemed *friend Mr.D.M. at his house at F.Ch.* in London." Reprinted in Hamor, *A True Discourse*, 51–9. (Originally written in 1614.)

Fuller, Thomas. *The Worthies of England*. Ed. John Freeman. London: Allen & Unwin, 1952. (Originally published in 1662.)

Hamor, Ralph. *A True Discourse of the Present State of Virginia*. London: Printed by John Beale for William Welby. 1615; reprint, Richmond: Virginia State Library Press, 1957. Intro. by A. L. Rowse.

Hening, William Waller. *Statutes at Large; Being a Compilation of All the Laws of Virginia from the First Session of the Legislature in the Year 1619*. Richmond, 1810–23.

Proceedings of the First Assembly of Virginia, 1619. Intro. by George Bancroft. In *Collections of New York Historical Society*, 2nd series, vol. 3, part I (New York: D. Appleton, 1857), 329–58.

Records of the Governor and Company of the Massachusetts Bay in New England. Ed. Nathaniel B. Shurtleff. Boston: William White, 1853.

Rolfe, John. Letter to Sir Thomas Dale. Reprinted in Hamor, *A True Discourse*, 61–9. (Originally written in 1614.)

Rowlandson, Mary. *The Soveraignty and Goodness of God, Together with the Faithfulness of His Promises Displayed: Being a Narrative of the Captivity and Restauration of Mrs. Mary Rowlandson*. Cambridge, Mass.: Samuel Green, 1682.

Slotkin, Richard, and James K. Folsom, eds. *So Dreadfull a Judgment: Puritan Responses to King Philip's War, 1676–1677*. Middletown, Conn.: Wesleyan University Press, 1978.

Smith, John. *The Complete Works of Captain John Smith*. Ed. Philip L. Barbour. 3 vols. Chapel Hill: University of North Carolina Press, 1986. The texts that I use in this project are vol. 1: *A True Relation* (1608); *The Proceedings of the English Colony in Virginia* (1612); *New England's Trials* (1622); vol. 2: *The Generall Historie of Virginia* (1624); vol. 3: *The True Travels* (1630).

A True Relation, ed. Charles Deane. Boston: Wiggins & Hunt, 1866.

Strachey, William. *The Historie of Travaile Into Virginia Britannia.* Ed. R. H. Major. London: Printed for the Hakluyt Society, 1849. (Originally written in 1612.)

    Lawes Divine, Morall and Martiall. Ed. David H. Flaherty. Charlottesville: University of Virginia Press, 1969. (Originally published in 1612.)

Symonds, William. *Virginia. A Sermon Preached at White-Chappell, In the Presence of the Adventurers and Planters for Virginia.* London: Printed by I. Windet for Eleazar Edgar and William Welby, 1609.

Wharton, Henry. *The Life of John Smith, English Soldier.* Trans. (from the Latin) with an introductory essay by Laura Polanyi Striker. Chapel Hill: University of North Carolina Press, 1957. (Originally published in 1685.)

Whitaker, Alexander. *Good News From Virginia.* Imprinted by Felix Kyngston for William Welby, 1613.

    "To my verie deere and loving *Cosen* M.G. *Minister of the* B.F. in London." 1614; reprinted in Hamor . . . *A True Discourse,* 59–61.

Wingfield, Edward Maria. *A Discourse of Virginia,* c. 1608. Ed. Charles Deane. Transactions and Collections of the American Antiquarian Society, vol. 4, 67–103. Worcester, Mass.: American Antiquarian Society, 1860.

II. Eighteenth Century

Barlow, Joel. *The Vision of Columbus.* Hartford: Printed by Hudson and Goodwin for the author, 1787.

Belknap, Jeremy. *American Biography.* Published According to Act of Congress. Boston: Printed by Isaiah Thomas and Ebenezer T. Andrews, 1794.

Beverley, Robert. *The History and Present State of Virginia.* Ed. Louis B. Wright. Chapel Hill: University of North Carolina Press for The Institute of Early American History and Culture, 1947. (Originally published in 1705.)

Brown, Charles Brockden. *Edgar Huntly, or, Memoirs of a Sleepwalker.* Ed. David Lee Brown. New York: Macmillan, 1928. (Orig. published in 1799.)

Byrd, William. *The History of the Dividing Line.* In *The Prose Works of William Byrd of Westover,* ed. Louis B. Wright. Cambridge, Mass.: Harvard University Press (Belknap Press), 1966, 160–1. (Originally published in 1738.)

Castiglioni, Luigi. *Viaggio.* Ed. and trans. Antonio Pace. Syracuse: Syracuse University Press, 1983. (Originally published in 1790.)

Chastellux, Marquis de. *Travels in North America in the Years 1780, 1781, and 1782.* 2 Vols. Translated from the French by an English Gentleman. London: G. G. J. and J. Robinson, 1787. Reprint: New York: New York Times and Arno Press, 1968.

    Travels in North America in the Years 1780, 1781, and 1782. 2 vols. A revised translation, with introduction and notes by Howard C. Rice, Jr. Chapel Hill: University of North Carolina Press, 1963. (Originally published in Paris in 1786.)

Fontaine, Peter. Letter to Moses Fontaine, March 30, 1757. Reprinted in Ann Maury, *Memoirs of a Huguenot Family.* New York: Putnam, 1872, 349.

Jefferson, Thomas. The Declaration of Independence. In *The Life and Selected Writings of Thomas Jefferson.* Adrienne Koch and William Peden, eds. New York: Random House, 1944, 22–8.

    Letter to Benjamin Hawkins, February 18, 1803. In *Writings of Jefferson.* Vol. 10, 369–70.

    Notes on the State of Virginia. New York: Harper & Row, 1964. (Originally published in 1785.)

"To Captain Hendrick, the Delawares, Mohicans, and Munries." In *Writings of Jefferson*. Vol. 16, 450–4.

The Writings of Thomas Jefferson. Andrew A. Lipscomb and Albert E. Bergh, eds. 20 Volumes. Washington, D.C.: The Thomas Jefferson Memorial Association, 1903–4.

Keith, Sir William. *The History of the British Plantations in America*. London: Printed at the expense of the Society for the encouragement of Learning, by S. Richardson, 1738.

Kimber, Edward. "A Short Account of the British Plantations in America." *London Magazine* 24 (July 1755), 307–12.

Latrobe, Benjamin. *The Virginia Journals of Benjamin Latrobe, 1795–1798*. Ed. Edward C. Carter II, et al. New Haven: Yale University Press for Maryland Historical Society, 1977.

Lawson, John. *A New Voyage to Carolina*. Ed. Hugh Talmage Lefler. Chapel Hill: University of North Carolina Press, 1967. (Originally published in 1709.)

Oldmixon, John. *The British Empire in America*. London: Printed for John Nicholson at the King's Arms in Little Britain, Benjamin Tooke at the Middle-Temple Gate, Fleetstreet, and Richard Parker and Ralph Smith Under the Piazza of the Royal Exchange, 1708.

The British Empire in America. London: Printed for J. Brotherton, J. Clarke in Duck-Lane, A. Ward, J. Clarke at the Royal Exchange, C. Hitch, J. Osbourn, E. Wicksteed, C. Bathurst, Timothy Saunders and T. Harris, 1741. Reprint, New York: Kelley, 1969.

Randolph, Edmund. *History of Virginia*. Ed. Arthur H. Shaffer. Charlottesville: University of Virginia Press, 1970. (Originally written c. 1809–13.)

"Resolution on Unclaimed Western Lands," March 3, 1791. Reprinted in *Legislative Histories*. Eds. Charlene Bangs Bickford and Helen E. Veit. Baltimore: Johns Hopkins University Press, 1986. Vol. 6, 2127–8.

Robertson, William. *The History of America, Books IX and X: Containing the History of Virginia to the Year 1688; and of New England to the year 1652*. Philadelphia: Printed from the London edition by James Humphries, 1799. Reprinted in *The History of the Discovery and Settlement of America*. New York: J. & J. Harper, 1828.

Sewall, Samuel. *The Diary of Samuel Sewall, 1674–1729*. Ed. M. Halsey Thomas. New York: Farrar, Straus & Giroux, 1973.

Smith, Samuel Stanhope. *An Essay on the Causes of the Variety of Complexion and Figure in the Human Species*. Ed. Winthrop D. Jordan. Cambridge, Mass.: Harvard University Press (Belknap Press). 1965.

Stith, William. *The History of the First Discovery and Settlement of Virginia*. Williamsburg: Printed by William Parks, 1747.

Weems, Mason Locke. Letter to Mathew Carey, January 20, 1797. In Skeel, ed. *Weems*. Vol. 2, 70.

III. Nineteenth Century

Adams, Henry. "Captain John Smith." *North American Review* 104, 214 (January 1867), 1–30.

Adams, John Quincy. *Memoirs of John Quincy Adams*. Ed. Charles Francis Adams. Philadelphia: Lippincott, 1876. Vol. 9.

"Oration on the anniversary Festival of the sons of the Pilgrims. Plymouth, Dec. 22, 1802." Reprinted in Jedidiah Morse, *A Report To The Secretary of War Of The United States, On Indian Affairs*. New Haven: S. Converse, 1822, 281.

Allen, William. *An American Biographical and Historical Dictionary.* Cambridge, Mass.: William Hilliard, 1809.

"American Historical Paintings." *New-York Mirror* 14, 36 (March 4, 1837), 288.

Baldwin, Ebenezer. *Observations on the Physical, Intellectual, and Moral Qualities of Our Colored Population.* New Haven: L. H. Young, 1834.

Baldwin, Joseph G. *The Flush Times of Alabama and Mississippi.* Intro. William A. Owens. New York: Sagamore Press, 1957. (Originally published in 1853.)

Bandelier, Adolphe F. *The Unpublished Letters of Adolphe F. Bandelier.* El Paso: Carl Hertzog, 1942.

Barber, John Warner. *Interesting Events in the History of the United States.* New-Haven: J. W. Barber, 1829.

Barker, James Nelson. *The Indian Princess; or, La Belle Sauvage.* Philadelphia: T. & G. Palmer, 1808. Reprinted in *The Romantic Indian.* Ed. Charles M. Lombard. Delmar, N.Y.: Scholars' Facsimiles and Reprints, 1981. Vol. 2, 1–74.

Barlow, Joel. *The Columbiad.* Reprinted in *The Works of Joel Barlow.* 2 vols. Facsimile, intro. William K. Bottorff and Arthur L. Ford. Vol. 2. Gainesville: Scholars' Facsimiles and Reprints, 1970. (Originally published in 1807.)

Barnes, Charlotte. *The Forest Princess, or Two Centuries Ago* in *Plays, Prose, and Poetry.* Philadelphia: E. H. Butler, 1848, 145–270.

Bird, Robert Montgomery. *Nick of the Woods.* Ed. Curtis Dahl. New Haven: College and University Press, 1967. (Originally published in 1837.)

Brandburn, George. "Remarks," in "House Report, No. 7, Commonwealth of Massachusetts, House of Representatives, January 19, 1841. Quoted in James Hugo Johnston, *Race Relations in Virginia and Miscegenation in the South.* Amherst: University of Massachusetts Press, 1970. 338.

Brougham, John. *Po-ca-hon-tas, or The Gentle Savage.* Reprinted in *Dramas From the American Theatre, 1762–1909.* Ed. Richard Moody. Cleveland: World, 1966, 397–421. (Originally staged in 1855.)

Bryant, William Cullen. "The Prairies." In *The Complete Poems of William Cullen Bryant.* Ed. H. C. Edwards. New York: Stokes, 1894. 131.

Burk, John. *The History of Virginia From Its First Settlement to The Present Day.* Vol. 1. Petersburg, Va.: Dickson & Pescud, 1804.

Caruthers, William A. *The Cavaliers of Virginia.* New York: Harper & Brothers, 1834. Reprint, Ridgewood, N.J.: Gregg, 1968.

Chapman, John Gadsby. *The Picture Of The Baptism Of Pocahontas.* Washington: Peter Force, 1840.

Chateaubriand, François-René de. *Atala / René.* Trans. Irving Putter. Berkeley and Los Angeles: University of California Press, 1952. (*Atala* was originally published in 1801, *René* in 1802.)

  Chateaubriand's Travels in America. Trans. and intro. Richard Switzer. Lexington: University of Kentucky Press, 1969. (Originally published in 1828.)

Child, Lydia Maria. *An Appeal for the Indians.* New York: W. P. Tomlinson, 1868.

  Hobomok, A Tale of Early Times. Ed. Carolyn L. Karcher. New Brunswick, N.J.: Rutgers University Press, 1986. (Originally published in 1824.)

Cooke, John Esten. "A Dream of the Cavaliers." *Harper's New Monthly Magazine* 22, 128 (January 1861), 252–4.

  My Lady Pokahontas. Boston: Houghton Mifflin, 1885.

"Wanderings on the Banks of the York." *Southern Literary Messenger* 26, 26 (June 1858), 457–65.

Cooper, James Fenimore. *The Last of the Mohicans.* New York: New American Library, 1962. (Originally published in 1826.)

The Letters and Journals of James Fenimore Cooper. 6 vols. Ed. James Franklin Beard. Cambridge, Mass.: Harvard University Press (Belknap Press), 1960.

The Pioneers. New York: New American Library, 1964. (Originally published in 1823.)

The Prairie. New York: New American Library, 1964. (Originally published in 1827.)

The Spy. New York: Heritage Press, 1963. (Originally published in 1821.)

The Wept of Wish Ton-Wish. Philadelphia: Carey, Lea & Carey, 1829. First American edition.

The Wept of Wish-Ton-Wish. Text of the revised edition. Intro. by Richard Beale Davis. Columbus, Ohio: Merrill, 1970.

Crawford, William H. "Statement of March 13, 1816." Reprinted in *Documents of United States Indian Policy.* Ed. Francis Paul Prucha. Lincoln: University of Nebraska Press, 1975. 26–8.

Croly, David Goodman. *Miscegenation: The Theory of the Blending of the Races, Applied to the American White Man and Negro.* New York, 1863; reprint, London: Trübner & Co., 1864.

Croswell, Joseph. *A New World Planted.* Boston: Gilbert and Dean, 1802.

Custis, George Washington Parke. *Pocahontas, or The Settlers of Virginia* (1830). Reprinted in *Representative American Plays from 1767 to the Present,* 7th ed. Ed. Arthur Hobson Quinn. New York: Appleton-Century-Crofts, 1953. 165–92.

Davis, John. *Captain Smith and Princess Pocahontas.* Philadelphia: T. C. Plowman, 1805.

The Farmer of New-Jersey, or, A Picture of Domestic Life. New York: Furman and Loudon's Type, 1800.

The First Settlers of Virginia, An Historical Novel. New York: Printed for I. Riley and Co. by Southwick & Hardcastle, 1805.

Travels Of Four Years And A Half In The United States Of America During 1798, 1799, 1800, 1801, and 1802. Ed. A. J. Morrison. New York: Holt, 1909. (Originally published in 1803.)

The First Settlers of Virginia, An Historical Novel. 2nd. ed. New York: Printed for I. Riley and Co., 1806.

Deffebach, Lewis. *Oolaita; or, The Indian Heroine. A Melo Drama in Three Acts.* Philadelphia: Printed for the author, 1821.

"The Difference of Race between the Northern and Southern People." *Southern Literary Messenger* 30 (June 1860), 401–9.

Eastburn, James Wallis, and His Friend [Robert Sands]. *Yamoyden, A Tale of the Wars of King Philip.* New York: Published by James Eastburn; Clayton & Kingsland, Printers, 1820.

"Editor's Table." *Southern Literary Messenger* 28 (May 1859), 395–7.

Frost, John. *Pictorial Life of Andrew Jackson.* Hartford: Wm. Jas. Hamersley, 1846.

Gardiner, W. H. Rev. of *The Spy,* by James Fenimore Cooper, *North American Review* 15, 36 (n.s. 6, 11), (July 1822), 250–82.

Hall, James. *A Memoir of the Public Services of William Henry Harrison.* Philadelphia: Key & Biddle, 1836.

Sketches of History, Life and Manners in the West. 2 vols. Philadelphia: Harrison Hall, 1835.

Hawthorne, Nathaniel. *The French and Italian Notebooks.* Ed. Thomas Woodson. Columbus: Ohio State University Press, 1980.

The Scarlet Letter. Eds. Sculley Bradley, Richmond Groom Beatty, E. Hudson
Long, and Seymour Gross. New York: Norton, 1978. (Originally published in 1850.)

Henry, William Wirt. "The Rescue of Captain John Smith by Pocahontas."
Potters American Monthly 4–5 (1875), 523–8, 591–2.

"The Settlement at Jamestown, with Particular Reference to the Late Attacks upon Captain Smith, Pocahontas, and John Rolfe." *Proceedings of
the Virginia Historical Society.* Richmond: Published for the Society, February 24, 1882, 10–62.

"A Defense of Captain John Smith." *Magazine of American History* 25
(1891), 300–13.

"Did Percy Denounce Smith's History of Virginia?" *Virginia Magazine of
History and Biography* 1 (1893–4), 473–6.

Hillhouse, William. *Pocahontas; A Proclamation: With Plates.* New Haven: J.
Clyme, 1820.

"The Indians in American Art." *The Crayon* 3 (January 1856), 28.

Irving, Washington. "Traits of Indian Character" and "Philip of Pokanoket." In *The Sketch Book of Geoffrey Crayon, Gent.* New York: New American Library, 1981. 272–82. (Originally published in 1819.)

Kennedy, John Pendleton. *Horse-shoe Robinson; A Tale of the Tory Ascendency.*
Philadelphia: Carey, Lea & Blanchard, 1835.

Swallow Barn; or, A Sojourn in the Old Dominion. 2 vols. Philadelphia: Carey
and Lea, 1832.

Swallow Barn. Intro. by Lucinda H. MacKethen. Baton Rouge: Louisiana
State University Press, 1986. (This text is based on Kennedy's revised
1851 edition.)

Knapp, Samuel Lorenzo. *Lectures on American Literature.* New York: Elam Bliss,
1829. Reprinted in *American Cultural History, 1607–1829,* ed. Richard
Beale Davis and Ben Harris McClary. Gainesville, Fla. Scholars' Facsimiles & Reprints, 1961. 145.

Landscape [pseud.]. "Mr. Chapman's Picture – The Baptism of Pocahontas." *Daily National Intelligencer* 28, 8690 (December 21, 1840), 3.

Latrobe, Benjamin. "Account of the descendants of Pocahontas, daughter
of Powhatan, king or chief of the tribe of Powhatan, who inhabited the
country about the falls of the James River, Virginia." *Proceedings of the
American Philosophical Society* 22 (1885), 333.

"The Launch of the Powhatan." *Virginia Historical Register* 3, 1 (1850), 111.

Lincoln, Abraham. "Address Delivered at the Dedication of the Cemetery
at Gettysburg." In *The Norton Anthology of American Literature.* Eds., Nina
Baym et al. 2nd ed. New York: Norton, 1985. Vol. 1, 1464–5 (Originally
delivered in 1863.)

Marshall, John. Publisher's Preface. In *The Life of George Washington.* Vol. 1.
New York: Wise, 1925. (Originally published 1804–7.)

Maury, Ann. *Memoirs of a Huguenot Family.* New York: Putnam, 1872.

McKenney, Thomas, and James Hall. *The History of the Indian Tribes of North
America.* 3 vols. Philadelphia: Daniel Rice & J. G. Clarke, 1836–44.

Meade, William. *Old Churches, Ministers and Families Of Virginia.* Philadelphia:
Lippincott, 1891. (Originally published in 1857.)

Melville, Herman. *The Confidence-Man.* Eds. Harrison Hayford, Hershel Parker, and G. Thomas Tanselle. Evanston and Chicago: Northwestern University Press and Newberry Library, 1984. (Originally published in
1857.)

Moby-Dick or, The Whale. Ed. Charles Feidelson, Jr. Indianapolis: Bobbs-Merrill, 1964. (Originally published in 1851.)

Pierre or The Ambiguities. Eds. Harrison Hayford, Hershel Parker, and G. Thomas Tanselle. Evanston and Chicago: Northwestern University Press and Newberry Library, 1971. (Originally published in 1852.)

White-Jacket or The World in a Man-of-War. Eds. Harrison Hayford, Hershel Parker, and G. Thomas Tanselle. Evanston and Chicago: Northwestern University Press and Newberry Library, 1970. (Originally published in 1850.)

"Mr. Chapman's Painting Of the Baptism of Pocahontas." *Daily National Intelligencer* 28, 8673 (December 1, 1840), 3.

Morse, Edward Lind. *Samuel F. B. Morse: His Letters and Journals*. Boston: Houghton Mifflin Company, 1914, Vol. 2.

Morse, Jedidiah. *A Report to the Secretary of War of the United States, on Indian Affairs*. New Haven: S. Converse, 1822.

Mosby, Mary Webster [Mrs. M. M. Webster]. *Pocahontas: A Legend*. Philadelphia: H. Hooker, 1840.

Official Records of the Union and Confederate Navies in the War of the Rebellion. Published under the direction of The Hon. H. A. Herbert. Secretary of the Navy, by Lieut. Commander Richard Rush, U.S.N. and Mr. Robert H. Woods. Ser. 1, vol. 4. Washington: U.S. Government Printing Office, 1896. 236.

[O'Sullivan, John L.] "Annexation." *United States Magazine and Democratic Review* 17 (July / August 1845), 5–10.

"The True Title." Editorial. *New York Morning News* (December 27, 1845).

Owen, Robert Dale. *Pocahontas: A Historical Drama*. New York: George Dearborn, 1837.

"Paintings For The Rotundo." *Report of the Select Committee to the House of Representatives*. H.R. Rep. No. 294, 24th Congress, 2nd Session, February 28, 1837. Washington, D.C.: Blair & Rives.

Palfrey, John Gorham. *History of New England*. 3 vols. Boston: Little, Brown, 1899. (Originally published in 5 volumes, 1858–1890.)

Paulding, James Kirke. *Koningsmarke, the Long Finne*. Ed. Daniel A. Wells. Schenectady, NY: Union College Press, 1988. (Originally published in 1823.)

Letters From the South. vols. New York: Harper & Brothers, 1835. (Originally published in 1817.)

The Letters of James Kirke Paulding. Ed. Ralph M. Aderman. Madison: University of Wisconsin Press, 1962.

Pearson Emily Clemens [Emily Catharine Pierson]. *Jamie Parker, The Fugitive*. Hartford: Brockett, Fuller, and Co., 1851.

Pearson, Emily Clemens [Pocahontas, pseud.]. *Cousin Franck's Household, or, Scenes in the Old Dominion*. 4th ed. Boston: Upham, Ford and Olmstead, 1853; reprint, Freeport, N.Y.: Books for Libraries, 1972.

The Poor White; or, The Rebel Conscript. Boston: Graves and Young, 1864.

Ruth's Sacrifice. Boston: C.H. Pearson, 1863.

Pickett, James Chamberlayne. *The Memory of Pocahontas Vindicated Against the Erroneous Judgment of the Hon. Waddy Thompson*. Washington: Printed by J. and G. S. Gideon, 1847.

"Preparations in the Capitol – Paintings in the Rotunda." Letter from a "correspondent," dated November 30, 1840. *New York Herald* 6, 64, whole no. 1629, (December 3, 1840), 2.

Prescott, William Hickling. *History of the Conquest of Mexico*. Ed. John Foster Kirk 3 vols. Denver: Tandy, Wheeler, 1873. (Originally published in 1843.)

"The President and the Union." *New Orleans Bee* (December 10, 1860). Reprinted in Southern Editorials on Secession. Ed. Dwight Lowell Dumond. New York: Century, 1931. 315–16.

"Presidential Election." *Daily National Intelligencer* 28, 8673 (December 1, 1840), 3.

Register of Debates in Congress. 23rd Congress, 2nd Session (December 1, 1834 – March 3, 1835), vol. 11, pt. 1. Washington, D.C.: Gales & Seaton, 1835.

Rev. of Samuel G. Drake, *Biography and History of the Indians of North America.* North American Review 44, (n.s. 35), 95 (April 1837), 301–34.

Rev. of *Gleanings in Europe*, by James Fenimore Cooper. North American Review 46, (n.s. 37), 98 (January 1838), 3.

Rev. of *The Last of the Mohicans,* by James Fenimore Cooper. United States Literary Gazette 4 (May 1826), 87–94.

Rev. of *The Wept of Wish-Ton-Wish.* Southern Review (February 1830), 207–26.

Robertson, Wyndham. "The Marriage of Pocahontas." *Southern Literary Messenger* 31, 6 (July 1859), 81–91.

   Pocahontas alias Matoaka and Her Descendants. Richmond: J. W. Randolph & English, 1887.

Scott, Walter. *Ivanhoe.* London: Penguin Books, 1986. (Originally published in 1820.)

Seaver, James A. *The Life of Mary Jemison.* Reprint of 5th ed. Jersey Shore, Pa.: Zebrowski, 1991. (Originally published in 1824.)

Sedgwick, Catharine Maria. *Hope Leslie, or Early Times in the Massachusetts.* Ed. Mary Kelley. New Brunswick, N.J.: Rutgers University Press, 1987. (Originally published in 1827.)

Shourds, Thomas. *History and Genealogy of Fenwick's Colony.* Reprint, Baltimore: Genealogical Publishing, 1976. (Originally published in 1876.)

Simms, William Gilmore. *The Life of Capt. John Smith.* New York: Geo. F. Cooledge & Brother, 1846.

   The Partisan: A Tale of the Revolution. New York: Harper & Brothers, 1835.

   "Pocahontas: A Subject For The Historical Painter." In *Views and Reviews in American Literature, History and Fiction.* New York: John Wiley, 1848, 88–101. (Originally published in *Southern and Western Magazine* 2 (September 1845), 145–54.)

Smythe, Clem T. "The Burial of Pocahontas." *Virginia Historical Register* 2 (1849), 187–9.

Sparks, Jared. *Lives of Alexander Wilson and Captain John Smith.* In *The Library of American Biography.* Vol. 2. Boston: Hilliard, Gray, and Co., 1839. 239–41.

Spencer, Jesse Ames. *History of the United States from the Earliest Period to the Administration of President Johnson.* New York: Johnson, Fry and Company, 1866.

Stephens, Ann S. *Malaeska: The Indian Wife of the White Hunter.* Reprint, New York: Day, 1929. (First published as a novel in 1860.)

Stone, John Augustus. *Metamora; or The Last of the Wampanoags.* In *Favorite American Plays of the Nineteenth Century.* Ed. Barrett H. Clark. Princeton: Princeton University Press, 1943.

Thompson, Waddy. *Recollections of Mexico.* New York: Wiley & Putnam, 1846.

Timrod, Henry. "Ethnogenesis." In *Poems of Henry Timrod.* Richmond: B. F. Johnson, 1901. 150–54.

Trollope, Frances. *Domestic Manners of the Americans.* Ed. Donald Smalley. New York: Random House, 1949. (Originally published in 1832.)

"The True Question: A Contest for the Supremacy of Race, as Between the

Saxon Puritan of the North, and the Norman of the South.'' *Southern Literary Messenger* 30 (July 1861), 19–27.

U.S. House of Representatives Executive Document no. 315 (41st Congress, 2nd Session). In Charles E. Fairman, *Art and Artists of the Capitol of the United States of America*. Washington, D.C.: U.S. Government Printing Office, 1927, 245.

''W.'' ''Chapman's Painting.'' *Daily National Intelligencer* 28, 8686 (December 16, 1840), 3.

Waldron, William Watson. *Pocahontas, Princess of Virginia: and Other Poems*. New York: Dean & Trevett, 1841.

Weems, Mason Locke. *Mason Locke Weems, His Works and Ways*. Ed. Emily Ellsworth (Ford) Skeel. New York, 1929; Printed for the Plimpton Press, Norwood, MA.

   The Life of Washington. Ed. Marcus Cunliffe. Cambridge, Mass.: Harvard University Press (Belknap Press), 1962. (Cunliffe uses the text of the ninth edition – Philadelphia: Mathew Carey, 1809.)

The Wept of Wish-Ton-Wish. A Drama, in Two Acts, From J. Fennimore [*sic*] Cooper's Novel of the Same Name. New York: Samuel French, n.d. [1856?].

Whitcomb, Samuel Jr. ''Copy of an Interview with Thomas Jefferson by My Father, the Late Samuel Whitcomb, Formerly of Dorchester Mass., June 1, 1824.'' Jefferson Papers, Alderman Library, University of Virginia, Charlottesville, Va.

Whittier, John Greenleaf. Rev. of *Cousin Franck's Household*, by [Emily Clemens Pearson]. (Her name is not mentioned in the review.) *National Era* 7, 319 (February 10, 1853), 1.

Windle, Mary Jane, *Life At the White Sulpher Springs*. Philadelphia: Lippincott, 1857.

Wirt, William. *The Letters of the British Spy*. Richmond: Printed by Samuel Pleasants, Jr., 1803. (Originally published in the *Virginia Argus*, August/September 1803.)

   Sketches of the Life and Character of Patrick Henry. 15th ed. Hartford: Silas Andrus & Son, 1832.

IV. Twentieth Century

Acts and Joint Resolutions of the General Assembly of the Commonwealth of Virginia. Chapter 318. Richmond: Department of Purchases and Supply, Commonwealth of Virginia, 1968.

Adams, Henry. *The Education of Henry Adams*. Boston: Houghton Mifflin, 1918.

   The Letters of Henry Adams. Ed. J. C. Levenson et al. Cambridge, Mass.: Harvard University Press (Belknap Press), 1982.

Allen, Paula Gunn. *C'Koy'u, Old Woman*. In *Skins and Bones: Poems 1979–87*. Albuquerque: West End Press, 1988, 1–23.

Barth, John. *The Sot-Weed Factor*. New York: Doubleday, 1960.

Campbell, William P. The William P. Campbell Papers. Archives of American Art, Smithsonian Institution, Washington D.C.

Cliff, Michelle. *No Telephone to Heaven*. New York: Dutton, 1987.

Crane, Hart. *The Bridge*. New York: Liveright, 1970. (Originally published in 1930.)

Davenport, John, and Eddie Cooley. "Fever." Fort Knox Music, Inc., and Trio Music Company, Inc., 1956.

Ford, Ford Madox. *The Good Soldier.* New York: Bantam, 1991. (Originally published in 1915.)

Garnett, David. *Pocahontas, or the Nonpareil of Virginia.* London: Chatto & Windus, 1972. (Originally published in 1933.)

Islas, Arturo. *Migrant Souls.* New York: Avon, 1990.

Lindsay, Vachel. "Our Mother Pocahontas." In *The Chinese Nightingale and Other Poems.* New York: Macmillan, 1917. 39–42.

Sandburg, Carl. "Cool Tombs." In *Cornhuskers.* New York: Holt, 1918.

Vizenor, Gerald. *The Heirs of Columbus.* Hanover: Published by University Press of New England (Wesleyan University Press), 1991.

Williams, William Carlos. In *The American Grain.* New York: New Directions, 1956. (Originally published in 1925.)

Young, Neil. "Pocahontas." Silver Fiddle-BMI, 1977.

Secondary Sources

Abrams, Ann Uhry. "The Pocahontas Paradox: Southern Pride, Yankee Voyeurism, Ethnic Identity or Feminine Heroics." Paper delivered at the annual meeting of the American Studies Association, October 1988.

Arpad, Joseph J. "Between Folklore and Literature: Popular Culture as Anomaly." *Journal of Popular Culture* 9, 2 (Fall 1975), 403–23.

Ayres, B. Drummond, Jr. "Last Stand Nears for Tiny Indian Tribe's Identity." *New York Times,* January 16, 1989, natl. ed., 8.

Baigell, Matthew. "Territory, Race, Religion: Images of Manifest Destiny." *Smithsonian Studies in American Art* 4, 3–4 (Summer / Fall 1990), 3–21.

Barbour, Philip L. *Pocahontas and Her World.* Boston: Houghton Mifflin, 1970.
The Three Worlds of Captain John Smith. Boston: Houghton Mifflin, 1964.

Bell, Michael Davitt. "History and Romance in Catharine Sedgwick's *Hope Leslie.*" *American Quarterly* 22, 2 (Summer 1970), 213–21.

Bercovitch, Sacvan. *The American Jeremiad.* Madison: University of Wisconsin Press, 1978.

Bercovitch, Sacvan, and Myra Jehlen, eds. *Ideology and Classic American Literature.* Cambridge: Cambridge University Press, 1986.

Berkhofer, Robert, Jr. *The White Man's Indian.* New York: Random House, 1979.

Bieder, Robert E. *Science Encounters the Indian, 1820–1880.* Norman: University of Oklahoma Press, 1986.

Billington, Ray Allen, and Martin Ridge. *Westward Expansion: A History of the American Frontier.* 5th ed. New York: Macmillan, 1982.

Bowden, Henry Warner. *American Indians and Christian Missions.* Chicago: University of Chicago Press, 1981.

Brown, Sterling. *The Negro in American Fiction.* Port Washington, N.Y.: Kennikat Press, 1968 (originally published in 1937).

Brown, Stuart E., Jr., Lorraine F. Myers, and Eileen M. Chappel. *Pocahontas' Descendants.* Berryville, Va.: Pocahontas Foundation, 1985.

Bryant, Loy Y. "The Pocahontas Theme in American Literature." M.A. thesis, University of North Carolina, 1935.

Burns, Marilyn J. *Pocahontas Blood.* Silver Spring, Md.: Virginia Tree, 1983.

Campbell, William P. *John Gadsby Chapman: Painter and Illustrator.* Exhibit catalogue, National Gallery. Washington D.C.: H. K. Press for National Gallery of Art, 1962.

Castro, Michael. *Interpreting the Indian.* Albuquerque: University of New Mexico Press, 1983.

Chamberlain, Georgia Stamm. " 'The Baptism of Pocahontas': John Gadsby Chapman's Gigantic Mural in the Rotunda of the National Capitol." *Iron Worker* (Lynchburg, Va.: Lynchburg Foundry Co.), 23, 3 (Summer 1959), 15–22.

———. "John Gadsby Chapman, Painter of Virginia." *Art Quarterly* (Detroit Museum of Arts Founders Society) 24, 4 (Winter 1961), 378–90.

———. *Studies on John Gadsby Chapman.* Annandale, Va.: Turnpike Press, 1963.

Chapin, Bradley. *Criminal Justice in Colonial America, 1606–1660.* Athens: University of Georgia Press, 1983.

Christensen, Edwin O. *Early American Wood Carving.* Cleveland: World, 1952.

Colacurcio, Michael J. "Footsteps of Anne Hutchinson." *ELH* 39 (1972), 459–94.

Compilation of Works of Art and Other Objects in the United States Capitol. Prepared by the Architect of the Capitol Under the Direction of the Joint Committee on the Library. Washington, D.C.: U.S. Government Printing Office, 1965.

Cowden, Gerald S. "The Randolphs of Turkey Island." Ph.D. diss., William and Mary, 1977.

Cronon, William. *Changes in the Land: Indians, Colonists, and the Ecology of New England.* New York: Hill & Wang, 1983.

Daniels, Jonathan. *The Randolphs of Virginia.* Garden City, N.Y.: Doubleday, 1972.

Davis, Curtis Carroll. *Chronicler of the Cavaliers: A Life of Virginia Novelist Dr. William A. Caruthers.* Richmond: Dietz, 1953.

Davis, Richard Beale. *Intellectual Life in Jefferson's Virginia.* Chapel Hill: University of North Carolina Press, 1964.

Dearborn, Mary V. *Pocahontas's Daughters.* New York: Oxford University Press, 1986.

Debo, Angie. *A History of the Indians of the United States.* Norman: University of Oklahoma Press, 1970.

Dekker, George. *James Fenimore Cooper: The American Scott.* New York: Barnes & Noble, 1967.

Dekker, George, and John P. McWilliams, eds. *Fenimore Cooper: The Critical Heritage.* London: Routledge & Kegan Paul, 1973.

Deloria, Vine, Jr. *Custer Died for Your Sins.* New York: Avon, 1969.

Dictionary of American Naval Fighting Ships. 8 Vols. Washington D.C.: Navy Department, Office of the Chief of Naval Operations, Naval History Division, 1959–81.

Dippie, Brian W. *The Vanishing American.* Middletown, Conn.: Wesleyan University Press, 1982.

Dorsey, Ella Loraine. *Pocahontas.* Washington, D.C.: Howard Press, 1906.

Dumond, Dwight Howell, ed. *Southern Editorials on Secession.* New York: Century, 1931.

Edmunds, R. David. *The Shawnee Prophet.* Lincoln: University of Nebraska Press, 1983.

Enloe, Cynthia. *Bananas Beaches and Bases.* Berkeley and Los Angeles: University of California Press, 1990.

Evans, J. Martin. *America: The View from Europe.* New York: Norton, 1976.

Fairburn, William Armstrong. *Merchant Sail.* 6 Vols. Center Lovell, Maine: Fairburn Marine Educational Foundation, 1945–55. Vol. 2, 1026–7.

Fairman, Charles E. *Art and Artists of the Capitol of the United States of America.* Washington, D.C.: U.S. Government Printing Office, 1927.

Faust, Drew Gilpin. *The Creation of Confederate Nationalism.* Baton Rouge: Louisiana State University Press, 1988.

Faust, J. Frederick. "An 'Abundance of Blood Shed on Both Sides': England's First Indian War, 1609–1614." *Virginia Magazine of History and Biography* 98, 1 (January 1990), 3–56.

Feest, Christian F. "The Indian in Non-English Literature." In *History of Indian-White Relations,* ed. Wilcolm E. Washburn. Vol. 4 of *Handbook of North American Indians,* genl. ed. William C. Sturtevant. Washington: Smithsonian Institution, 1988, 582–6.

Fiedler, Leslie A. "The Indian in Literature in English." In *History of Indian-White Relations,* ed. Wilcolm E. Washburn. Vol. 4 of *Handbook of North American Indians,* genl. ed. William C. Sturtevant. Washington: Smithsonian Institution, 1988, 573–81.

Love and Death in the American Novel. Rev. ed. New York: Stein & Day, 1975.

The Return of the Vanishing American. New York: Stein & Day, 1969.

Fletcher, John Gould. *John Smith – Also Pocahontas.* New York: Brentano's, 1928; Reprint, New York: Kraus Reprint, 1972.

Fliegelman, Jay. *Prodigals and Pilgrims: The American Revolution against Patriarchal Authority, 1750–1800.* Cambridge: Cambridge University Press, 1982.

Florida Historical Quarterly 33, 3–4 (January–April 1955). (This issue is dedicated solely to the great Seminole chief Osceola.)

Fowler, David H. *Northern Attitudes toward Interracial Marriage.* New York: Garland, 1987.

Fox, Velda M. "The Development of the Pocahontas Story in American Literature, 1607–1927." M.A. thesis, State University of Iowa, 1927.

Fredrickson, George M. *The Black Image in the White Mind.* New York: Harper & Row, 1972.

Free, William J. *The* Columbian Magazine *and American Literary Nationalism.* The Hague: Mouton, 1968.

Fritz, Jean. *The Double Life of Pocahontas.* New York: Putnam, 1983.

Fryd, Vivien Green. "Two Sculptures for the Capitol: Horatio Greenough's *Rescue* and Luigi Persico's *Discovery of America.*" *American Art Journal* 19, 2 (1987), 16–39.

Gerdts, William H. *American Neo-Classic Sculpture.* New York: Viking, 1973.

Gibbs, Linda Joans. *One Hundred and Fifty Years of American Painting: An Exhibition from the Permanent Collection of the Museum of Art at Brigham Young University.* Provo, Utah: Brigham Young University Press, 1994.

Gilliam, Charles Edgar. "His Dearest Daughter's Names." *William and Mary Quarterly,* ser. 2, vol. 21, no. 3 (July 1941), 239–42.

Glasrud, Bruce A., and Alan M. Smith, eds. *Race Relations in British North America, 1607–1783.* Chicago: Nelson-Hall, 1982.

Gordon, Barry and Richard Meth, "Men As Husbands." In Richard L. Meth and Robert S. Pasick, eds., *Men in Therapy: The Challenge of Change.* New York: Guilford Press, 1990, 54–87.

Gossett, Thomas F. *Race: The History of an Idea in America.* New York: Schocken, 1965.

Green, Rayna. "The Only Good Indian: The Image of the Indian in American Vernacular Culture." Ph.D. diss., Indiana University, 1973.

"The Pocahontas Perplex: The Image of Indian Women in American Culture." *Massachusetts Review* 16, 4 (1975), 698–714.

"Traits of Indian Character." *Southern Folklore Quarterly* 39 (1975), 233–62.

Hall, David. D. *The Antinomian Controversy, 1636–1638.* Middletown, Conn.: Wesleyan University Press, 1968.

Hamilton, Wynette L. "The Correlation between Societal Attitudes and

Those of American Authors in the Depiction of American Indians, 1607–1860." *American Indian Quarterly* 1, 1 (Spring 1974), 1–26.

Hatch, Charles E., Jr. "Robert Sully at Jamestown, 1854." *William and Mary Quarterly* 22, 4 (October 1942), 343–52.

Hayes, Kevin J. *Captain John Smith: A Reference Guide*. Boston: Hall, 1991.

Hendricks, Margo. "Civility, Barbarism, and Aphra Behn's The Widow Ranter." In Margo Hendricks and Patricia Parker, eds. *Women, "Race," and Writing in the Early Modern Period*. London: Routledge, 1994, 225–39.

Hendricks, Margo and Patricia Parker, eds. *Women, "Race," and Writing in the Early Modern Period*. London: Routledge, 1994.

Henriques, Fernando. *Children of Conflict*. New York: Dutton, 1975.

Henry, Robert Selph. *The Story of the Confederacy*. New York: Grosset & Dunlap, 1936.

Heyl, Erik. *Early American Steamers*. Vol. 3. Buffalo: published by the Author, 1964, 291–4.

Horan, James D. *The McKenney-Hall Portrait Gallery of American Indians*. New York: Bramhall House, 1986.

Horowitz, David. *The First Frontier: The Indian Wars and America's Origins – 1607–1776*. New York: Simon & Schuster, 1978.

Horsman, Reginald. *Expansion and American Indian Policy, 1783–1812*. Lansing: Michigan State University Press, 1967.

 Race and Manifest Destiny. Cambridge, Mass.: Harvard University Press, 1981.

Hubbell, Jay B. "The Smith-Pocahontas Story in Literature." *Virginia Magazine of History and Biography* 65, 3 (July 1957), 274–300.

Hulme, Peter. *Colonial Encounters: Europe and the Native Caribbean, 1492–1797*. London: Methuen, 1986.

Jackson, Richard. *Popular Songs of Nineteenth-Century America*. New York: Dover, 1976.

Jacobs, Wilbur R. *Dispossessing the American Indian*. New York: Scribner, 1972.

Jacobs, Wilbur R., ed. *The Appalachian Indian Frontier: The Edmond Atkin Report and Plan of 1755*. Lincoln: University of Nebraska Press, 1967.

Jenkins, William Warren. "Three Centuries in the Development of the Pocahontas Story in American Literature: 1608–1908." Ph.D. diss., University of Tennessee, 1977.

Johnston, James Hugo. *Race Relations in Virginia and Miscegenation in the South*. Amherst: University of Massachusetts Press, 1970.

Jones, Howard Mumford. *O Strange New World*. New York: Viking, 1964.

Josephy, Alvin M., Jr. *The Patriot Chiefs*. New York: Viking, 1958.

Kasson, Joy S. "Power and Powerlessness: Death, Sexuality and the Demonic in Nineteenth-Century American Sculpture." *Women's Studies* 15 (1988), 343–67.

Keiser, Albert. *The Indian in American Literature*. New York: Oxford University Press, 1933.

Kellogg, Louise Phelps. "Pocahontas and Jamestown." *Wisconsin Magazine of History and Biography* XXV (September 1941), 38–42.

Kellogg, Thelma Louise. "The Life and Works of John Davis." *University of Maine Studies*, ser. 2, no. 1. Orono, Maine: University Press, 1924.

Kolodny, Annette. *The Lay of the Land*. Chapel Hill: University of North Carolina Press, 1975.

Krythe, Maymie R. *Sampler of American Songs*. New York: Harper & Row, 1969.

Kupperman, Karen Ordahl. *Captain John Smith: A Collection of His Writings*. Chapel Hill: University of North Carolina Press, 1988.

 Settling with the Indians. Totowa, N.J.: Rowman & Littlefield, 1980.

Lair, John. *Songs Lincoln Loved.* New York: Duell, Sloan, & Pearce, 1954.

Larkins, Sharon. "Using Trade Books to Teach about Pocahontas." *Georgia Social Sciences Journal* 19, 1 (1988), 21–25.

Larson, Charles R. *American Indian Fiction.* Albuquerque: University of New Mexico Press, 1978.

Leach, Douglas Edward. *Flintlock and Tomahawk: New England in King Philip's War.* New York: Macmillan, 1958.

Lemay, J. A. Leo. *The American Dream of Captain John Smith.* Charlottesville: University of Virginia Press, 1991.

Lerner, Sidney. Letter to the author, July 4, 1990. (See also, *Wallace's American Trotting Register,* vol. 3, 1879.)

Levine, Robert. *Conspiracy and Romance.* Cambridge: Cambridge University Press, 1989.

Lincoln, Charles H., ed. *Narratives of the Indian Wars, 1675–1699.* New York: Scribner, 1913.

Lindsey, David. "Perry in Japan." *American History Illustrated* 13, 5 (August 1978), 4–8, 44–9.

Lombard, Charles M. "Chateaubriand's American Reception." In *Chateaubriand Today,* ed. Richard Switzer. Madison: University of Wisconsin Press, 1970, 221–8.

Lombard, Charles M., ed. *The Romantic Indian.* Vol. 2. Delmar, N.Y.: Scholars' Facsimiles and Reprints, 1981.

Lukács, Georg. *The Historical Novel.* Trans. Hannah Mitchell and Stanley Mitchell. Intro. Fredric Jameson. Lincoln: University of Nebraska Press, 1983.

Lynes, Russell. *The Art-Makers.* New York: Dover, 1970.

Macleod, William Christie. *The American Indian Frontier.* New York: Knopf, 1928.

"Malee – Pocahontas of Florida." *National Republic* 21, 4 (August 1933), 5–6; 21, 5 (September 1933), 21–2, 32.

Marx, Leo. *The Machine in the Garden: Technology and the Pastoral Ideal in America.* New York: Oxford University Press, 1964.

McEvedy, Colin. *The Penguin Atlas of North American History to 1870.* London: Penguin, 1988.

McWilliams, John P. *Political Justice in a Republic.* Berkeley and Los Angeles: University of California Press, 1972.

Meth, Richard L., and Robert S. Pasick, eds. *Men in Therapy: The Challenge of Change.* New York: Guilford Press, 1990.

Miller, Perry. "Religion and Society in the Early Literature of Virginia." In Miller, *Errand into the Wilderness.* New York: Harper & Row, 1956, 99–140.

Moody, Richard. *Dramas from the American Theatre, 1762–1909.* Cleveland: World, 1966.

Mossiker, Frances. *Pocahontas.* New York: Knopf, 1976.

Murphy, Sharon. "American Indians and the Media." *Journalism History* 6 (1979), 39–43.

Nathan, Hans. *Dan Emmett and the Rise of Early Negro Minstrelsy.* Norman: University of Oklahoma Press, 1962.

"The New England Pocahontas." Reprinted in G. Waldo Browne, *Real Legends of New England.* Chicago: Whitman, 1930, 28–34.

Norton, Anne. *Alternative Americas: A Reading of Antebellum Political Culture.* Chicago: University of Chicago Press, 1986.

O'Gorman, James F. *Aspects of American Printmaking, 1800–1950.* Syracuse: Syracuse University Press, 1988.

O'Meara, Walter. *Daughters of the Country.* New York: Harcourt, Brace & World, 1968.

Parry, Ellwood. *The Image of the Indian and the Black Man in American Art.* New York: Braziller, 1974.

Pearce, Roy Harvey. *Savagism and Civilization: A Study of the Indian and the American Mind.* 1953; reprint, Baltimore: Johns Hopkins University Press, 1967.

Peden, William. "A Book Peddler Invades Monticello." *William and Mary Quarterly,* ser. 3 vol. 6, no. 4 (October 1949), 631–6.

Petter, Henri. *The Early American Novel.* Columbus: Ohio State University Press, 1971.

Pleckman, H. "The New Family and Health Improvement." *Virginia Health Bulletin Extra,* no. 12, *New Family Series* no. 5 (1925), 25–6.

Poesch, Jessie. *The Art of the Old South.* New York: Knopf, 1983.

Potter, David M. *The Impending Crisis, 1848–1861.* Completed and edited by Don E. Fehrenbacher. New York: Harper & Row, 1976.

Pratt, Julius W. "The Origin of 'Manifest Destiny.'" *American Historical Review* 32 (July 1927), 795–8.

Prucha, Francis Paul. *American Indian Policy in the Formative Years.* Lincoln: University of Nebraska Press, 1962.

Quinn, Arthur Hobson, ed. *Representative American Plays from 1767 to the Present.* 7th ed. New York: Appleton-Century-Crofts, 1953.

Rans, Geoffrey. "Inaudible Man: The Indian in the Theory and Practice of White Fiction." *Canadian Review of American Studies* 7 (Fall 1977), 103–15.

Ransome, David R. "Pocahontas and the Mission to the Indians." *Virginia Magazine of History and Biography* 99, 1 (January 1991), 81–94.

Rasmussen, William, and Robert S. Tilton. *Pocahontas: The Life and Legend.* Forthcoming publication of the Virginia Historical Society, Richmond, 1994.

Reep, Diana. *The Rescue and Romance.* Bowling Green, Ohio: Bowling Green State University Popular Press, 1982.

Reynolds, Patrick M. "The Unofficial Confederate Anthem." In "Flash-backs," comics section, *Washington Post,* May 16 and 23, 1993.

Rice, Howard C. Jr. Introduction to Marquis de Chastellux, *Travels in North America in the Years 1780, 1781, and 1782.* A revised translation, with introduction and notes by Howard C. Rice, Jr. Chapel Hill: University of North Carolina Press, 1963. Vol. 1, 28.

Ringe, Donald A. *James Fenimore Cooper.* New York: Twayne, 1962.

Robertson, Karen. "Pocahontas at the Masque." Paper delivered at the meeting of the Shakespeare Association of America, Philadelphia, April 12, 1990.

Rogin, Michael Paul. *Fathers and Children.* New York: Knopf, 1975.

Rountree, Helen C. *Pocahontas's People.* Norman: University of Oklahoma Press, 1990.

The Powhatan Indians of Virginia: Their Traditional Culture. Norman: University of Oklahoma Press, 1989.

Ruf, Barbara. "John Davis: Poet, Novelist, and Traveler." Ph.D. diss., University of Tennessee, 1974.

Sachs, Howard L., and Judith Rose Sachs. *Way up North in Dixie.* Washington, D.C.: Smithsonian Institution Press, 1993.

Salisbury, Neal. "Red Puritans: The 'Praying Indians' of Massachusetts Bay and John Eliot." *William and Mary Quarterly,* ser. 3, vol. 31, no.1 (January 1974), 27–54.

Samuels, Ernest. *The Young Henry Adams.* Cambridge, Mass.: Harvard University Press, 1948.

Scapp, Ron. "Lack and Violence: Towards a Speculative Sociology of the Homeless." *Practice* 6, 2 (Fall 1988), 34–47.

Scheick, William J. *The Half-Blood: A Cultural Symbol in Nineteenth-Century American Fiction.* Lexington: University Press of Kentucky, 1979,

Schimmel, Julie. "Inventing 'the Indian.' " In *The West as America,* ed. William H. Truettner. Washington, D.C.: Smithsonian Institution Press, 1991, 148–89.

Segal, Charles M., and David C. Stineback. *Puritans, Indians, and Manifest Destiny.* New York: Putnam, 1977.

Sheehan, Bernard W. *Seeds of Extinction: Jeffersonian Philanthropy and the American Indian.* New York: Norton, 1973.

Slotkin, Richard. "Myth and the Production of History." In *Ideology and Classic American Literature.* Eds. Sacvan Bercovitch and Myra Jehlen. Cambridge: Cambridge University Press, 1986, 86.

    Regeneration through Violence. Middletown, Conn.: Wesleyan University Press, 1973.

Smith, Bradford. *Captain John Smith.* Philadelphia: Lippincott, 1953.

Smith, Henry Nash. *Virgin Land: The American West as Symbol and Myth.* New York: Random House, 1950.

Sollars, Werner. *Beyond Ethnicity: Consent and Descent in American Culture.* New York: Oxford University Press, 1986.

Stampp, Kenneth M. *The Peculiar Institution.* New York: Random House, 1956.

Striker, Laura Polanyi, and Bradford Smith. "The Rehabilitation of Captain John Smith." *Journal of Southern History* 38, 4 (November 1962), 480–1.

Sundquist, Asebrit. *Pocahontas & Co.* Atlantic Highlands, N.J.: Humanities, 1987.

Tate, Thad W., and David L. Ammerman, eds. *The Chesapeake in the Seventeenth Century.* New York: Norton, 1979.

Taylor, Joshua C. *America as Art.* New York: Harper & Row, 1976.

Taylor, William R. *Cavalier and Yankee.* New York: Harper & Row, 1969.

Thompson, Henry Tazewell. *Henry Timrod: Laureate of the Confederacy.* Columbia, S.C: State, 1928.

Towner, Lawrence W. "*Ars Poetica et Sculptura:* Pocahontas on the Boston Common." *Journal of Southern History* 28, 4 (November 1962), 484–5.

Trennert, Robert A. "Popular Imagery and the American Indian." *New Mexico Historical Review* 51 (1976), 215–32.

Trenton, Patricia, and Patrick T. Houlihan. *Native Americans: Five Centuries of Changing Images.* New York: Abrams, 1989.

Truettner, William H. "Prelude to Expansion." In *The West as America,* ed. William H. Truettner. Washington, D.C.: Smithsonian Institution Press for National Museum of American Art, 1991, 55–95.

Truettner, William H., ed. *The West as America: Reinterpreting Images of the Frontier, 1820–1920.* Washington, D.C.: Smithsonian Institution Press, 1991.

VanDerBeets, Richard, ed. *Held Captive by Indians: Selected Narratives, 1642–1836.* Knoxville: University of Tennessee Press, 1973.

Vaughan, Alden T. *American Genesis: Captain John Smith and the Founding of Virginia.* Boston: Little, Brown, 1975.

Vaughan, Alden T., and Edward W. Clark, eds. *Puritans among the Indians: Accounts of Captivity and Redemption, 1676–1724.* Cambridge, Mass.: Harvard University Press (Belknap Press), 1981.

Viola, Herman J. *The Indian Legacy of Charles Bird King.* Washington, D.C.: Smithsonian Institution Press and Doubleday, 1976.

Wadlington, Walter. "The *Loving* Case: Virginia's Anti-Miscegenation Stature in Historical Perspective." *Virginia Law Review* 52B, 5 (1966), 1202.

Washburn, Wilcolm E., ed. *History of Indian-White Relations.* Volume 4 of *Handbook of North American Indians,* genl. ed. William C. Sturtevant. Washington, D.C.: Smithsonian Institution, 1988.

Washington, Joseph R., Jr. *Race and Religion in Early Nineteenth-Century America.* 2 vols. Lewiston, Queenston. Lampeter: Edwin Mellen Press, 1988.

Webb, Stephen Saunders. *1676 – The End of American Independence.* New York: Knopf, 1984.

Wecter, Dixon. *The Saga of American Society.* New York: Scribner, 1937.

Wernick, Jon S. "Indians in Almanacs, 1783–1815." *Indian History* 8 (1975), 36–42.

Woodward, Grace Steele. *Pocahontas.* Norman: University of Oklahoma Press, 1969.

Wyatt-Brown, Bertram. *Southern Honor.* New York: Oxford University Press, 1982.

Young, Neil. "Pocahontas." Silver Fiddle (BMI), 1977.

Young, Philip. "The Mother of Us All: Pocahontas Reconsidered." *Kenyon Review* 24, 3 (Summer 1962), 391–415.

Zolla, Elémire. *The Writer and the Shaman: A Morphology of the American Indian.* Trans. Raymond Rosenthal. New York: Harcourt Brace Jovanovich, 1973.

Index

Abrams, Ann Uhry, 94, 119, 124
Adams, Henry, 4, 87, 89, 173–5
Adams, John, 56
Adams, John Quincy, 97, 104, 108
Aeneas and Lavinia, 6
Alexander, William, 15–17, 24
Allen, Paula Gunn
    C'koy'u, Old Woman, 180
Allen, William
    American Biographical and Historical
        Dictionary, 54
Allston, Washington, 97, 104, 117
"An Act to Preserve Racial Integrity"
    (Virginia), 30
Anderson, Robert, 145
Anne, Queen of England, 8, 17–18, 20,
    128
Argall (Argal), Samuel, 7, 16

Baigell, Matthew, 133–5
Baldwin, Ebenezer
    Observations on the Physical, Intellectual,
        and Moral Qualities of Our Colored
        Population, 30–1
Baldwin, Joseph, 174–5
Bandelier, Adolphe, 4, 88–9, 174
Barber, John Warner
    Interesting Events in the History of the
        United States, 96 (Fig. 2)
Barbour, Philip, 16
    The Three Worlds of Captain John Smith,
        16
    Pocahontas and Her World, 110
Barker, James Nelson, 26, 48, 55
    The Indian Princess, 26, 59, 74
Barlow, Joel
    Columbiad, 49–51
    The Vision of Columbus, 49
Barnes, Charlotte
    The Forest Princess, 30, 72
Barth, John
    The Sot-Weed Factor, 180
Beauregard, P. G. T., 145
Belknap, Jeremy
    American Biography, 38, 54

Bell, Michael Davitt, 78
Berkhofer, Robert, 67
Beverley, Robert
    History and Present State of Virginia, 3,
        16–18, 23, 37, 39, 45, 94
Bierstadt, Albert, 143
Blanchard, C. K., 51
Bolling family, 11, 45
    Bolling, Anne, 9
    Bolling, John, 108
    Bolling, Mary Marshall Tabb, 9
    Bolling, Mary Burton, 9–10, 12
    Bolling, Robert, 9
    Bolling, Robert, Jr., 9
    Bolling, Thomas, 108
    Bolling, William, 106, 108, 110–12,
        125
Boone, Daniel, 1, 19
The Booton Hall Portrait (of Pocahontas),
    92, 105, 106 (Fig. 9), 108
Brackenridge, Hugh Henry, 40
Bradford, William, 89
    History of Plymouth Plantation, 165
Brandburn, George, 29
Brant, Joseph, 23
Brant, Molly, 23, 67, 180
Brougham, John
    Po-ca-hon-tas, or The Gentle Savage, 74–
        6, 175
Brown, Charles Brockden
    Edgar Huntly, 56
Brown, Sterling, 154
Brown, Stuart E., Jr. et al.
    Pocahontas' Descendants, 2, 32
Brueckner, Henry
    The Marriage of Pocahontas, 130
Bryant, William Cullen, 60, 136–7
    "An Indian at the Burial-Place of His
        Fathers," 136
    "Indian Girl's Lament," 136
    "The Disinterred Warrior," 136
    "The Prairies," 136–7
Bryant Minstrels, 175
Buffon, Georges
    Histoire Naturelle, 47

245

Bumppo, Natty, 19
Burk, John, 26–7, 28–9, 94, 143
   The History of Virginia, 26–7, 28–9, 94
Byrd, William
   History of the Dividing Line, 18–20

Cadmus, Paul
   *Pocahontas Saving the Life of Captain
     John Smith*, 180, 182 (Fig. 34)
Capellano, Antonio, 95, 100 (Fig. 5)
Carey, Mathew, 38
Caruthers, William A.
   The Cavaliers of Virginia, 4, 76, 77–8,
     80–1
Catlin, George, 130, 134, 137
   *Pigeon's Egg Head (The Light) Going to
     and Returning from Washington*, 130,
     132 (Fig. 22)
Chamberlain, Georgia Stamm, 105, 112
Channing, William Ellery, 29
Chapman, John Gadsby, 4, 92, 93, 96,
   99 *passim*, 184
   The Baptism of Pocahontas, 4, 93, 96,
     101 (Fig. 7), 105 *passim*
   The Crowning of Powhatan, 105
   The First Ship, 105
   Hagar Fainting in the Wilderness, 103
     (Fig. 8)
   *Hagar and Ishmael Fainting in the
     Wilderness*, 102
   The Landing at Jamestown, 105
   The Picture of the Baptism of Pocahontas
     (pamphlet) 118–20
   *Pocahontas Saving the Life of Captain
     John Smith*, 105, 112, 118 (Fig. 19)
   The Warning of Pocahontas, 105
Chappell, Alonzo
   *Pocahontas Saving the Life of Capt. John
     Smith*, 99 (Fig. 4), 112
Charbonneau, Toussaint and Sacajawea,
   67
Chastellux, Marquis de, 9–11, 31, 36,
   43, 45, 47
   Travels, 9, 36–41, 47
Chateaubriand, François-René de, 57,
   59–62
   Atala, 59–62, 79
   Genie du Christianisme, 59
   Réné, 60–2
Child, Lydia Maria, 60
   Hobomok, 64, 65–6, 70, 79
Choate, Rufus, 87
Church, Frederic, 143
Cliff, Michele
   No Telephone to Heaven, 183–5
Cole, Thomas, 60, 132–3
   The Course of Empire, 132–3
Columbus, Christopher, 50

*Compilation of Works of Art and Other
   Objects in the United States Capitol*,
   179
"Conflict of Northern and Southern
   Races," 171
Connecticut Wits, 49
Cooke, George, 112
Cooke, John Esten
   "A Dream of the Cavaliers," 166,
     168–9
   My Lady Pokahontas, 166, 179
Cooper, James Fenimore, 60, 64, 70–2,
   79, 88, 89, 136
   Gleanings in Europe, 90
   The Last of the Mohicans, 63, 66–7, 79,
     136
   The Pilot, 47
   The Prairies, 64
   The Spy, 58, 89
   The Wept of Wish-Ton-Wish, 64, 67–72, 79
Corbould, Edward
   Pocahontas Rescues Captain John Smith,
     98 (Fig. 3)
Cortez, Hernando, 82–7, 122
Crane, Hart
   The Bridge ("Powhatan's Daughter"),
     180
Crockett, Davy, 102
Croswell, Joseph
   A New World Planted, 48–9, 94
Custis, George Washington Parke, 72,
   102
   Pocahontas, or the Settlers of Virginia,
     72–4

Dale, Thomas, 14, 15, 16, 105, 112,
   115–16
   proposed marriage to another of
     Powhatan's daughters, 16
Davis, Curtis Carroll, 80
Davis, Jefferson, 175
Davis, John, 3, 26, 32–3, 35 *passim*, 58,
   94, 120
   Captain Smith and Princess Pocahontas,
     32, 46, 95 (Fig. 1)
   The Farmer of New-Jersey, 32, 40
   The First Settlers of Virginia 32, 46
   Travels, 32, 34–6, 38, 40–8
Davis, Richard Beale, 41, 54
Deane, Charles, 4, 5, 87, 89, 164–9,
   173–5
Dearborn, Mary
   Pocahontas's Daughters, 2
Debo, Angie, 27–8
Deloria, Vine, Jr., 176, 178–9
"The Difference of Race Between the
   Northern and Southern People,"
   171

"Doña Marina" ("La Malinche") 82–7, 122, 180
Drake, Samuel, 57
Drayton, Percival, 148
Drayton, Thomas F., 148

Eastburn, James Wallis and Robert Sands
    Yamoyden, 64–5, 70, 79
Edmunds, R. David, 140
Elizabeth I of England, 169
Ellis, Powhattan, 104
Emmett, Daniel Decatur
    "Dixie," 175
Evans, J. Martin, 182

"Father William," 31
Faust, Drew Gilpin, 170, 171
Ferguson, Adam
    Essay on the History of Civil Society, 19
Fiedler, Leslie, 62–3, 83, 89
"Flag of the Powhatan Guards," 127, 170
Fletcher, John Gould, 52
Fliegelman, Jay, 53
Fontaine, Rev. Peter, 21–3, 31
Ford, Ford Madox
    The Good Soldier, 183
Fowler, David H.
    on "cultural disparities" between the races, 15
Franklin, Benjamin, 89
Free, William J., 48, 49
Fritz, Jean, 5
Fryd, Vivien Green, 176

Gadsby, John, 100
Gardiner, C. K., 112
Gardiner, W. H., 58–9, 87
Garnett, David
    Pocahontas, 180
Gilliam, Albert, M.
    Virginia, or Love and Bravery, 72
Girard, Stephen, 147
Green, Rayna, 27, 146
Greenough, Horatio, 97, 176–8
    George Washington, 176
    The Rescue, 176–8 (177 - Fig. 32)
Grieve, George, 40

Hall, James (*see also* McKenney, Thomas), 108–9
    Sketches of History, Life, and Manners in the West, 108–9
Harrison, William Henry, 140–2
Hamor, Ralph, 2, 10, 16
Hawkins, Benjamin, 24

Hawthorne, Nathaniel, 89, 126, 127
    The French and Italian Notebooks, 127
    The Scarlet Letter, 89, 126
Henry, Patrick, 37, 170
Henry, Robert Selph, 148
Henry, William Wirt, 174
Hillhouse, William ("Old Pocahontas"), 158–9, 161, 162
    Pocahontas; A Proclamation, 149–53 (150–1 - Fig. 28)
Hobomoc (*see also* Child *Hobomoc*), 51
Howe, Henry
    Historical Collections of Virginia, 163 (Fig. 29)
Hulme, Peter, 5

"The Indians in American Art," 143
Intermarriage (*see also* Miscegenation)
    between blacks and whites, 22–3, 31
    between Indians and whites, 3, 11–27, 55, 59, 63 *passim*, 136
Irving, Washington, 67
    Life of Washington, 89
Islas, Arturo
    Migrant Souls, 184–5

Jackson, Andrew, 108, 142
Jacob and Esau, 131
James I of England, 8, 18, 20, 30, 45, 48, 93, 128,, 161
Jamestown Colony, 2, 5, 6, 7, 11, 12, 14, 41, 48, 57, 73, 105, 118, 123, 124–5, 143–4, 165, 169, 170–1, 173, 174, 184
Janvier, Thomas, 88
Jason and Medea, 6, 50
Jefferson, Thomas, 11, 24–5, 37, 45, 46–7, 51, 73, 89, 158, 162, 170, 173
    Notes on the State of Virginia, 24, 46–7, 158
    The Declaration of Independence, 25
Jenkins, William Warren, 42, 86, 165
Johnson, Sir William, 23, (and Moll Brant) 67
Johnston, Josiah Stoddard, 102, 104
Jones, John Paul, 89, 104
Jonson, Ben
    The Vision of Delight, 8

Kames, Lord, 10
Karcher, Carolyn, 65
Keiser, Albert, 11
Kennedy, John Pendleton, 154–5
    Horse-Shoe Robinson, 159
    Swallow Barn, 154–5, 157, 158
Kimber, Edward
    A Short Account of the British Plantations in America, 41

King, Charles Bird, 112, 117, 134
  Hayne Hudjihini, 112, 117 (Fig. 18)
  Tenskwatawa (engraving), 141
Kolodny, Annette
  The Lay of the Land, 181
Kupperman, Karen Ordahl, 5, 16

"Landscape," 121–2
Larkins, Sharon, 7
Latrobe, Benjamin, 28
Lawson, Charles R., 180
Lemay, J. A. Leo, 5
Leutze, Emanuel
  *The Storming of Teocalli by Cortez and His
    Troops*, 86
Levine, Robert, 87
Lewis, Lorenzo, 100
Lewis, Nelly Parke Custis, 100, 102
Lincoln, Abraham, 126–7, 175
  "Gettysburg Address," 126–7
Lindsay, Vachel
  "Our Mother Pocahontas," 30
Logan, 88
Lombard, Charles, M., 59
Louisiana Purchase, 25, 152–3

Madison, James, 37, 102, 108, 170
"Malee - The Pocahontas of Florida,"
  (Milly) 67
Manifest Destiny, 4, 7, 133–9
Marshall, John, 34–5, 42, 47, 52, 55, 57
  The Life of George Washington, 34–5
Mason, George, 37
Massachusetts Bay Colony, 6, 14, 165
Massasoit, 48–9, 51, 88
Matteson, Tompkins H., 137, 139
  The Last of the Race, 137, 139 (Fig. 25)
McEvedy, Colin, 152
McKenney, Thomas and James Hall
  The Indian Tribes of North America, 108,
    113 (Fig. 14)
McNall, David
  Pocahontas, 180, 183 (Fig. 35)
McRae, John, 130
Melville, Herman
  "Bartleby the Scrivener," 46
  The Confidence Man, 58, 87–8, 109
  Israel Potter, 89
  Moby-Dick, 30, 146
  Typee, 63
  Pierre, 30
  White-Jacket, 30
Mercer, Samuel, 145
Miles, William, 32
Miscegenation, (see also Intermarriage),
  4, 7, 9 *passim*, 11–17, 55, 59, 61,
  63, 69, 72
  laws against, 14–15

repeal of anti-miscegenation statutes,
  29–30
Missouri Compromise, 150–3
Monceaux, R. L. Morgan
  Matowaka, 185 (Fig. 36)
Monroe, James, 108
Morgan, Lewis Henry, 4, 88–9, 174
Morse, Samuel F. B., 102, 104
Morton, Thomas, 14,
Mosby, Mary Webster (*see* Mrs. M. M.
  Webster)
Mossiker, Frances, 5
Mound Builders, 131–3, 136–7
Mozier, Joseph, 127, 129, 136, 138
  Indian Girl's Lament, 136, 138 (Fig.
    24)
  Pocahontas, 127, 129 (Fig. 21)
Murray, William and Rebecca (Bolling),
  28

Nehlig, Victor
  Pocahontas and John Smith, 179, 181
    (Fig. 33)
"New England Pocahontas," 76
Neill, Edward, 87, 175
Norton, Anne, 162, 172, 181
  Alternative Americas, 162

Oldmixon, John
  The British Empire in America (1708),
    21
  The British Empire in America (1741),
    20–1
O'Meara, Walter, 84–5
Opechancanough, 41
Osceola, 128
Owen, Robert Dale, 74, 105–6
  Pocahontas, 59, 74, 91–2

Palfrey, John Gorham, 4, 87, 162–4,
  173–5
  History of New England, 162–4
Pamunkey Indians, 31–2
Paulding, James Kirke, 104, 169
  Koningsmarke, 4, 76–7
  Letters From the South, 28, 76
  "Ode to Jamestown," 76
Peale, Charles Willson, 102
Pearce, Roy Harvey, 19
Pearson, Emile Clemens (Emily
  Catherine Pearson), 145, 153–4,
  155, 156–62
  Cousin Franck's Household, 145, 153,
    154, 156–62
  Jamie Parker, The Fugitive, 153–4, 156
Perry, Matthew C., 145, 147–8
Petter, Henri, 38
Philip, King (Metacom), 65, 67, 68, 88

Pickett, James Chamberlayne
   The Memory of Pocahontas Vindicated . . .
      Waddy Thompson, 86
Plymouth Colony, 6, 14, 48, 165
Pocahontas
   as a convert to Christianity, (*see also*
      Chapman, *The Baptism of Pocahontas*)
      7, 12, 15, 96, 118–20, 121, 124
      passim, 161, 170
   as Matowaka (Matoaks), 14, 74, 91–2
   as Rebecca, 14, 18, 92, 96, 131, 144
   descendants of, 2, 4, 9–11, 17–18, 20,
      21, 23, 28–32, 33, 52, 55, 71, 108,
      131, 138, 139, 153, 156, 161, 165,
      172
   kidnapping by Argall, 7, 16, 34
   marriage to John Rolfe, 3, 7, 11–18,
      21–4, 26–7, 29–30, 34, 42, 51, 55,
      62, 64, 67, 72, 78, 90, 93, 118,
      125, 130, 161, 165, 179, 180–2
   rescue of John Smith, 1, 3, 5–6, 7,
      11, 13, 26–7, 30, 32, 34–5, 40–8,
      50–1, 52–7, 58–9, 62, 72–3, 74, 75,
      76 *passim*, 93, 94–7, 98, 99, 100,
      105, 112, 118–21, 123–4, 125–6,
      127, 128, 134–5, 143, 144, 148–9,
      162, 173, 178, 184, 186
   rescue of Smith doubted, 5, 122,
      148–9, 162–9, 173–5
The "Pocahontas Fan," 167 (Fig. 30)
Pocahontas (film), 185
Pocahontas (rowboat), 146
Pocahontas (steamer - *see also* U.S.S.
   Pocahontas), 144, 148
Pocahontas (whaler), 146
"Pocahontas" (pacing mare), 175
Poe, Edgar Allan, 64
Pollard, J. G., 31
Potter, David M., 152
Powell, William H., 133
   Discovery of the Mississippi River, 131,
      133 (Fig. 23)
Powers, Hiram
   The Last of the Tribes, 137
Powhatan, 7, 21, 28, 39, 41–6, 48, 56,
   57, 83, 105, 144, 173, 180, 186
   quoted by Smith in *Proceedings*, 9
Prescott, William Hickling, 4,
   The History of the Conquest of Mexico, 82–7
Prucha, Francis Paul, 20

Quinn, Arthur Hobson, 72

Randolph family, 11, 28–9, 30, 31, 45
   Randolph, Edmund, 52
   Randolph, Joh, 28, 29, 30, 98, 162,
      172, 174
   Randolph, William, 172

Red Jacket, 88
Reep, Diana, 82
Richardson, Samuel, 42–3, 62
Robertson, Bolling, 28
Robertson, Karen, 186
Robertson, William
   *A History of the Discovery and Settlement of
      America*, 23–4
Robertson, Wyndham, 165–6
Rolfe, John (*see also* Pocahontas,
   marriage to John Rolfe) 2, 3, 7,
      11–19, 21–4, 26–7, 29–30, 38–9,
      42, 45, 52, 58–9, 62, 67, 72, 74,
      75, 78, 81, 89, 105, 108, 115–16,
      117, 118, 125, 130, 138, 156, 169,
      179, 180–2, 186
Rolfe, Thomas (*see also* Pocahontas,
   descendant of), 2, 7, 13, 17, 23,
      26, 45, 59, 63, 74, 90, 108, 125,
      186
Rose, Johann Wilhelm
   Pocahontas, 60
Rountree, Helen C., 2, 5
   Pocahontas's People, 2, 31
Ruf, Barbara, 47
Rush, William, attr.
   Pocahontas (figurehead), 147 (Fig. 27)

Sacajawea, 67, 180
Samoset, 51
Sandburg, Carl
   "Cool Tombs," 180
Scapp, Ron, 182
Scheibler, Carl Friedrich
   *Reisen . . . des Schiffs — Captain J.
      Schmidt*, 60
Scheick, William, 11, 13
Schimmel, Julie, 136–7
Schoolcraft, Henry, 67
Scott, Sir Walter, 71, 76–7, 81, 90, 131,
   171
   Ivanhoe, 131, 171
The Sedgeford Hall Portrait (of
   Pocahontas), 108, 110 (Fig. 12)
Sedgwick, Catharine Maria, 77–9, 81
   Hope Leslie, 4, 31, 76, 77–81
Sewall, Samuel, 14
Shaffer, Arthur H., 52
Sheehan, Bernard W., 12
Shill, Steve
   Pocahontas, 185
Simms, William Gilmore, 64, 89, 122–4,
   143
   Life of Captain John Smith, 89, 123–4
   Mellichampe, 64
   The Partisan, 64, 159
   "Pocahontas: A Subject For The
      Historical Painter," 122–4

Slotkin, Richard, 1, 27
  Regeneration Through Violence, 1
Smith, John, 2, 5, 10, 17–18, 20, 26–7,
    38–9, 40–8, 76, 83, 88, 89, 105,
    119–20, 121, 123–4, 125–6, 127,
    128, 134–5, 144 162–9, 173–5,
    176, 178, 185–6
  Generall Historie, xv, 3, 38–9, 59, 83,
    164–5, 173
  "Letter" to Queen Anne, xv, 17–18,
    20, 128
  True Relation, 164–5, 173, 174
  rescued by Pocahontas, *see*
  Pocahontas, rescue of John Smith
Smith, Samuel Stanhope, 10–11, 24, 28,
    31
  *An Essay on the Causes . . . Human
    Species*, 10
Southworth, Mrs. E.D.E.N.
  The Three Beauties, 82
Squanto, 51
Sparks, Jared, 178
  *Lives of Alexander Wilson and Captain
    John Smith*, xvi
Spencer, Jesse. A.
  History of the United States, 99
Stith, William, 24
Stowe, Harriet Beecher
  Unle Tom's Cabin, 154, 155–6, 157
Strachey, William, 2–3, 174, 179–80
Striker, Laura Polanyi, 169
Sully, Robert Matthew, 106, 108, 110,
    113, 170
  Pocahontas (Virginia), 115 (Fig. 16)
  Pocahontas (Wisconsin), 116 (Fig. 17)
Sully, Thomas, 108
  Pocahontas, 114 (Fig. 15)
Sumter, Fort, 145
Sundquist, Åsabrit
  Pocahontas and Co., 2
Symonds, William, 13
  *Virginia. A Sermon Preached At White-
    Chappel*, 13

Taylor, William R., 155–6
Tecumseh, 88, 140–2
Tenskwatawa ("Open Door,"
    "Propet"), 140–2
Thompson, Waddy, 85–6, 122
  Recollections of Mexico, 85–6
Timrod, Henry
  "Ethnogenesis," 171
Tippicanoe, 140–2
Towner, Lawrence W., 94
Trollope, Frances, 102, 103
Trumbull, John, 96, 97
  *George Washington Resigning His
    Commission*, 96

Signing of the Declaration of Independence,
    96, 98, 100 (Fig. 6)
Surrender of General Burgoyne, 96
Surrender of Lord Cornwallis, 96
The *Turkey Island Portrait* (of
    Pocahontas), 108–12, 113–6 (Figs.
    14–17)
Tyler, John, 140, 146

U.S.S. *King Philip*, 146
U.S.S. *Mohawk*, 146
U.S.S. *Mohican*, 146
U.S.S. *Nansemond*, 146
U.S.S. *Narragansett*, 146
U.S.S. *Osage*, 146
U.S.S. *Osceola*, 146
U.S.S. *Pawnee*, 146
U.S.S. *Pequot*, 146
U.S.S. *Pocahontas*, 145–6, 148
U.S.S. *Powhatan*, 145–8
U.S.S. *Seminole*, 146
U.S.S. *Wampanoag*, 146
U.S.S. *Wyandotte*, 146

Van Buren, Martin, 140, 142
Vanderlyn, John, 56
Van de Passe, Simon, 8, 43, 92, 106,
    107 (Fig. 10), 108, 109 (Fig. 11 -
    Engraving after Van de Passe), 111
Vaughan, Alden T., 5
Virgil
  Aeneid, 6, 49–51
Virginia, 2, 4, 9–16, 18, 23, 29–30, 34,
    37, 38, 48, 52, 54, 55, 78, 89, 102,
    105, 118, 119, 121, 144, 149–53,
    161–2, 163
  vs. New England (*see also* Pocahontas,
    rescue of Smith doubted), 6, 58–9,
    143–4, 164–5, 170, 171, 172, 173
Vizenor, Gerald
  The Heirs of Columbus, 180

"W.," 120–1
Wadlington, Walter, 29–30
Waldron, William Watson
  Pocahontas, Princess of Virginia, xvi, 187,
    note 1
Washington, Augustine, 53–4
Washington, Bushrod, 34
Washington, George, 3, 34, 37, 52–4,
    56, 89, 102, 147, 170, 173, 176
Washington, Hannah Lee, 102
Washington, Mrs. John A., 102
Washington, Martha, 72, 100
Webster, Daniel, 87
Webster, Mrs. M.M. (Mary Webster
    Mosby), 57, 124, 126
  Pocahontas: A Legend, 57, 124

Webster, Noah
  An American Selection, 38, 40, 54
Weems, Mason Locke, 3, 38–9, 53
  Life of Washington, 53–4
The Wept of Wish-ton-Wish (drama), 81–2
Weir, Robert W., 124
  Embarkation of the Pilgrims, 124 (Fig. 20), 130
Welles, Gideon, 145
West, Benjamin, 120
Wheatley, Phillis, 56
Whitaker, Alexander, 3, 15, 105, 112–13, 115–16, 117
Whitman, Walt
  The Half-Breed, 64
Wilde, Richard Henry, 104
Williams, Eunice, 31,
Williams, John
  Redeemed Captive Returning to Zion, 78
Williams, William Carlos

  In the American Grain, 180
Windle, Mary Jane
  Life At The White Sulpher Springs, 30
Wingfield, Edward Maria, 3
  A Discourse of Virginia, 164–5
Winkfield, Unca Eliza
  The Female American, 60
Winthrop, John, 89
Wirt, William, 52
  The Letters of the British Spy, xv, 9, 37
Wise, Henry Alexander, 97–100, 103, 104
Woodbury, Mary
  Pocahontas, 108, 111 (Fig. 13)
Woodward, Grace Steele, 5

Young, Neil
  "Pocahontas," 180
Young, Philip, 6, 178

Continued from the front of the book

62. Victoria Harrison, *Elizabeth Bishop's Poetics of Intimacy*
61. Edwin Still Fussell, *The Catholic Side of Henry James*
60. Thomas Gustafson, *Representative Words: Politics, Literature, and the American Language, 1776–1865*
59. Peter Quartermain, *Disjunctive Poetics: From Gertrude Stein and Louis Zukovsky to Susan Howe*
58. Paul Giles, *American Catholic Arts and Fictions: Culture, Ideology, Aesthetics*
57. Ann-Janine Morey, *Religion and Sexuality in American Literature*
56. Philip M. Weinstein, *Faulkner's Subject: A Cosmos No One Owns*
55. Stephen Fender, *Sea Changes: British Emigration and American Literature*
54. Peter Stoneley, *Mark Twain and the Feminine Aesthetic*
53. Joel Porte, *In Respect to Egotism: Studies in American Romantic Writing*
52. Charles Swann, *Nathaniel Hawthorne: Tradition and Revolution*
51. Ronald Bush (ed.), *T. S. Eliot: The Modernist in History*
50. Russell Goodman, *American Philosophy and the Romantic Tradition*
49. Eric J. Sundquist (ed.), *Frederick Douglass: New Literary and Historical Essays*
48. Susan Stanford Friedman, *Penelope's Web: Gender, Modernity, H. D.'s Fiction*
47. Timothy Redman, *Ezra Pound and Italian Fascism*
46. Ezra Greenspan, *Walt Whitman and the American Reader*
45. Michael Oriard, *Sporting with the Gods: The Rhetoric of Play and Game in American Culture*
44. Stephen Fredman, *Poet's.Prose: The Crisis in American Verse*, Second edition
43. David C. Miller, *Dark Eden: The Swamp in Nineteenth-Century American Culture*
42. Susan K. Harris, *Nineteenth-Century American Women's Novels: Interpretive Strategies*
41. Susan Manning, *The Puritan-Provincial Vision: Scottish and American Literature in the Nineteenth Century*
40. Richard Godden, *Fictions of Capital: Essays on the American Novel from James to Mailer*
39. John Limon, *The Place of Fiction in the Time of Science: A Disciplinary History of American Writing*
38. Douglas Anderson, *A House Undivided: Domesticity and Community in American Literature*
37. Charles Altieri, *Painterly Abstraction in Modernist American Poetry*
36. John P. McWilliams, Jr., *The American Epic: Transforming a Genre, 1770–1860*
35. Michael Davidson, *The San Francisco Renaissance: Poetics and Community at Mid-Century*
34. Eric Sigg, *The American T. S. Eliot: A Study of the Early Writings*
33. Robert S. Levine, *Conspiracy and Romance: Studies in Brockden Brown, Cooper, Hawthorne, and Melville*

32. Alfred Habegger, *Henry James and the "Woman Business"*

31. Tony Tanner, *Scenes of Nature, Signs of Man*

30. David Halliburton, *The Color of the Sky: A Study of Stephen Crane*

29. Steven Gould Axelrod and Helen Deese (eds.), *Robert Lowell: Essays on the Poetry*

28. Robert Lawson-Peebles, *Landscape and Written Expression in Revolutionary America: The World Turned Upside Down*

27. Warren Motley, *The American Abraham: James Fenimore Cooper and the Frontier Patriarch*

26. Lyn Keller, *Re-making It New: Contemporary American Poetry and the Modernist Tradition*

25. Margaret Holley, *The Poetry of Marianne Moore: A Study in Voice and Value*

24. Lothar Hönnighausen, *William Faulkner: The Art of Stylization in His Early Graphic and Literary Work*

23. George Dekker, *The American Historical Romance*

22. Brenda Murphy, *American Realism and American Drama, 1880–1940*

21. Brook Thomas, *Cross-Examinations of Law and Literature: Cooper, Hawthorne and Melville*

20. Jerome Loving, *Emily Dickinson: The Poet on the Second Story*

19. Richard Gray, *Writing the South: Ideas of an American Region*

18. Karen E. Rowe, *Saint and Singer: Edward Taylor's Typology and the Poetics of Meditation*

17. Ann Kibbey, *The Interpretation of Material Shapes in Puritanism: A Study of Rhetoric, Prejudice, and Violence*

16. Sacvan Bercovitch and Myra Jehlen (eds.), *Ideology and Classic American Literature*

15. Lawrence Buell, *New England Literary Culture: From Revolution through Renaissance*

14. Paul Giles, *Hart Crane: The Contexts of "The Bridge"*

13. Albert Gelpi (ed.), *Wallace Stevens: The Poetics of Modernism*

12. Albert J. von Frank, *The Sacred Game: Provincialism and Frontier Consciousness in American Literature, 1630–1860*

11. David Wyatt, *The Fall into Eden: Landscape and Imagination in California*

10. Elizabeth McKinsey, *Niagara Falls: Icon of the American Sublime*

9. Barton Levi St. Armand, *Emily Dickinson and Her Culture: The Soul's Society*

8. Mitchell Breitwieser, *Cotton Mather and Benjamin Franklin: The Price of Representative Personality*

7. Peter Conn, *The Divided Mind: Ideology and Imagination in America, 1898–1917*

6. Marjorie Perloff, *The Dance of the Intellect: Studies in Poetry of the Pound Tradition*

The following titles are out of print

5. Stephen Fredman, *Poet's Prose: The Crisis in American Verse*, First edition

4. Patricia Caldwell, *The Puritan Conversion Narrative: The Beginnings of American Expression*

3. John McWilliams, Jr., *Hawthorne, Melville, and the American Character: A Looking-Glass Business*
2. Charles Altieri, *Self and Sensibility in Contemporary American Poetry*
1. Robert Zaller, *The Cliffs of Solitude: A Reading of Robinson Jeffers*